The Politics of Urban Public Services

The Politics of Urban Public Services

Edited by
Richard C. Rich
Virginia Polytechnic Institute
and State University

LexingtonBooks
D.C. Heath and Company
Lexington, Massachusetts
Toronto

Library of Congress Cataloging in Publication Data
Main entry under title:

The Politics of urban public services.

Includes index.
1. Municipal services—Addresses, essays, lectures. 2. Municipal government—Addresses, essays, lectures. I. Rich, Richard C.
HD4431.P66   352'.00724   80–7689
ISBN 0–669–03765–6   AACR2

Published simultaneously in Canada

Printed in the United States of America

International Standard Book Number: 0-669-03765-6

Library of Congress Catalog Card Number: 80-7689

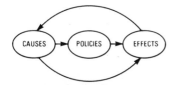

Policy Studies
Organization Series

General Approaches to Policy Studies

Policy Studies in America and Elsewhere
  edited by Stuart S. Nagel
Policy Studies and the Social Studies
  edited by Stuart S. Nagel
Methodology for Analyzing Public Policies
  edited by Frank P. Scioli, Jr., and Thomas J. Cook
Urban Problems and Public Policy
  edited by Robert L. Lineberry and Louis H. Masoti
Problems of Theory in Policy Analysis
  edited by Philip M. Gregg
Using Social Research for Public Policy-Making
  edited by Carol H. Weiss
Public Administration and Public Policy
  edited by H. George Frederickson and Charles Wise
Policy Analysis and Deductive Reasoning
  edited by Gordon Tullock and Richard Wagner
Legislative Reform
  edited by Leroy N. Rieselbach
Teaching Policy Studies
  edited by William D. Coplin
Paths to Political Reform
  edited by William J. Crotty
Determinants of Public Policy
  edited by Thomas Dye and Virginia Gray
Effective Policy Implementation
  edited by Daniel Mazmanian and Paul Sabatier
Taxing and Spending Policy
  edited by Warren J. Samuels and Larry L. Wade
The Politics of Urban Public Services
  edited by Richard C. Rich
Analayzing Urban Service Distributions
  edited by Richard C. Rich
The Analysis of Policy Impact
  edited by John Grumm and Stephen Washby
Public Policies for Distressed Communities
  edited by F. Stevens Redburn and Terry F. Buss
Implementing Public Policy
  edited by Dennis J. Palumbo and Marvin A. Harder
Evaluating and Optimizing Public Policy
  edited by Dennis J. Palumbo, Stephen B. Fawcett, and Paula Wright
Representation and Redistricting Issues
  edited by Bernard Grofman, Arend Lijphart, Robert McKay, and
  Howard Scarrow
Administrative Reform Strategies
  edited by Gerald E. Caiden and Heinrich Siedentopf

Specific Policy Problems

Analyzing Poverty Policy
  edited by Dorothy Buckton James
Crime and Criminal Justice
  edited by John A. Gardiner and Michael Mulkey
Civil Liberties
  edited by Stephen L. Wasby
Foreign Policy Analysis
  edited by Richard L. Merritt
Economic Regulatory Policies
  edited by James E. Anderson
Political Science and School Politics
  edited by Samuel K. Gove and Frederick M. Wirt
Science and Technology Policy
  edited by Joseph Haberer
Population Policy Analysis
  edited by Michael E. Kraft and Mark Schneider
The New Politics of Food
  edited by Don F. Hadwiger and William P. Browne
New Dimensions to Energy Policy
  edited by Robert Lawrence
Race, Sex, and Policy Problems
  edited by Marian Lief Palley and Michael Preston
American Security Policy and Policy-Making
  edited by Robert Harkavy and Edward Kolodziej
Current Issues in Transportation Policy
  edited by Alan Altshuler
Security Policies of Developing Countries
  edited by Edward Kolodziej and Robert Harkavy
Determinants of Law-Enforcement Policies
  edited by Fred A. Meyer, Jr., and Ralph Baker
Evaluating Alternative Law-Enforcement Policies
  edited by Ralph Baker and Fred A. Meyer, Jr.
International Energy Policy
  edited by Robert M. Lawrence and Martin O. Heisler
Employment and Labor-Relations Policy
  edited by Charles Bulmer and John L. Carmichael, Jr.
Housing Policy for the 1980s
  edited by Roger Montgomery and Dale Rogers Marshall
Environmental Policy Formation
  edited by Dean E. Mann
Environmental Policy Implementation
  edited by Dean E. Mann
The Analysis of Judicial Reform
  edited by Philip L. Dubois
The Politics of Judicial Reform
  edited by Philip L. Dubois
Critical Issues in Health Policy
  edited by Ralph Straetz, Marvin Lieberman, and Alice Sardell

*For Lila who taught me to care about people
and the politics that shape their lives.*

Contents

List of Figures
and Tables

Acknowledgments

I want to express my deep appreciation of the cooperation I have received from the authors of the chapters in this book. Their responsiveness to my many requests and patience with the countless delays that occurred between idea and publication made my task easier and improved the final product. Their conduct stands as tribute to their professionalism. I thank them for being willing to share their insights.

I am also grateful for the generous support provided for this project by my department at Virginia Polytechnic Institute. It is testimony to its commitment to advancing the field of policy studies and scholarly inquiry in general. I am proud to be associated with such an organization.

Acknowledgment is due my friend and teacher David Olson who excited me about urban politics and stands behind all of my work in that field in ways even he probably does not realize.

Finally, the editor and Policy Studies Organization would like to thank the Ford Foundation for its financial aid to the symposium on which this book is based. Thanks are particularly owed to Louis Winnick, the director of the National Affairs Division. However, no one other than the individual authors is responsible for the ideas advocated here.

1 The Political Economy of Urban-Service Distribution

Richard C. Rich

All too often cities have been studied as isolated, service-providing governmental units. This orientation emphasizes internal processes of administration and political decision making, leading to proposals intended to further apolitical, efficient service provision.

—J.J. Kirklin and S.P. Erie, "The Study of City Government," p. 173.

Are local public services of any political significance? Most of us who think about the subject recognize in a general way that certain public services are essential to the very existence of urban life. Yet most observers also feel that local services are mundane, largely technical matters of limited political import. Although citizens may become exercised over specific service-delivery issues—the closing of a school, the location of a garbage dump, the widening of a street— most realize even in the heat of their anger that these issues are unimportant compared with policies on, for example, civil liberties, the environment, or national defense. Local service delivery is the backwater of public-policy analysis.

Perhaps a central reason for this attitude is that we have virtually no generally acceptable evidence that minor variations in public services make significant differences in people's lives. Where is the evidence that crime is reduced by increased rates of police patrol? Where is the clear evidence that what a city spends on its schools is related to the quality of the education children receive or to the jobs they ultimately fill? Although it is clear that terminating police or education services would have profound effects on the city's residents, the effects of adding a few police officers to the force or of marginally reducing the student/teacher ratio in the public schools are not known. As a result, we do not know the political significance of the fact that some citizens receive measurably more or better public services than others.

A second reason for the highly limited nature of concern about service distribution can probably be traced to the widely held belief that services are distributed according to professionally determined, politically neutral bureaucratic decision rules. Numerous studies have demonstrated the existence and explored the impact of such rules for deciding which neighborhoods get how much and what quality of service (Antunes and Plumlee 1977; Jones et al. 1978; Jones 1980; Nivola 1978).

Such rules are generally established in the name of efficiency and effectiveness. They direct a distribution of services that either eases the task of

1

administration (as when a rule calls for the repair of city streets on a predetermined schedule rather than in response to individual complaints) or promotes effective and efficient utilization of resources by corresponding to professional standards (as when fire stations are located so as to minimize the time any given unit would require to reach a destination within its service zone). These decision rules almost inevitably favor some groups over others, but each rule may favor a different group. Taken together, the rules that direct the distribution of the various services a city provides thus produce what Robert Lineberry (1977) terms an "unpatterned inequality." All areas and population groups may not receive the same services, but there is no consistent bias against any group or area across services.

This explanation of how services get distributed is consistent with the broad impression derived from reading the reports of research on service distribution (Rich 1979). This empirically identified "unpatterned equality" is, however, at odds with casual observation of life in our cities. A tour of any city's neighborhoods will reveal marked, often startling, differences in the physical character and apparent quality of life in different areas. So noticeable are the differences in the conditions of streets and public facilities, the nature of the housing stock, and so forth, from one neighborhood to another, that it is difficult to believe that residents enjoy even roughly equal public services.

Clearly, the major differences in the physical characteristics of U.S. neighborhoods are attributable to differences in the private wealth of their inhabitants. Such a large proportion of goods and services are privately purchased in the United States that the basic quality of life in a neighborhood is necessarily intimately related to residents' personal income. Yet even the relatively narrow range of public services provided by U.S. cities *do* shape the quality of life. Some, like the siting of public facilities or the quality of neighborhood schools, affect the distribution of populations with different private resources. Others, like police and fire protection and trash collection, contribute more directly to the quality of life in an area.

The various chapters of this book are predicated on the assumption that public services are politically important—that their impact on the quality of urban life is great enough to make it worthwhile to try to understand them. Each chapter explores some aspect of the political processes that determine the distribution of local services and the differences distributional decisions make.

This introduction, besides previewing the subsequent chapters and highlighting their relationships to one another, is intended to suggest a conceptual framework within which to analyze and understand service distribution. In doing so, it will take a more macro approach than the other chapters, addressing the most general political context of public services.

I do not propose to offer firm answers to the foregoing questions about the nature of public services that make their distribution seem unimportant to many citizens and scholars. The evidence necessary for such answers is not yet available. I do hope to suggest a conceptual perspective from which we can see how even though both these reservations about public services (that they have relatively little impact on urban conditions, and that their distribution is largely in the hands of rule-governed bureaucrats) may be valid, service-delivery patterns are nevertheless of great political significance.

Public Services and the Local State

Construction of the conceptual framework begins with the question: Why do we have public services? What purpose do they serve? The popular perception, supported by academic orthodoxy, is probably that public services are provided in response to human needs and are designed to remedy problems or create desirable states (Advisory Commission on Intergovernmental Relations [ACIR] 1973). Public services often have these effects, but they often do not. This perspective does not take us very far in understanding the selectivity local governments demonstrate in responding to apparent human needs, the woefully inadequate quantity and quality of some services that are provided, or the frequent failure to supply the types of services actually needed to meet human needs or bring about desired changes.

We would do better to begin with a theory of the state, the mechanism by which social and economic relationships are ordered through lawmaking and implementation. County governments, municipal governments, and special districts are the state at the local level, and their behavior can be explained from the conceptual scheme developed by critical theorists to deal with the state at the national level. Although there is certainly no consensus among critical theorists on the details of a theory of the state, they do generally agree on two points.[1] The first is that the state evolved as a result of the need for a sector of a society that is nominally independent of the economic sector and can legitimate decisions made by economic institutions and mediate the conflicts those decisions create. Second, there is general agreement that state action serves two broad purposes: to facilitate the accumulation and circulation of capital, and to maintain the social control necessary for production processes and the reproduction of economic classes (see, for example, Hirsch 1981).

In plain English, and in the context of this chapter, this means simply that top priorities for local governments are (1) ensuring that industrial and commercial activities can go on by, for example, providing the necessary infrastructure (transportation nets, utilities, and so forth), and (2) keeping the effects of those human problems not resolved (or exacerbated) by the operation of the market system (crime, poverty, and so on) within acceptable limits so that urban life and commercial activity are possible. One need not be a critical or Marxist theorist to accept this basic proposition and recognize the centrality of business concerns to local policymaking (Barnekov and Rich 1977; Peterson 1979).

What does this miniature theory of the state tell us about public services and their distribution? To begin with, it provides a theoretical basis for expecting exactly the patterns that have been documented by most previous research on the subject. Lineberry (1977) has identified five primary explanations for observed service distributions. His own research and his reading of other studies leads him to conclude that none of these explanations satisfactorily accounts for observed patterns, though he argues that the "bureaucratic decision rule" thesis is probably the most promising approach to this task.

The most thoroughly discredited of the alternative explanations is that group that Lineberry collectively labels "the underclass hypothesis." This hypothesis states that services will be distributed in a fashion that discriminates against low-income and nonwhite citizens. Although some research has found evidence of such a distribution of certain services in particular cities (see, for example, Martin 1969; Weicher 1971), other research has revealed the opposite pattern in the same or other services in other cities (for example, Gold 1974; Lineberry 1977). The finding that services are equally distributed or provided in a compensatory fashion (going disproportionately to lower-income people) is always greeted with some surprise by analysts.

This result, however, should not be considered either remarkable or evidence of the humanitarian impact of state action. Critical theories of the state would lead us to expect an equal or compensatory distribution of services as a product of the function state action serves in a capitalist system.

To understand this we must recognize a distinction between public services that support commerce, the circulation of capital, and the production process (for example, street maintenance, sewers, and fire protection), and services that are oriented more toward class-reproduction processes and maintenance of the social control required for those processes to function (for example, welfare, housing, and education). The former, infrastructure services must be available to everyone (though not necessarily equally used by or of benefit to everyone) if they are to be effective; they are generally considered essential services. In fact, most research on these services has revealed a tendency toward equal distribution (Boots 1972; Levy, Meltsner, and Wildavsky 1974; Antunes and Plumlee 1977).

The latter or class-reproductive services need not be equally distributed among segments of the population; indeed, they often depend for their effectiveness on being carefully targeted to specific groups. Thus we should not be at all surprised to find that low-income people are disproportionately the recipients of locally provided welfare or social services, or that poor neighborhoods have more police patrol, public-housing facilities, or low-interest housing-rehabilitation loans. If the function of state action is, as critical theory claims, to counterbalance the destabilizing human problems created by the operation of the market (Harvey 1978; Hill 1978), then it is logical for those populations among whom these problems are concentrated to be the targets of ameliorative state action. Again, empirical research has generally revealed such a concentration (see chapter 2 by Wolch).

State action not only *facilitates* class reproduction by maintaining social control, but also more directly contributes to that reproduction. Thus we should not be surprised to find, for example, that the poorest schools are concentrated in low-income and working-class neighborhoods, whereas better schools dominate middle- and upper-income areas; that children of lower- and working-class families are tracked into blue-collar-oriented curricula, whereas middle- and upper-class children are designated "college material"; that welfare institutions seem only to contribute to recipients' inability to escape poverty; that many services that would contribute to the economic mobility of the lower classes (adequate day care, effective job training, certain types of small-business assistance, and so on) are not provided or not provided in adequate quantity or quality by local governments; or that middle- and upper-class persons are allowed to isolate themselves into political jurisdictions in which they can escape heavy tax burdens that inhibit the accumulation of capital. Nor should we be surprised to find that the unintended consequences of state actions seem to perpetuate the problems they are nominally intended to remedy, as when the siting of subsidized housing reinforces the concentration of low-income groups into neighborhoods in which children acquire educational and economic handicaps, or when public-housing reinvestment programs lead to the displacement and further impoverishment of the poor. These and many other phenomena are examples of the class-reproductive functions of state action at the local level and illustrate the intimate link between the political and the economic systems.

Service Distribution and the Political Economy

The "proper" distribution of services is a crucial prerequisite to state action effectively performing its twin economic functions of supporting production and reproduction. Although specific service decisions (such as the repair of a pothole or the handling of a complaint) may be subject to random forces, the broad distribution of public energies among service types and of services among population groups must *not* be random if it is to be functional for the economic system. If we see public-service distributions as capricious (and there are serious methodological questions about how accurately our research allows us to see them (Rich 1979), it is probably because of the theoretical lens through which we view them, not because of the character of the distributions.

If we begin with the liberal welfare-state assumption that public services are designed to remedy human problems, then research to date does present a perplexing picture of random inequalities. Critical theory, however, helps us discern the logic in these findings.

A useful point of departure in this task is the recognition that the concept of service distribution has at least two broad dimensions. The first is the allocation of public funds among alternative types of services. This decision, made in the budgetary process, determines which among an array of potential services the state will produce, and at what level each will be provided. The second dimension of service distribution is reflected in the allocation of those services that *are* to be provided among population groups. This allocation determines who will get how much of the available public services. Although it is influenced by decisions in the budgetary process, this allocation occurs primarily in the administrative process, with all levels of the bureaucracy playing a role.

Of the two distributive decisions, the former has far more impact. Decisions about what services to fund (I will call them *legislative decisions,* for convenience) set the broad framework within which all other distributive decisions are made, and set constraints on the impact of those decisions on people's lives. To illustrate, the decision about which of several eligible individuals is to receive some welfare benefit is of less social significance than the decision about what group will be eligible for benefits; the decision about how to distribute bus routes about the city has less impact on the transportation mix in that city than the decisions that determine how many bus routes there will be and what carrying capacity they will have. In each of these examples, the more crucial decisions are those made at the legislative rather than the administrative stage.

In many instances the effective decision about who will benefit from public services is made before public resources are ever mobilized for service delivery. Although basic public services (police and fire protection, sewers, street lighting, and so on) benefit a wide spectrum of the population, many specialized services provide direct benefits only to specific subgroups within the population. (Consider, for example, the clientele for senior citizens' centers, job-training programs, day-care facilities, public housing, or summer jobs for unemployed youths.) Thus when public officials select the mix of public services that is to be provided, they also determine to a large extent the distribution of benefits from public action. The implication is that the most significant politics of urban-service distribution probably takes place in the local (and, to the extent that localities respond to initiatives from higher-level governments, in the state and national) budgetary process.

By choosing to concentrate public resources on those services that confer roughly equal benefits on a broad segment of the public, local political elites can ensure that the impact of public expenditure will essentially maintain or reinforce the existing distribution of wealth and opportunity. An examination of the distribution of city expenditures among functional areas shows clearly that they have, in fact, selected this option (Bureau of the Census 1979), concentrating their funds on distributive rather than redistributive services, and on services for which there were few private-sector substitutes. Such decisions restrict both the potential impact of public services on societal problems and the redistributive effect of public provision of goods and services.

The central point here is as follows. The most significant decisions about public services are made before any services ever reach "the street," and any study that examines only the distribution of those services cities actually decide to deliver can provide only a highly limited basis for judging the equity of service distribution or understanding the politics of public services.

Recognizing the significance of legislative service decisions helps us examine the twin reservations about the study of public services cited at the outset of this chapter. The first was that public services have a very limited impact on urban conditions. If they have little impact, it is probably at least as much because they are designed to have little impact as because of any lack of knowledge about social processes. Critical theory would lead us to expect relatively little impact on social problems since the purpose of state action is to keep the conflict caused by those problems within acceptable limits in order to preserve the very social relationships that created the problems, not to effect changes that remove root causes of social disorder.

This observation takes on added significance in light of the fact that most citizen involvement in service-delivery decisions is focused on the administrative aspect of distribution rather than the legislative. Although citizens frequently protest individual service failures (defective street lights, poor snow removal, inconvenient hours at a public clinic), they seldom mobilize to influence the local budgetary decisions that determine the scope of the local public sector.[2] This is unfortunate since it is these legislative decisions that have the most profound impact of the distribution of benefits from state action. In fact, in recent years there has been a growing effort to call attention to the potential for bringing about social change by expanding the local state (Case, Goldberg, and Shearer 1976; Institute for Policy Studies 1975; Kirshner and Morey 1973).

The second reservation about the study of service distributions is that they are controlled by bureaucrats following technically determined rules. If, as an increasing number of students of the subject are arguing, bureaucratic decision rules are the principal determinant of the street-level distribution of locally provided services, the simplified critical theory of the state cited at the outset of this chapter is again useful in demonstrating the political significance of public services. If political elites have set the rules of the service-delivery game through decisions made at the legislative stage, they have every reason to be content to leave the calling of individual plays to bureaucratic umpires. Indeed, it is to their great advantage to have routine distributional decisions made by professional bureaucrats guided by technically determined rules. This tends to depoliticize local state action and, in a society valuing professionalism and scientific management, to legitimate the social relations sustained by the resulting service-delivery patterns, allowing the local state to fulfill important ideological functions in the capitalist system (Gold, Lo, and Wright 1975; Harvey 1978).

Urban Form and Service Distributions

The second or administrative aspect of service distribution involves the allocation of existing services among groups and individuals. This allocation is made
principally through decisions about the *geographic* distribution of service resources. The geographic spread of service benefits is politically significant only
because the extensive class and racial segregation that characterizes U.S. cities
causes decisions about the physical location of services to be generally tanta-
mount to decisions about the class and racial composition of service beneficiaries.

Critical scholars have extensively documented the intimate relationship that
exists between capitalist economics and the political organization and distribution of population in urban space (Gordon 1976; Harvey 1977; Mollenkopf
1978; Walker 1981). To the extent that population distributions reflect the
structure of the economic system, it is capitalism that gives political meaning to
the geographic distribution of services.

Most previous research on service distribution has focused on the administrative face of the phenomenon and has examined it *within* given local jurisdictions. This research has produced the empirical picture of public-service distribution in the United States as dominated by the unpatterned inequalities referred
to earlier (for a review, see Rich 1979).

This research has largely ignored what is arguably the most politically and
economically important aspect of urban-service distributions—the distribution
of services *among* jurisdictions within metropolitan areas. The combination of
political fragmentation and class and racial clustering in U.S. metropolitan areas
creates situations in which local jurisdictions (municipalities, counties, and—
perhaps most important in this context—special districts) can "specialize" in
service packages that cater to narrow bands of the class spectrum (Cox and
Nartowicz 1980; Neiman 1975; Newton 1975).

Through judicious use of tools such as municipal incorporation, special
districts, and zoning laws, middle- and upper-class communities can effectively
isolate themselves from working- and lower-class persons, thereby freeing themselves of much of the social cost of ensuring order and providing for class reproduction (Danielson 1976). Their efforts in this respect produce a legal separation
of public resources from public needs, which in the absence of extensive state
and federal funding of public services effectively limits the redistributive impact
of state action and ensures poor services for impoverished communities.

Although political fragmentation and the attendant separation of public
resources from public needs may bestow short-term benefits on some middle-
and upper-class suburbanites and certain elements of the capitalist community
(Cox and Nartowicz 1980), it contributes directly to the fiscal crisis con-
fronting so many jurisdictions (Research Planning Group on Urban Social
Services 1978). Fiscally stressed cities find it increasingly difficult to perform
either of the central functions of the local state, and public services become

increasingly both the focus of efforts to manage the political economy, and the source of class confrontation as capital attempts to restrict the state's interference with the accumulation process by cutting back public services (Rich 1980).

The politics that ensue (those we observe in the United States today) are instructive. For capital the secret to success in this case lies in reducing the costs of the state's social-control and reproductive activities to a minimum while preserving as much of the state's accumulation- and production-supporting function as possible. The organizational structure of local government is well suited to this. Social-control and reproduction activities are generally carried out by highly visible, politically exposed public agencies ("main-line" city departments, boards of education, and so on) whose programs are funded principally by local property taxation, whereas those activities supporting accumulation and reproduction are more often performed through insulated, politically invisible government agencies and special authorities (Friedland, Piven, and Alford 1977). Thus in an era of cutbacks those services with redistributive impacts become highly politicized and are often slashed, whereas "basic" infrastructural services are held sacrosanct in all but the most distressed cities.

In addition to this functional specialization, local government, by virtue of its geographic fragmentation, is also well suited to serve the interests of capital in conflicts over public-service levels. Given the way in which classes and firms are sorted into jurisdictions within metropolitan areas, production- and reproduction-supporting state functions are often performed to a large degree by different units of government. This means that state activity can be reduced across the full range of government services in those jurisdictions that have become less crucial to accumulation processes without endangering the production-support function of the state, whereas higher levels of services can be maintained in other, more fiscally sound jurisdictions without stressing the accumulation process with heavy costs for the state's social-control and reproductive activities. The tension between state activity and accumulation is therefore never crystallized as a class conflict but appears as a conflict between the residents of declining cities and their own governments. Although this may have the effect of politicizing service issues, it also contributes to the continued depoliticization of the economic structure and urban spatial organization that created the stress on public services in the first place.

The most crucial politics of urban-service delivery may, then, be the politics surrounding the processes of local-government fragmentation, for they largely set the fiscal capacity of local governments for providing services, and thereby delimit the legislative and administrative distributional decisions examined early in this chapter. If we are to understand the politics of urban services, we must explore in greater depth the implications of the geopolitical organization of our cities for both service-delivery patterns and the overall functioning of local political economies.

Organization of the Book

The authors of subsequent chapters in this book do not approach their subjects from the perspective of critical theory. They do, however, address many of the questions raised by this perspective; and each chapter advances the study of public-service distributions beyond earlier research in some significant way. The chapters are grouped into three sections to reflect commonalities.

The first of these sections, part I, contains the most diverse set of chapters. Each explores some aspect of the causes and consequences of public-service distributions. In chapter 2 Jennifer Wolch addresses more directly than any other contributor the question of what political significance we should attach to public services. Reversing the logic common to studies of service distribution, she treats service decisions as independent variables affecting urban development patterns. She finds that the distribution of social services can have substantial impact on population patterns in urban areas and, subsequently, on both the need for services in given jurisdictions and the capacity of those jurisdictions to provided needed services.

Chapters 3 and 4 examine aspects of the influence of bureaucratic decision rules on service delivery. Mary Bryna Sanger's analysis of the New York City case demonstrates the pervasive influence of such rules but also suggests how they and the processes by which they are articulated can be opened to political examination and debate. An especially noteworthy aspect of her work is the way in which it suggests the source of the explanatory power of the bureaucratic-decision-rule (BDR) thesis. Other hypotheses about how public-service distributions are determined are largely outcome oriented. They predict specific distributional patterns and can be discredited by contrary evidence. The BDR thesis, however, is essentially process oriented. It describes *how* distributions occur, not what patterns will develop. Accordingly, the BDR hypothesis is compatible with almost any empirically observed distribution pattern and is difficult to discredit. In fact, the BDR hypothesis is compatible with other explanations of observed distributions. BDRs may well be the mechanism through which distributions that are dictated by other than bureaucratic considerations are actually arranged.

Joseph Viteritti, in chapter 4, explores the assumptions that underlie most treatments of BDRs as distributive mechanisms, and relates administrative processes to political issues of equity. His work complements the critical theoretical framework outlined in this introduction by delineating the role and latitude of administrative processes in carrying out legislatively determined service distributions. He makes the important point that efficiency and equity, so often viewed as incompatible goals in service agencies, are in fact complementary, and that the logic of bureaucratic organization will tend to harmonize the two under proper conditions. The implication is that we need not make a political choice between efficient services and equitable ones, but that achieving more of one will give us more of the other.

In chapter 5 James Button investigates the relationship between a variety of political behaviors and service-distribution patterns. He finds that under certain conditions the allocation of the two services he examines are responsive to political influence. Although the generalizability of this result is not clear from Button's sample, his work is especially valuable for its methodological contribution. Most research in this field relies on aggregate data and a cross-sectional approach. In contrast, Button employs objective, aggregate data along with subjective or judgmental interview data, and historical analysis to ferret out the relationship between service patterns and black political activism. This labor-intensive research strategy is probably the type of study that will be required to understand the subtle dynamics of the service-distribution phenomenon so often wrongly treated as if it were static.

In the final chapter of part I, Russell Harrison takes on the topic of inter-jurisdictional service distributions through an empirical test of so-called fiscal-zoning theory. This theory explains the sharp differences in the quality of the services and the service packages offered by various jurisdictions in metropolitan areas by reference to the influence municipalities can exercise over the kind of residents and businesses they attract. Harrison's test of this thesis is, as he recognizes, far from complete. It does, however, lend credence to the important role assigned to governmental fragmentation in the critical analysis of public services presented earlier in this chapter.

Part II contains five chapters united by a concern for the budgetary aspects of service distribution. Terrence Jones's chapter sets the stage for this analysis by exploring the impact of fiscal stress on the geographic, class, and racial distribution of services in St. Louis. His longitudinal analysis, which shows only a slight tendency for nonwhite and low-income areas to bear a disproportionate burden in times of service cutbacks, thus lends only weak support to the underclass hypothesis cited earlier. This result, however, should be interpreted in recognition of the fact that the services Jones studied, police patrol and street maintenance, are not redistributive in nature. The critical perspective outlined earlier, in fact, would lead us to expect relatively equal distribution of an infrastructure service like street maintenance and an equal or even compensatory distribution of a social-control service like police patrol. The fact that Jones finds even slight discrimination against lower-socioeconomic-status (SES) areas in these services suggests that the degree of inequality may be a good deal worse in other services.

Harold Wolman extends the focus on the service impacts of budgetary cutbacks in chapter 8. He combines conceptual and empirical analyses to derive a set of expectations about the distributional consequences of service reductions, reaching the conclusion that without the intervention of higher levels of government, the burden can be expected to fall disproportionately on low-income and minority neighborhoods. The succeeding two chapters take on special significance in light of Wolman's persuasive case that for cities to manage service cutbacks equitably depends heavily on the incentives for equitable service distribution and the resources made available under the Community Development Block Grant (CDBG) program.

If we can generalize from the Denver case, the analysis in chapter 9 by Dennis Judd and Alvin Mushkatel suggests that the administration of even the CDBG program has produced a bias *against* allocating services to the most needy urban neighborhoods. Similarly, in chapter 10 John Sacco finds in his examination of a national sample of cities that federal efforts at encouraging the targeting of CDBG monies to high-need areas has had limited success at best. These analyses do not bode well for the equity-inducing impact of federal intervention in local service delivery under the even broader block-grant program envisioned by the Reagan administration.

In the final chapter in this section, David Cingranelli asks what it would cost to achieve an equitable distribution of local services. His examination of data from Boston indicates that more equitable distribution of existing services can be achieved without massive increases in local expenditures and should be possible even for fiscally stressed cities. This finding may reflect the validity of Viteritti's argument in chapter 4 about the complementarity of equity and efficiency as goals of service bureaucracies.

It is important to note, however, that Cingranelli's work focuses on the distribution of *existing* services *within* a jurisdiction. It would be useful to replicate this analysis in asking about the costs of equalizing services across municipalities within metropolitan areas, with special attention to the changes that might occur in local government's fiscal capacity/service-need ratio if entire metropolitan areas were treated as fiscal units. Would broadening the local tax base in this way provide the infusion of funds that would be required to provide new or more adequate services, rather than just more equitable distribution of existing services?

The source of many of the service-distribution patterns described in chapters 2 through 11 can be traced at least in part to some aspect of the structural organization of government in the United States. Arguments for service equity often lead to arguments for structural reform (for an example, see Rich 1977). Most such calls for reform are based on logic rather than empirical evidence, since it is impossible to know the impact of a political form on service delivery in advance of its institution. However, other nations have governmental arrangements that differ significantly from those in the United States, and it may be possible to learn something about the relationship of structural arrangements to service distributions that cannot be discerned from examination of the U.S. system alone.

Political fragmentation, through both federal arrangements and the geopolitical organization of urban areas, is commonly cited as a major source of service inequities. Accordingly, each of the chapters in part III examines a political system that is marked by a good deal less formal fragmentation than that of the United States. Each has the potential of telling us something about the likely impact of reforms frequently suggested for the United States. For example, Ronald Aqua's examination in chapter 12 of the determinants of service distributions in Japan's highly centralized system shows that local politics and local bureaucrats' decisions play a significant role even in the face of extensive national financing of services and nationally articulated service standards. This result should caution us about the need to understand the local sources of service distributions in order to regulate them even through structural reforms relying on the intervention of higher levels.

This caution is inverted in chapter 13, in which Alan Burnett and Dilys Hill report on the impact of neighborhood organizations on service distribution in England. They find that the centralized, highly professionalized nature of English local-government decision making combines with the nonparticipatory political culture of the nation to restrict the influence of neighborhood associations over local policy even more dramatically than is true in the United States. The implication is that structural arrangements that facilitate citizen access to decision making about services and foster public debate of service rules and standards are crucial to achieving popular control of public-service distributions.

The two concluding chapters return to the subject of structural determinants of service distributions. Frederick Lazin's description of welfare and education services in the formally centralized Israeli system highlights the capacity of local political leaders and bureaucrats to circumvent structural efforts to achieve service equality across and within local jurisdictions. He identifies a variety of design flaws in Israeli governmental organization that lead to inequitable service distributions despite a national commitment to equity—flaws that U.S. reformers would be well advised to avoid in their programmatic and structural proposals.

The Australian system described by Andrew Parkin in chapter 15 provides a contrast. Careful program design has allowed the Australians to achieve a significant degree of interjurisdictional service equality without sacrificing responsiveness to local demands. The similarities between Australian and U.S. urbanization may make this an especially useful comparison, since the stark differences in service distributions found in the two nations may more reasonably be attributed to differences in their governmental structures.

As is so often the case in the social sciences, the studies reported in this collection probably raise more questions about urban-service delivery than they answer. They do, however, advance our understanding of the subject not only by offering partial answers, but also by asking more appropriate questions about the often ignored political aspects of service distributions and by suggesting productive methods of seeking more complete answers. I am confident that the authors share my hope that this book will further stimulate the already growing debate over the role of public services in our society. In all, their work helps to move our discipline closer to answering Kirklin and Erie's (1972, p. 181) decade-old, but still largely unheaded, call to elevate the analysis of municipal-service delivery to a higher level of theoretical sophistication.

Notes

1. Marxist scholars in both Europe and the United States have been deeply divided over the nature and functions of the state in capitalist societies and the conceptual role of the state in critical theory. This is not the place to review or attempt to resolve that debate. I might direct interested readers to the reviews of this issue found in Dear and Clark (1978); Fainstein and Fainstein (1979); Gold, Lo, and Wright (1975); Holloway and Picciotto (1978); Jessop (1977); and Poulantzas (1976). An attempt to resolve some of the points of conflict in this debate in the context of urban analysis is found in Research Planning Group on Urban Social Services (1978).

For purposes of this chapter I will attempt to make only those assumptions about the nature of the state on which there is widespread agreement, and will essentially ignore the complex and subtle theoretical issues raised by many of my statements about the functions of state action. My objective here is to draw out the relevance of critical theory for analyses of urban-service distributions and to set knowledge of those distributions in a larger context. I do not see this as primarily a contribution to the critical theory of the local state in capitalist systems.

2. Obviously, interest groups lobby the federal and, to a lesser degree, state governments for budgetary decisions that will affect locally delivered services (especially education and welfare). Extensive citizen involvement in distinctly local budgetary processes is rare, however.

References

Advisory Commission on Intergovernmental Relations (ACIR). 1973. *City Financial Emergencies.* Washington, D.C.: U.S. Government Printing Office.

Antunes, G., and Plumlee, J. 1977. "The Distribution of an Urban Public Service: Ethnicity, Socioeconomic Status and Bureaucracy as Determinants of the Quality of Neighborhood Streets." *Urban Affairs Quarterly* 12:312-332.

Barnekov, T.K., and Rich, D. 1977. "Privitism and Urban Development: An Analysis of the Organized Influence of Urban Business Elites." *Urban Affairs Quarterly* 12:431-460.

Boots, A., et al. 1972. *Inequality in Local Government Services.* Washington, D.C.: Urban Institute.

Bureau of the Census. 1979. *Government Finances and Employment at a Glance.* Washington, D.C.: U.S. Government Printing Office.

Case, J.; Goldberg, L.; and Shearer, D. 1976. "State Business." *Working Papers for a New Society* 4:67-75.

Cox, K.R., and Nartowicz, F.Z. 1980. "Jurisdictional Fragmentation in the American Metropolis: Alternative Perspectives." *International Journal of Urban and Regional Research* 4:196-211.

Danielson, M.N. 1976. *The Politics of Exclusion.* New York: Columbia University Press.

Dear, M., and Clark, G. 1978. "The State and Geographic Process: A Critical Review." *Environment and Planning* 10:173–183.

Fainstein, N.I., and Fainstein, S.S. 1979. "New Debates in Urban Planning: The Impact of Marxist Theory within the United States." *International Journal of Urban and Regional Research* 3:381–403.

Friedland, R.; Piven, F.F.; and Alford, R.R. 1977. "Political Conflict, Urban Structure and the Fiscal Crisis." *International Journal of Urban and Regional Research* 1:447–472.

Gold, D.A.; Lo, C.Y.H.; and Wright, E.O. 1975. "Recent Developments in Marxist Theories of the Capitalist State." *Monthly Review* 27:29–43.

Gold, S.D. 1974. "The Distribution of Urban Government Services in Theory and Practice: The Case of Recreation in Detroit." *Public Finance Quarterly* 2:107–130.

Gordon, D. 1976. "Capitalism and the Roots of the Urban Crisis." In *The Fiscal Crisis of American Cities,* eds. R.E. Alcaly and D. Mermelstein. New York: Vintage Books, pp. 82–112.

Harvey, D. 1977. "Government Policies, Financial Institutions and Neighborhood Change in the United States." In *Captive Cities,* ed. Michael Harloe. New York: Wiley, pp. 123–139.

———. 1978. "On Planning the Ideology of Planning." In *Planning Theory in the 1980s,* eds. R.W. Burchell and G. Sterlieb. New Brunswick, N.J.: Rutgers University.

Hill, R.C. 1978. "Fiscal Collapse and Political Struggle in Decaying Central Cities in the United States." In *Marxism and the Metropolis,* eds. W.K. Tabb and L. Sawers. New York: Oxford University Press.

Hirsch, J. 1981. "The Apparatus of the State, the Reproduction of Capital and Urban Conflicts." In *Urbanization and Urban Planning in Capitalist Society,* eds. M. Dear and A.J. Scott. New York: Methuen, pp. 593–607.

Holloway, J., and Picciotto, S., eds. 1978. *State and Capital.* London: Edward Arnold.

Institute for Policy Studies. 1975. *What Do I Do Now?: A Reader on Public Policy.* Washington, D.C.: Institute for Policy Studies.

Jessop, R. 1977. "Recent Theories of the Capitalist State." *Cambridge Journal of Economics* 1:353–374.

Jones, B.D. 1980. *Service Delivery in the City.* New York: Longman.

Jones, B., et al. 1978. "Service Delivery Rules and the Distribution of Local Government Services: Three Detroit Bureaucracies." *Journal of Politics* 40:332–368.

Kirklin, J.J., and Erie, S.P. 1972. "The Study of City Government and Public Policy Making: A Critical Appraisal." *Public Administration Review* 32:173–184.

Kirshner, E.M., and Morey, J. 1973. "Controlling a City's Wealth." *Working Papers for a New Society* 1:9–19.

Levy, F.S.; Meltsner, J.; and Wildavsky, A. 1974. *Urban Outcomes*. Berkeley: University of California Press.

Lineberry, R.L. 1977. *Equality and Urban Policy*. Beverly Hills, Calif.: Sage Publications.

Martin, L. 1969. *Library Response to Urban Change*. Chicago: American Library Association.

Mollenkopf, J.A. 1978. "The Postwar Politics of Urban Development." In *Marxism and the Metropolis*, eds. W.K. Tabb and L. Sawers. New York: Oxford University Press, pp. 117-152.

Neiman, M. 1975. "From Plato's Philosopher King to Bish's Tough Purchasing Agent: The Premature Public Choice Paradigm." *Journal of the American Institute of Planners* 41:55-73.

Newton, K. 1975. "American Urban Politics: Social Class, Political Structure and Public Goods." *Urban Affairs Quarterly* 11:241-264.

Nivola, P. 1978. "Distributing a Municipal Service: A Case Study of Housing Inspection." *Journal of Politics* 40:58-81.

Peterson, P.E. 1979. "A Unitary Model of Local Taxation and Expenditure Policies." In *Urban Policy-Making*, ed. D.R. Marshall. Beverly Hills, Calif.: Sage Publications.

Poulantzas, N. 1976. "The Capitalist State: A Reply to Miliband and Laclau." *New Left Review* 95:63-83.

Research Planning Group on Urban Social Services. 1978. "The Political Management of the Urban Fiscal Crisis." *Comparative Urban Research* 5:71-84.

Rich, R.C. 1977. "Equity and Institutional Design in Urban Service Delivery." *Urban Affairs Quarterly* 12:383-410.

———. 1979. "Distribution of Services: Studying the Products of Urban Policy Making." In *Urban Policy Making*, ed. D.R. Marshall. Beverly Hills, Calif.: Sage Publications.

———. 1980. "The Complex Web of Urban Governance, Gossamer or Iron?" *American Behavioral Scientist* 24:277-298.

Walker, R.A. 1981. "A Theory of Suburbanization: Capitalism and the Construction of Urban Space in the United States." In *Urbanization and Urban Planning in Capitalist Society*, eds. M. Dear and A.J. Scott. New York: Methuen, pp. 383-429.

Weicher, J.C. 1971. "The Allocation of Police Protection by Income Class." *Urban Studies* 8:207-220.

Part I
Impacts and Determinants of Public-Service Distributions

2

Spatial Consequences of Social Policy: The Role of Service-Facility Location in Urban Development Patterns

Jennifer R. Wolch

Recent analyses have shown that human-service-dependent populations are increasingly concentrated in poverty-ridden inner-city neighborhoods. Conversely, more affluent parts of cities and suburban communities have relatively few service-dependent residents. This development of service-dependent ghettos appears to have deleterious side-effects, threatening central-city fiscal viability and urban-revitalization efforts and seriously deepening the disparity in quality of life between service-dependent and non-service-dependent populations.

Although our understanding of the complex structural causes of service-dependent ghettos is incomplete, it is clear that social-policy arrangements influence the geographic patterns of service-dependent populations. The current income-maintenance program, with its dual system of cash and in-kind service benefits, implies a network of public facilities designed to distribute human services to persons in need of support. Within major metropolitan areas, particularly central cities in decline, the service-facility network has evolved into a set of service "hubs" that result from the interplay of public policy and professional practices of human-service delivery and care giving. Besides serving existing service-dependent populations, such hubs also attract service users to nearby areas, intensifying ghettoization.

Despite the potentially profound effect of service hubs on urban populations, issues surrounding the distribution of facilities are seldom considered in the national social policymaking process. There appears to be no distribution policy for service support and only faint recognition of the role service-policy measures and programs play in the exacerbation or mitigation of urban social problems.

This chapter presents evidence concerning the nature and magnitude of service-dependent groups and the structure of their public support system. It also provides a general framework for explaining the development of service-dependent ghettos, which focuses on the roles of service-dependent location

I greatly acknowledge the research support from the National Science Foundation, Program in Geography and Regional Science, and extend my thanks to Michael J. Dear and Julian Wolpert for their valuable comments.

choice, community-based service provision, and local responses to the service-dependent minority. This framework supports the argument that social policy and planning at both national and subnational levels must both account for and mitigate undesirable influences of policy on the geographic distribution of service-dependent groups, service opportunities, and the quality of the urban environment.

Service-Dependent Populations in Urban Areas

Social programs such as cash income assistance and provision of in-kind benefits are targeted to the low-income population. This low-income population is not a monolithic block but consists instead of several subgroups having different support requirements and transfer-eligibility characteristics. One major distinction with respect to support needs and opportunities is between the working and nonworking poor. Whereas the working poor rely on earnings from employment to fill their consumption needs, the nonworking groups are service dependent because of their heavy reliance on both human-service supports and cash transfers provided under existing social-welfare programs.

The service-dependent population includes the chronically unemployed; the needy elderly; the mentally ill, retarded, and physically handicapped in poverty; prisoners and ex-prisoners; low-income persons with drug or alcohol addiction problems; and special juvenile population groups such as court wards. The trend toward deinstitutionalization of many service-dependent groups, along with a move toward community-based residential treatment, has swelled the ranks of the service-dependent population. In some central cities, welfare populations and the aged and disabled receiving public support make up more than 18 percent of the population (U.S. Department of Health, Education, and Welfare [DHEW] 1978a).

Numerous public programs exist to support service-dependent persons. The broad structure and targeting of support is defined at the federal level, where primary program goals reflect concerns for economic efficiency and social equity. Four federal programs provide cash assistance to eligible applicants: Aid to Families with Dependent Children (AFDC), Supplemental Security Income (SSI), Social Security (SS), and Veteran's Compensation. Also at the federal level are five programs that supply specific services rather than cash: food stamps; public-housing/rental assistance; Medicare; Medicaid; and Title XX social services, a program providing such services as protective services; in-home supportive services; casework management; employment-related services; home-health services; nutritional supplements; day care; counseling; and community mental-health and social services to AFDC and SSI recipients and to income-eligible groups. The annual public expenditure for in-kind services is considerable, with funds for food stamps, Medicare, Medicaid, and four federal housing programs alone exceeding expenditures for cash-transfer programs by 120 percent in 1975. Cash-equivalent values of in-kind services to recipients are also substantial; Smeeding (1977), for example, estimates that in 1972 the average cash-equivalent value for food stamps ranged from $375 to $418 (depending on household income), whereas the average subsidy from Medicaid or Medicare varied between $317 and $468, and the value of public-housing residence was between $214 and $683.[1]

Although these programs originate at the federal level, most are mediated through state- and local-government structures. States have the option to: (1) supplement federal support levels; (2) extend eligibility to more groups; (3) define modes of service to be delivered; (4) specify institutional arrangements between service agencies and the state; and (5) provide their own programs.

Most federal and state programs are administered by the bottom rungs on the social-policy hierarchy—counties and cities. In addition to their role as channeling agency, local governments often provide cash relief to indigent populations not eligible for other support, provide emergency medical assistance, and have the option to supplement Title XX funds. Moreover, local governments define the level and mix of services provided to community residents, including those who are service dependent. These decisions have important implications for the welfare of service-dependent persons.

The objectives of local social programming are distinct from those of federal and state agencies and often serve to modify the redistributive intent built into program superstructures. Local policymakers and social planners are highly constrained by non-service-dependent groups competing for limited public resources. Their primary focus is on fulfillment of mandated responsibilities, but in ways most acceptable to community residents. This may entail adjusting the distribution of federal and state program benefits by channeling intergovernmental funds to specific ends or by minimizing service-program opportunities, expansion, or coverage. In the absence of a federal or state service-distribution policy, local agencies can also target services to specific neighborhoods to placate demands or to meet obligations in the most expedient and least controversial fashion. The spatial organization of service support as determined by local governments may conflict with national social-policy objectives, combining with other forces to ensure the development of service-dependent ghettos.

Service-Dependent-Population Patterns and the Human-Service Network

The distribution of service-dependent groups and service facilities stems from mutual locational dependence of clients and facilities and from the interdependence of service-delivery goals. These interdependencies and constraints play a crucial role in the dynamics of urban deterioration and potential community change. A two-way linkage ties service dependents, who seek to minimize the expense of service consumption through residential-location choices, to functionally linked service facilities designed to provide accessible service to dependent clients. This linkage becomes translated into a tendency for service facilities to agglomerate in service-dependent areas of cities. In turn, the concentration of services can operate to attract those in need of service support to these same service-rich zones, leading to a recursive cycle of facility and service-dependent-population concentration. This agglomeration produces negative spillover effects that influence community attitudes toward service-dependent groups and support facilities, prompting the exclusion of service-dependent persons from many residential areas and the consequent intensification of ghettoization.

Typically, a service-dependent person receives more than one support service, consuming instead a package or bundle of services available within the structure of social-welfare programs. This service package may be of substantial economic value and may represent an essential supplement to minimal cash allowances (Lyons et al. 1976; Smith and Howitt 1976; Smeeding 1977). Moreover, the elements of the service package directly affect the residential-location choices of service-dependent populations.

Individual services in a service package can be distinguished on the basis of two characteristics affecting the degree to which services affect the location of service users:

1. *Place specificity,* which indicates whether support is delivered to clients at their residences or is supplied from a place-specific facility to which clients must travel.
2. *Convertibility,* a characteristic distinguishing between *cash* or services that can be converted to cash, and those services that must be consumed *in-kind*.

The service package is likely to consist of a mix of place-specific, delivered, cash, and in-kind transfers. The types of services contained in the package imply different constraints for the service-dependent user. Consumption of place-specific services (for example, drug treatment or legal aid) requires that the client travel to the service facility. A delivered service, such as meals-on-wheels, implies no such inconvenience or expense. Constraints connected with convertibility are somewhat different. Unrestricted cash grants allow free choice in the selection of consumer goods and services by the service-dependent recipient. In-kind transfers, such as public housing, are indivisible and cannot be utilized for any other item of consumption. Hence lack of convertibility implies less choice regarding the level of goods or services to consume, with the potential that an excess of the in-kind service will be used while other needs go unmet.[2]

In combination, the degree of place specificity and convertibility of the service package defines the extent to which that package restricts the locational choices of its consumer. Within each service-dependent subpopulation (needy elderly, mentally ill, physically disabled, and so on), individuals span a continuum reflecting their support requirements and the degree of autonomy dependence of residential location choice implied by their service package (see figure 2-1).

At the dependent end of the residential autonomy–dependence continuum, high levels of need for service support are associated with restrictive service packages, dominated by residential-care services that are by definition place-specific and not convertible. Residential-care facilities include group homes, halfway houses, and convalescent homes. Although inmates of such facilities may utilize services external to the institution and receive cash grants to pay for their residential-care needs, their location is a function of the distribution of residential-care facilities.

Service-dependent persons falling on the autonomous end of the residential autonomy–dependence continuum have relatively few in-kind service needs and consume highly convertible services such as "mailbox" income grants. Such people appear to be the least constrained by their service packages. Restrictions

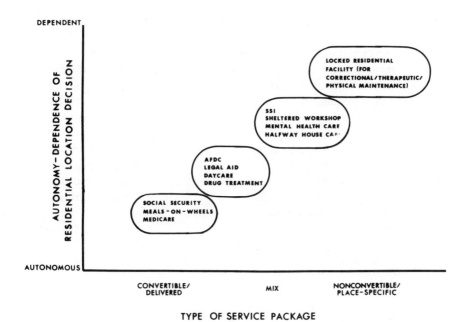

Figure 2-1. Continuum of Autonomy-Dependence of Service-Dependent Residential Location Choice

imposed on location and housing consumption are due solely to the level of cash transfer they receive. These restrictions serve to constrain the autonomous group to relatively low-income, low-rent zones within metropolitan areas.

In contrast to the residentially autonomous groups, service dependents with moderate needs for service support typically rely not only on cash transfers but also on less convertible and/or place-specific services. For this subpopulation, which appears to represent a sizable proportion of the service-dependent group, service packages restrict location choices more severely (Wolpert and Wolpert 1976; Dear and Taylor 1979; Dear 1974; Wolpert, Dear, and Crawford 1975; Wolch 1978, 1980). This occurs in two ways. First, low convertibility of services implies less discretionary cash for the service-dependent household, limiting their ability to purchase favorable locations and housing. Second, available cash income is further reduced by expenditures for transportation to service facilities. Transportation expenses necessitate consideration of the distribution of service opportunities in the choice of residential location and attract service dependents to the locus of service provision. The observable result of minimal cash-income allowances and a reliance on service facilities is a localization of many service dependents in low-cost residential areas accessible to service-facility sites.

Spatial Patterns of Caregiving

Given the linkages between service opportunities and the residential-location choices of many service-dependent persons, knowledge of the spatial distribution of service supply is crucial if we are to unravel the spatial consequences of service policy. The little evidence that is available indicates that caregiving facilities tend to concentrate in decaying portions of inner-city areas, forming service-rich areas or service hubs.

Service hubs, comprising both residential and nonresidential service facilities, form in response to the goals and requirements of such institutions. First, the pattern of community-based residential-care services reflects their needs for low-rent, multifamily residential structures or small-scale facilities, appropriately zoned to allow service operations and/or residence of several single unrelated individuals (Lauber and Bangs 1974; McKinnon 1976). Low rents are crucial because the budgets of publicly operated community-based facilities tend to be limited, and levels of cash assistance to private-facility operators on behalf of service-dependent clients (SSI and Medicaid, for instance) are extremely modest and cannot sustain high capital or operating expenditures. Such requirements provide a rationale for siting residential-care facilities for service dependents in deteriorated inner-city zones in which the availability of low-rent, multifamily structures coming under relatively loose zoning controls creates a noncontroversial situation for such facilities.

Second, the location of nonresidential human services in service hubs results from basic service-delivery goals of providing accessible services that minimize client transportation costs, subject to budgetary constraints. This type of facility-location framework is similar to those developed to explain the distribution of other types of public facilities and used in practice to site certain facilities (Scott 1970; Toregas et al. 1971; A. White 1976; Holmes, Williams, and Brown 1972; Shurman, Hardwick, and Hubers 1973). Since place-specific services are targeted to particular types of clients (for example, the disabled, mentally ill, or elderly), service providers must consider the spatial distribution of their target populations carefully in order to minimize the probability of unmet needs. In the absence of explicit demand for services, service locators would be expected to be sensitive to indirect indicators or correlates of service need, such as income, education, family size, age, and so forth.

Empirically, the representation of nonresidential service facilities is frequently related to a variety of indirect indicators of need for service, although other factors certainly affect siting decisions (Coughlin, Bieri, and Plaut 1976; Naples 1976, Wolch 1978). Wolch (1978), for example, found that variables descriptive of the service-dependent group itself—such as proportion of welfare households, persons experiencing physical or mental disabilities, or needy elderly—influenced the distribution of Philadelphia services targeted toward their needs. Specifically, housing conditions, values, and rents; availability of rental accommodations; and sociodemographic indicators appear to be significant predictors of service-facility representation. The spatial clustering of service-dependent populations serves to attract facilities to particular zones, fostering the development of service hubs.

An additional factor affecting facility siting decisions stems from the nature of ancillary service-delivery goals. Services often have a shared or interdependent service objective, such as client normalization. Realization of the normalization goal, for example, often depends on the provision of a variety of services to clients, such as the provision of sheltered-workshop opportunities to group-home residents or of vocational training to the physically disabled. Service agencies with interdependent goal structures would be likely to locate in response to the distribution of linked facilities, thereby realizing agglomeration economies (Chin 1976; Couglin, Bieri, and Plaut 1976; A. White 1979).

Conflict in the Delivery of Human Services

The agglomeration of service facilities and service-dependent populations rarely goes unnoticed by nondependent community residents. Service hubs (and even single facilities) can generate sufficiently visible spillover effects to sensitize community organizations and political leadership, prompting community action regarding facility entry. The spillover effects of services and their clientele are of two basic varieties, common to any "noxious" facility:

1. *spatial impacts,* which vary with distance from the facility site, creating spatial externality fields (Dear 1974; Dear and Taylor 1979)
2. *aspatial impacts,* confined only by jurisdictional boundaries, termed here *local public-goods impacts*

Spatial Impacts

Three characteristics of service facilities affect community response toward facility entry and operation: (1) client type, (2) facility design, and (3) facility density. First, many client groups are perceived by local residents as deviant, dangerous, or socially unacceptable. Such clients may be feared as a threat to personal safety and well-being (Rabkin 1974; Fracchia et al. 1976; Handler and Hollingsworth 1971; Axinn and Levin 1975). Community attitudes toward different client groups mark their services as more or less wanted; the most unfavorable reactions are elicited by services for deinstitutionalized populations such as ex-mental patients, ex-convicts, or juvenile wards of the court, and by most types of residential-care service facilities. Second, the physical design of facilities—their scale, architectural character, visibility as service facilities, and level of maintenance—affect community perceptions of spillover effects. Third, the number or density of facilities located in any one neighborhood (the size of the service hub) affects traffic volume and congestion, as well as the overall perception of the neighborhood as safe or threatening. High facility densities also create concerns regarding dysfunctional client interactions. Such interactions can be expected when facilities cluster and incompatible client groups, such as ex-prisoners and frail elderly persons, reside in or frequent the same vicinity.

Local residents commonly relate the presence of unwanted service clients, unacceptable physical facilities, and high facility densities to property-value decline and neighborhood instability. Concrete assertions about economic losses attributable to facility siting are not necessarily based on fact; most research on this issue has failed to uncover any significant effects on either levels of real-estate market activity or property values as a result of facility siting (Breslow and Wolpert 1977; Wolpert 1975; Dear and Taylor 1979; Dear 1974). Nonetheless, predictions made by local residents concerning the negative impacts of facility and client presence on property values are widely used to marshal organized opposition to facility siting.

Local Public-Good Impacts:

These impacts are less direct than those mentioned earlier but nonetheless influence community attitudes and policies toward facilities and clients.

Three main local public-good impacts can be identified: (1) increased service provisions costs, (2) increased progressive intracommunity redistribution; and (3) changes in the mix of services in the local service package. First, costs of providing a specific package of urban goods are likely to rise as a result of any significant agglomeration of service dependents or facilities, for three reasons.

1. Cost hikes must be expected because of local responsibilities to provide basic services to service dependents and nondependents alike, even though they do not contribute to the tax base.
2. Any negative capitalization of facility or client impacts on property values jeopardizes existing local fiscal capacities, implying higher tax burdens for community residents.
3. Most services have tax-exempt status and thus occupy land and utilize local public services in place of land uses that would add to the tax base.

The second public-good impact concerns levels of intracommunity fiscal redistribution. Basically, significant service-dependent presence and facility entry precipitate a deviation from locally desired levels of redistribution. Redistribution in favor of the service-dependent population can stem from their consumption of local public goods financed out of a tax base to which they contribute only minimally, thus effecting a transfer from taxpayer to service dependent. Also, capital infrastructure financed by existing residents but used by incoming service-dependent groups and facilities constitutes an intertemporal redistribution from existing to new residents.

The third local public-good impact centers around the change in types of services provided that is likely to occur in a community with an expanding service-dependent population. The presence of service-dependent groups and their advocates typically (and increasingly) implies some political voice for the service-dependent sector. Demands for more "soft" human services (such as health, mental health, education, welfare, or social services) instead of "hard" services (such as police, fire, recreation, or public works) may be imposed on local public-sector representatives. This imposition, causing a change in the mix of hard and soft services, is essentially redistributive. Provision of hard services appears to be favored by non-service-dependent residents who have minimal public human-service requirements; soft services that provide opportunities and real income are in greater demand among service-dependent groups.

Strategies for Excluding the Service Dependent

Both negative spatial impacts and local public-good impacts are the basis for opposition to the entry of service facilities and their service-dependent users into neighborhoods and local jurisdictions. The tactics employed by neighborhood residents and the local public sector are quite different in nature; thus their strategies must be discussed in turn.

Neighborhoods within the spatial impact field of a facility or service hub typically mount several forms of opposition to facility siting. Such opposition can be considered a *conflict cost* of the human-service-facility location problem (Austin, Smith, and Wolpert 1970; Wolch 1978, 1980). At the neighborhood level, conflict costs are the effort and expense required by providers to overcome local opposition to siting fostered by real or perceived facility spillovers. Conflict costs may also persist after the onset of service delivery. Common conflict costs include:

1. additional planning costs and costs of community participation and educational programs designed to overcome opposition
2. legal expenditures required to circumvent or nullify existing zoning specifications or building codes that act as barriers to siting (McKinnon 1976; Lauber and Bangs 1974)
3. increased operation and maintenance costs necessary to implement special design features that serve to minimize the obtrusiveness of facilities, and to repair facility defacements perpetrated by local citizens against unwanted facilities.

The ability to impose conflict costs on service providers and thus to stave off an influx of service dependents and facilities, is strongly associated with neighborhood income levels (Wolpert 1975, 1976). Higher income groups and their attendant commercial services have greater resources to contribute to the maintenance of neighborhood character than do politically weak, low-income zones in which residents are often renters with minimal attachment to their current residential environment. Exclusion of facilities from more affluent neighborhoods can be contrasted to the attraction of facilities to low-income areas. Such attraction is rationalized on the basis of the availability of low-rent space for services, client-access advantages, and the minimal conflict costs of siting facilities in such low-income, often degraded zones. Spillover effects of service provision may drastically increase in low-income areas as a result of this siting pattern. However, such costs are external to the service provider and need not enter into the locational decision unless translated into conflict costs at some later time.

Local-government policies toward the service-dependent population affect the broader intrametropolitan distribution of this population and its associated service facilities. At the same time, the local public-goods impacts affecting the nondependent majority provide a rationale for local governments to use their power to control the entry of service-dependent groups. Exclusionary policies are in fact consistent with other local policies toward development and change designed to maximize the fiscal resources of the community by barring residential opportunities to low-income and ethnic minorities (Mills and Oates 1975; Hamilton 1975, 1976; M. White 1975; Portney and Sonstelie 1978). Strategies for local-government fiscal optimization lead to the implementation of two basic policy approaches for the exclusion of service dependents and associated facilities: *fiscal zoning* and *externality zoning.*

Fiscal zoning measures, such as residential-density controls, builder exactions, construction specifications, and growth-management practices influence the nature of development permitted within jurisdictional bounds. Such instruments have direct impacts on community property values and on the mix of owned and rental housing units. They thus act as a socioeconomic screen, effectively delimiting the range of prospective residents. Screening is likely to be particularly complete in the case of service dependents who subsist on minimal cash allowances and typically seek rental accommodations.

The use of fiscal-zoning tools to maintain community affluence and homogeneity also results in a self-reinforcing process affecting the mix of services in the local public-goods package. Preferences of higher-income residents support the design of service packages favoring hard services, thus minimizing intracommunity redistribution. Such service opportunities are not likely to attract service-dependent households seeking a wider range of soft as well as hard services. Low levels of soft services, notable in many non-central-city jurisdictions, therefore reinforce the segregation of service dependents from more affluent nondependent groups within metropolitan areas.

The second approach to the exclusion of service dependents and facilities is *externality zoning,* which acts to prevent noxious or externality-generating land uses from siting within jurisdictions or, at a minimum, to separate such uses from incompatible uses. Unwanted service facilities, which not only are noxious but also negatively affect the tax base, can be effectively denied entry into local jurisdictions by zoning ordinances that do not permit facility operation without special use permits or zoning variances. Such zoning procedures can place the facility-siting decision in the hands of neighborhood residents, since the variance or permit-issuing process is typically guided by public expression of approval or disapproval of the proposed zoning change. With respect to residential-care facilities such as group homes, zoning laws may even be explicitly structured to preclude facility siting and operation. In many jurisdictions, for example, there is a limit on the number of unrelated persons legally allowed to reside in the same housing unit. Also, local jurisdictions experiencing some facility entry have increasingly adopted zoning tools that specify the maximum allowable density of residential-care facilities. By excluding service facilities on which many service dependents rely, externality-zoning policies effectively exclude the service dependent themselves.

Clearly, jurisdictions within metropolitan regions pursue fiscal-resource maximization in different ways. Suburban communities, particularly those not yet built out, have considerable latitude to adopt fiscal- and externality-zoning approaches to the exclusion of service-dependent populations, among others. Not only have most suburban communities been developed as a result of out-migration of the affluent from central cities, but the structure of land-use controls and tax/expenditure package design also have been shaped by population groups seeking to escape the local public-goods impacts and spatial spillovers associated with large numbers of poor and service-dependent people.

Central cities and old, inner-ring suburbs, on the other hand, are constrained in their pursuit of fiscal-resource maximization. Their policies toward the service-dependent population are affected by ecological characteristics of their jurisdiction, such as the racial and income mix of population, and by physical condition of municipal infrastructure and the dwelling stock. Both social and physical characteristics imply significant rigidities in the service package provided. First, the political power of the poor, nonwhite, and service-dependent groups that have historically been concentrated in inner cities and deteriorating suburbs can be used to promote specific service demands and intracommunity redistribution. The condition of the built environment necessitates a certain minimum level of urban service, which may be forced upward if residents cannot individually assist in the maintenance of urban infrastructure and housing stock. In addition, long-term changes in the location of urban economic activity and high-quality housing services have transformed the nature of central-city land-use markets. Large portions of central-city areas now provide many of the attributes necessary for the support of service-dependent groups—in terms of physical and tenure characteristics of the housing stock, housing and facility prices, and levels of conflict costs and community opposition to service facilities and clients. As in the case of differential opposition to service-dependent presence in low- as opposed to high-income neighborhoods, lower overall levels of opposition to the service-dependent sector can be expected in central cities and inner-ring suburbs than in most newer suburban areas. Thus central-city–suburban differences in ecological, political, and economic characteristics sustain different local policy stances and reinforce the concentration and ghettoization of the service-dependent poor in deteriorating portions of metropolitan areas.

Social-Policy Issues

The urban service-dependent population is significant in size and is likely to continue to grow as a result of continuing trends toward deinstitutionalization and community-based human-service delivery. Close linkages between the residential-location opportunities of service consumers and their support facilities translate into a tendency for service facilities to agglomerate in low-income neighborhoods and jurisdictions. This tendency, which serves to increase the inequality of access to needed services within metropolitan areas, is reinforced by community opposition and exclusionary local policies toward service-dependent groups and facilities. Such local opposition, regulation, and control is strongest in affluent neighborhoods and suburban jurisdictions, and weakest in low-income zones, thus providing an additional rationale for the development of service hubs in these poor areas. The concentration of service facilities operates to attract additional populations coming in need of service care to these same poverty zones, initiating a cycle of colocation that ultimately results in the ghettoization of those who depend on publicly provided services.

Public policy at all levels of government has failed to tackle the problem of the service-dependent ghetto. In spite of the fundamental impact of the network of service facilities on the urban environment, the issues surrounding the pattern of human services are not given consideration in the design of social policy. For instance, major debates concerning population welfare and income maintenance have instead centered around income adequacy and poverty reduction, provision of cash versus in-kind assistance, and eligibility rules and work requirements for the receipt of service aid. These debates are fundamentally aspatial, ignoring issues concerning interdependencies between policy options, urban structure, and the well-being of service-dependent and nondependent populations. The observable consequences of public policy (ghettoization) have been persistently overlooked, and the core questions about the nature and magnitude of costs and benefits associated with service-dependent concentration and the development of service hubs remain unaddressed.

Social programs that *are* explicitly concerned with the quality of urban environments and the concentration of both working and nonworking poor in central cities are targeted to economic development of the urban core, or to opening up the suburbs through a variety of fair-share housing and mass-transportation programs. However, such policies have clearly failed to account adequately for the service needs of the dependent population and for the linkages between service availability and population location. They have, if anything, exacerbated the problem of service-dependent ghettos.

First, federal and state policies have led to the massive deinstitutionalization of service-dependent populations without adequate community-based aftercare programs and facilities. This so-called dumping of highly dependent populations in urban areas has stimulated ghettoization. Second, a fundamental conflict exists between the objectives of policies framed at the federal level and local policy objectives with respect to service provision and land development. Whereas federal policy provides support programs that enlarge metropolitan residential opportunities for service-dependent groups, local policies regarding service delivery and land use have been directed toward excluding these groups. Local-government policies are not required to account for the metropolitanwide consequences of their actions and are thus free to frustrate policies in aid of service-dependent populations, especially when their actions are supported by local-community attitudes of exclusion. Finally, low levels of program funding for economic development, income maintenance, and expansion of residential opportunities have severely limited the ability of such programs to promote the community integration and economic well-being of service-dependent groups.

The failings of social policy for service-dependent persons thus stem in part from poor program design and from a failure of policymakers to trace through and evaluate the spatial consequences of public policies. Serious conflicts between policies framed at the federal and local levels also underlie policy failure. Developments in social policy must begin to recognize the implications of social programs and policy conflict for the intraurban geographic distribution of both service facilities and service-dependent groups. Such consciousness is essential in order that social-policy-related deterioration in the quality of the urban environment be minimized. Moreover, evaluation of the spatial implications of policy actions is vital to the prevention of further inequities in an already skewed distribution of human welfare.

Notes

1. Cash-equivalent values represent the cash amount individuals would spend on a service if they were free to choose between that service and other consumption items. The current-year cash equivalents for the four programs examined by Smeeding would clearly be far in excess of the 1972 amounts given, as a result of rapid escalation in both general price levels and price levels for medical care and housing services in the post-1972 period.

2. The economic inefficiency of in-kind transfers to recipients is a well-known theoretical argument against their provision, although a consideration of the utility of both donors and recipients mitigates this inefficiency. See, for example, Williamson et al. (1975), Aaron and von Furstenberg (1971), or Olsen (1971).

References

Aaron, H.J., and von Furstenberg, G.M. "The Inefficiency of Transfers In-Kind: The Case of Housing Assistance." *Western Economic Journal* 9(1971):184–191.

Antunes, G., and Plumlee, J.P. "The Distribution of An Urban Service: Ethnicity, Socioeconomic Status and Bureaucracy as Determinants of the Quality of Neighborhood Streets." *Urban Affairs Quarterly* 12(1971):313–331.

Austin, M.; Smith, T.; and Wolpert, J. "The Implementation of Controversial Facility-Complex Programs." *Geographical Analysis* 2(1970):315–329.

Axinn, J., and Levin, H. *Social Welfare: A History of the American Response to Need.* New York: Harper and Row, 1975.

Breslow, S., and Wolpert, J. "The Effect of Siting Group Homes on the Surrounding Environs." Unpublished research report, Princeton University, Princeton, N.J., 1977.

Chin, S.P. "Locational Clustering of Service Facilities." Unpublished research paper, Princeton University, Princeton, N.J., 1976.

Coughlin, R.; Bieri, K.; and Plaut, T. "The Distribution of Social Services in the City of Philadelphia." Regional Science Research Institute Discussion Paper no. 93, Philadelphia, 1976.

Dear, M.J. "Locational Analysis for Public Mental Health Facilities." Ph.D. dissertation, University of Pennsylvania, 1974.

——. "Psychiatric Patients and the Inner City." *Annals, Association of American Geographers* 67(1977):588-594.

Dear, M.J., and Wolch, J.R. "The Optimal Assignment of Human Service Clients Public Facilities." Department of Geography, McMaster University, Hamilton, Ont., 1979.

Dear, M.J., and Woch, J.R. "The Optimal Assignment of Human Service Clients to Treatment Settings." In S.M. Golant, ed., *Location and Environment of Elderly Population.* New York: V.H. Winston and Sons, 1979.

Fracchia, J., et al. "Public Views of Ex-Mental Patients: A Note on Perceived Dangerousness and Unpredictability." *Psychological Reports* 38(1976):495-498.

Hamilton, B. "Zoning and Property Taxation in a System of Local Governments." *Urban Studies* 12(1975):215-221.

———. "Capitalization of Intrajurisdictional Differences in Local Tax Prices." *American Economic Review* 6(1976):743-753.

Handler, J.F., and Hollingsworth, E.J. "*The Deserving Poor.*" Chicago: Markham Publishing Company, 1971.

Holmes, J.; Williams, F.; and Brown, L. "Facility Location under Maximum Travel Restriction: An Example Using Day Care Facilities." *Geographical Analysis* 4(1972):258-266.

Lauber, D., and Bangs, F., Jr. *Zoning for Families and Group Care Facilities.* Chicago: American Society of Planning Officials, 1974.

Levy, F.; Meltsner, A.; and Wildavsky, A. *Urban Outcomes: Schools, Streets, Libraries,* Berkeley: University of California Press, 1974.

Lineberry, R. *Equality and Urban Policy: The Distribution of Municipal Public Services.* Beverly Hills, Calif.: Sage Publications, 1977.

Lyons, D., et al. *Multiple Welfare Benefits in New York City.* Rand Report no. 2002-HEW, 1976.

McKinnon, H. "Legal Barriers to the Siting of Human Service Facilities." Unpublished research report, Princeton University, Princeton, N.J., 1976.

Mills, E., and Oates, W. "The Theory of Local Public Services and Finance: Its Relevance to Urban Fiscal and Zoning Behavior." in E. Mills and W. Oates, eds., *Fiscal Zoning and Land-Use Controls.* Lexington, Mass.: Lexington Books, D.C. Heath and Company, 1975.

Naples, M. "Equity in the Representation of Social Service Facilities." Unpublished research paper, Princeton University, Princeton, N.J., 1976.

Olsen, E. "Transfers in Cash or In-Kind." *American Economic Review* 61(1971): 220–224.

Portney, P., and Sonstelie, J. "Profit-Maximizing Communities and the Theory of Local Public Expenditure." *Journal of Urban Economics* 5(1978):263–277.

Rabkin, J.G. "Public Attitudes toward Mental Illness: A Review of the Literature." *Schizophrenia Bulletin* 10(1974):9–33.

Scott, A.J. "Location-Allocation Systems: A Review." *Geographical Analysis* 2(1970):95–119.

Shurman, L.I.; Hardwick, C.P.; and Huber, G.A. "Location of Ambulatory Care Clinics in a Metropolitan Area." *Health Services Resaerch* (Summer 1973): 121–138.

Smeeding, T. "The Economic Well-Being of Low-Income Households: Implications for Income Inequality and Poverty." In M. Moon and E. Smolensky, eds., *Improving Measures of Economic Well-being.* New York: Academic Press, 1977.

Smith, V.K., and Howitt, G. *The Economic Status of Michigan AFDC Families: An Analysis of Income and Benefit Recipients.* Lansing: Department of Social Services, State of Michigan, 1976.

Smolensky, E.; Stiefel, L.; Schmundt, M.; and Plotnick, R. "In-Kind Transfers and the Size Distribution of Income." In M. Moon and E. Smolensky, eds. *Improving Measure of Economic Well-Being.* New York: Academic Press, 1977.

Toregas, C., et al. "The Location of Emergency Service Facilities." *Operations Research* 19(1971):1363–1373.

U.S. Department of Health, Education, and Welfare. Social Security Administration, Office of Policy, Office of Research and Statistics. *Public Assistance Recipients and Cash Payments, by State and County.* Washington, D.C.: U.S. Government Printing Office, 1978a.

——— . *Supplemental Security Income, State and County Data.* Washington, D.C.: U.S. Government Printing Office, 1978b.

White, A. "Locational Analysis for Public Facilities: Models, Patterns, and Processes." Ph.D. dissertation, University of Pennsylvania, 1976.

——— . "Accessibility and Public Facility Location." *Economic Geography* 55(1979):18–35.

White, M. "Fiscal Zoning in Fragmented Metropolitan Areas." In E. Mills and W. Oates, eds. *Fiscal Zoning and Land Use Controls.* Lexington, Mass.: Lexington Books, D.C. Heath and Company, 1975.

Williamson, J.B. "Beliefs about the Welfare Poor." *Sociology and Social Research* 2(1974):163–175.

Williamson, J.B., et al. *Strategies against Poverty in America.* New York: Schenkman, 1975.

Wolch, J.R. "The Residential Location Behavior of Service-Dependent House-holds." Ph.D. dissertation, Princeton University, 1978.

_____ . "The Residential Location of the Service-Dependent Poor." *Annals, Association of American Geography* 70(1970):330–341.

_____ . "The Location of Service-Dependent Households in Urban Areas." *Economic Geography* 57(1981):52–67.

Wolch, J.; Gabriel, S.; and Dear, M.J. "Intrametropolitan Disparities and the Service-Dependent Sector." Research Proposal to the National Science Foundation, University of Southern California, Los Angeles, 1980.

Wolpert, J. "The Agglomeration of Public Service Facilities in Urban Areas." Research Proposal to the National Science Foundation, Princeton University, Princeton, N.J., 1975.

Wolpert, J. "Regressive Siting of Public Facilities." *Natural Resources Journal* 16(1976):103–115.

Wolpert, J.; Dear, M.J.; and Crawford, R. "Satellite Mental Health Facilties." *Annals, Association of American Geographers* 65(1975):24–35.

Wolpert, J., and Wolpert, E. "The Relocation of Released Mental Hospital Patients into Residential Communities." *Policy Sciences* 7(1976):31–51.

3

Academic Models and Public Policy: The Distribution of City Services in New York

Mary Bryna Sanger

Questions about how public services are distributed within the city are increasingly addressed by academics, policy analysts, and most recently organized public interests. Over the last decade research designed to test hypotheses about the nature and determinants of service distributions has proliferated. Recent work has achieved substantial methodological refinement; major improvements in the range, type, and quality of data; and increasing sophistication in the specification of the research questions. In some respects, however, the results of these efforts have been disappointing. Academics had hoped to identify models capable of explaining existing distribution patterns that would have a high degree of generalizability. Instead, the preponderance of the literature shows a picture of unpatterned inequalities that vary profoundly by service and jurisdiction (Rich 1979).

The success of efforts to identify and explain the patterns of service allocations in cities has serious implications for academic theory and public policy. Patterned inequalities undermine social stability and may affect residential and commercial location decisions. Ultimately these factors have implications for a city's tax base. In a period of growing fiscal constraint and retrenchment at all levels of government, interest is increasingly focused on distributional issues. The question of who gets what, and why, is therefore a matter of great political, economic, and legal consequence.

Unprecedented budgetary retrenchment in many U.S. cities is having a significant impact on service delivery. Bureaucrats and politicians are under considerable pressure to control and justify aggregate service expenditures. Fewer resources mean that emphasis shifts to a concern with the efficiency of service-delivery systems. The response of organized public interests to fixed or reduced resources in their communities is increased concern about the determinants of relative shares and mix of available resources to different neighborhoods and social groups.

New York City provides a particularly salient example. Its budget contractions have been severe and obligatory. In addition, in 1975 the city's charter was revised, requiring the alteration of previously existing arrangements for service provision. The success of these reforms depends principally on the appropriateness of the description and diagnosis of previous methods used in determining service distributions.

Therefore, this chapter begins by introducing the recent charter reforms instituted in New York City and then presents the results of an analysis of the determinants of New York City's service distributions for fire, police, and sanitation in 1969-1970.[1] These results highlight some of the more important academic issues surrounding the prevailing models of urban-service distribution. The chapter concludes with an assessment of the usefulness of this literature for evaluating the potential effectiveness of New York City's reforms.

Charter Revision in New York City

In the late 1960s decentralization seemed to be an idea whose time had come. Grass-roots political activity and neighborhood concepts gained considerable support among disparate economic and political constituencies. A wide variety of experiments were initiated in cities around the country with varying degrees of success, including Little City Halls in Boston and the Office of Neighborhood Government in New York. (Nordlinger 1972; Yin and Yates 1975). These experiments attempted to respond to the pressures of a multitude of city constituencies claiming that the benefits of city services were not equally distributed. Early perceptions were that services varied in quality and/or quantity along racial, economic, and political lines.

Experiments in decentralization during this period therefore reflected a commonly held diagnosis of city ills: service bureaucracies were unresponsive, insulated, and unaccountable; and the benefits of city services were not equally enjoyed. A pilot program in New York called Command Decentralization (Shalala and Merget 1974) was initiated in response to these concerns and was administered by the Office of Neighborhood Government (Lindsay 1970). Shortly thereafter, in 1972, the state legislature created a Charter Revision Commission for New York City.

Inequitable distribution of services was not, to be sure, the only interest of those who sought to revise the New York City charter. There was also the view that the "superagencies" made bureaucrats too remote from their clients and that existing political structures remained recalcitrant and too rigid to permit meaningful community consultation on a myriad of service-delivery issues. Revising the charter was seen as a way of providing a new apparatus to promote meaningful citizen participation and ensure responsiveness by city bureaucracies. The view was that institutionalized structural changes were necessary to bring about the desired operational changes.

In the spring of 1975 the commission made public its preliminary recommendations. Following further revision and public hearings, the commission presented its recommendations to the electorate on the November ballot in the form of ten questions representing amendments to the existing city charter. Six passed emphatically and were subsequently adopted in what is now an essentially new charter. Although the revisions include a wide range of reforms, among them fiscal and budget reforms, as well as uniform land-use and planning changes, the following discussion will highlight only those innovations that specifically relate to service-delivery issues.

A key goal of the charter revisions—one that was strongly supported by the electorate—was the implementation of *coterminality*. The charter revisions created fifty-nine community boards of the previously existing sixty-two, broadened their mandate and required the use of identical geographic boundaries for these districts (or neighborhoods) and for specified service-delivery districts. No longer could police precincts, fire districts, and other service areas conform to their own historical or management configurations.[2] Coterminality makes each community or neighborhood within the city the relevant jurisdiction for the allocation of most city services. This eliminates the confusion caused by overlapping district lines of multiple service agencies, makes agency operations more visible, and enhances community identification. Further, coterminality provides a basis for better interaction and communication between neighborhoods and relevant agency personnel.

The charter revisions do not leave the question of communication between communities and agency personnel to chance. A central element is the mandate that each community district have a District Service Cabinet on which representatives from city service agencies and the community boards sit. The language of the charter calls specifically for the following:

> The head of each designated agency shall assign to each such local service district at least one official with managerial responsibilities involving the exercise of independent judgment in the scheduling, allocation and assignment of personnel and equipment and the evaluation of performance or the management and planning of programs. Each such official shall have operating or line authority over agency programs, personnel and facilities within the local service district. [New York City Charter, Section 2704.d]

These district supervisors, along with a community-appointed district service manager and the chairperson of the Community Board, serve together and consult on service-delivery issues (including community complaints and priorities) on a District Service Cabinet.

In addition to requiring District Service Cabinets and coterminality, the charter also requires agencies to commence geographic budgeting and to submit agency service statements. Geographic budgeting mandates that city service agencies include in the annual expense budget proposed expenditures for each unit of appropriations in each service district and that a service statement be provided that includes the basis for allocation to each local service district of each agency.

Finally, the last innovation relevant to service delivery concerns the increased participation and responsibility of the already existing Community

Boards. This is to be achieved partly through required informal consultation on the departmental budget estimates, as well as in board hearings and recommendations on the departmental estimates. Responsibility and participation are also strengthened by the board's authority to appoint the chairperson of the District Service Cabinet (the district service manager).

Considerable optimism accompanied the early work of the commission in developing the charter revisions. Since the time of their mandate, however, New York City has experienced tremendous fiscal upheavals resulting in changes of political legitimacy and public-policy priorities. The success of the adopted charter revisions depends therefore on two quite different conditions: first, whether or not the changes respond appropriately to the causes of existing disparities or inequities in service distributions and, second, whether or not in the present political climate any strong coalition exists capable of sustaining a meaningful commitment to achieving the charter's goals.

This chapter deals more directly with the first conditions for success, while hypothesizing on the degree to which the necessary political will actually exists to implement the changes properly. The next section, however, will present the results of a study I did on the distribution of city services in New York in an attempt to evaluate the usefulness of existing models of service distribution. I will then attempt to use that analysis to evaluate the future of the charter revisions and service delivery in New York.

City Services in New York City

In 1971 the city administrator's office in New York City released a study entitled "Municipal Expenditures by Neighborhood" (Marquez 1971). This study developed a methodology and translated citywide service allocations into sixty-two neighborhood components. These crude neighborhood expenditure figures were estimated by using the costs of major inputs of service and then allocating them to specific neighborhoods. These aggregate neighborhood expenditure figures for each city service provided the data I needed to derive my independent variables. I calculate per capita expenditures for police, fire, and sanitation services for each neighborhood and develop a model that explains the existing distributions as a function of supply and demand (the benefit principle), as well as of the political and public-policy goals of the executive.

The study treats demands as a function of service quality, individual income and wealth (ability or willingness to pay), indirect charges such as taxes, a vector of variables relating to an individual's tastes and preferences (socioeconomic characteristics), and another vector relating to the locational characteristics of the neighborhood (needs). Supply is treated as a function of service quanity, a vector of service conditions affecting input requirements, and a vector of quality characteristics (inherent quality dimensions specific to the service in question).

In addition, vectors of political and public-policy variables are included, testing the hypothesis that market criteria in the public sector are modified to include additional political and public-policy goals. For example, the policy variables tested the hypothesis that decision makers pursue public-policy goals such as compensation or redistribution in their allocation decisions.

The theoretical model tested, therefore, integrates two separate, yet related, components. One includes demand and supply variables predicting a result based on the benefit principle (market equity). Although actual allocations are not a result of such marketlike factors alone, they do offer a solution that decision makers consider along with political and public-policy goals. Therefore, I hypothesized that the knowledge of efficient service provision, in conjunction with more pragmatic political and public-policy goals, would determine the final service distributions to neighborhoods within the city.

The final estimating equations were derived using a stepwise regression with a large data pool. In order to provide the model with the greatest potential for success, the strongest predictors were selected for inclusion in each equation after I examined the correlation matrix and tested a large number of independent variables. Three major sources provided the data necessary to derive the independent variables: the New York City Planning Commission, the Service Delivery Component of the New York City Neighborhood Project (Barton et al. 1977), and the Official Canvass of Votes from the City Record. The final variables selected were service specific, suggested by the model and limited by the available data (for example, no quality variables or proxies were obtainable). The results are presented in table 3-1. The final equations explained over 70 percent of the variation in per capita police expenditures, over 80 percent in fire expenditures, and approximately 46 percent in sanitation expenditures.

Although the model proved useful in explaining service variations, the distributional patterns nonetheless were difficult to interpret. For example, it was impossible to conclude with any certainty whether a significant variable reflected demand- or supply-side considerations, since a single variable often related to both supply and demand. Further, the lack of service-quality proxies and the lack of confidence about the use of expenditures as a proxy for service level served to reduce the confidence one might have in the conclusions. Nevertheless, the findings are strongly suggestive and do provide an important opportunity to examine the central theoretical limitations of existing models of service distribution.

In New York City in 1969-1970, police and fire expenditures were found to be strongly related to income. Contrary to the expectation that an underclass existed—that low-income areas would fare worst—there was a strong negative relationship between median income of a neighborhood and its police and fire expenditures, and a strong positive relationship between high income and expenditures. This finding, for both police and fire expenditures, is consistent with a hypothesis that both high- and low-income groups were receiving favored treatment in the provision of the protective services. The implication here is

Table 3-1
Summary of Results: Regression of Independent Variables for Per Capita Police,
Fire, and Sanitation Expenditures for Sixty-one Neighborhoods, New York City,
Fiscal 1969-1970

Variable or Statistic	Regression Coefficients for Police Expenditures	Regression Coefficients for Fire Expenditures	Regression Coefficients for Sanitation Expenditures
Median family income	-.0205*** (-3.27)[a]	-.0106**** (-3.92)	-
Percentage of families $15,000+	3.3882** (2.40)	1.4852** (2.43)	-
Average assessed valuation	.0002**** (7.84)	.0001**** (12.60)	.0003**** (6.11)
Percentage change in population 1960-1970	-[b]	-.0001****	-
Nonresidential acres	-	-.0059*** (-3.42)	-
Population density	259.4663 (.25)	1611.5867** (2.43)	1006.0820*** (3.11)
Percentage residential acres	-1.0231*** (2.80)	-	-
Total acres	-	-	-0.0005 (-.65)
Political participation			-828.9141** (-2.48)
Constant	217.097	94.826	20.142
R^2	.704	.821	.458

[a]The coefficient in parenthesis is the value of T. The asterisks indicate the level of significance where: **** represents significance at the .001 level or higher; *** represents significance at the .01 level or higher; ** represents significance at the .02 level or higher; * represents significance at the .05 level or higher.

[b]Only those variables with values indicated were included in each regression equation so as to maximize the predictive potential of each model.

that middle-income areas fared the worst. Neither race nor political variables proved significant when the effects of income were taken into account. Findings for sanitation services did not support any conclusion that economic, political, or racial favoritism or discrimination were at work. Contrary to expectation, political participation proved to be significant and *negative,* suggesting a preference in service delivery to the politically disenfranchised.

For police and fire services, both of which are so centrally tied to property protection, we would expect ecological or service-condition variables to be significant. New York City police services were, in fact, strongly related to the average assessed valuation of the property. This was consistent with a notion of service needs that argues that highly valued property requires greater protection. Evidence of the highest assessed valuation was found in areas of commercial and industrial concentrations. City areas with high concentration of commercial activities are frequently areas with concentrations of high-income residential properties as well. Average assessed valuation was also highly significant and positive in explaining the distribution of both fire and sanitation services. Another indicator of service need, percentage of residential acres in the neighborhood, proved to be important for police services, having the expected negative coefficient.

Fire and sanitation expenditures were found to be strongly correlated with population density, another variable related to service conditions. Sanitation expenditures were also found to be negatively related to total acres in the neighborhood. However, the coefficient was not significant.

Findings for police and fire expenditures are consistent with the argument that differential service treatment by income class characterizes service patterns. This particular kind of service-distribution pattern (U-shaped by income) has been found elsewhere (Levy et al. 1974). All three services appear to have distribution patterns consistent with some notion of service "need." However, these findings were generated by an analysis based on market criteria. The success of the model in explaining the variance indicates that in New York City service allocations, as implied by neighborhood expenditures, *are* consistent with the model tested. These findings, however, might also support models that argue that overt discrimination or neighborhood conditions ("needs") determine allocations.

Prevailing Models

Most of the recent literature explains the distribution of city services as a function of one or more of three behavioral models (Lineberry 1977). The first stresses the importance of overt discrimination or, alternatively, of favoritism to certain groups in the city. Sometimes known as the *underclass hypothesis,* it posits that decision makers respond to economic, racial, and/or political power in their allocation decisions. Since these factors are often found together and generally have substantial sociospatial dimensions, researchers have attempted to separate out the joint effects of race, income, and political power to explain variations in service levels. The results of such research have been mixed, indicating different patterns for different jurisdictions. Even within jurisdictions different services appear to be distributed differently (Rich 1979).

The second model posits a rational allocative process that distributes services according to some notion of service need. Represented by more rational economic and technical criteria, this process considers some index of neighborhood conditions. Predictive variables tend to be service specific and reflect a variety of physical, social, and economic conditions that affect service delivery. Lineberry (1977) refers to this hypothesis as the *ecological hypothesis*. It is the attributes of neighborhoods themselves that explain observed patterns. As with the underclass model, research findings in support of this position have been far from conclusive.

The third model—and the one that appears to be enjoying the most academic popularity—posits a set of bureaucratic decision rules (BDRs) that dictates service-delivery patterns. Internally generated, these bureaucratic decision rules are seen as both organizationally and service specific and as varying by city and bureaucracy. Proponents of this view argue that the use of decision rules characterizes all large bureaucracies and that the content of these rules reflects the internal reward and incentive structure of the organization. Decision rules routinize behavior, simplify tasks, and provide a convenient and economical basis for action. Rules of this sort are devised by bureaucrats and service personnel with some consideration of professional norms, demand, need, equity, and perhaps even politics.

Neither the underclass nor the ecological hypothesis supplies a satisfactory explanation for the patterns observed in New York City or, for that matter, for patterns observed elsewhere (Rich 1979). Indeed, there are significant variables in my study that could be consistent with either hypothesis. The BDR model provides a more consistent and useful explanation of how services are distributed in many jurisdictions since both ecological and underclass explanations are largely subsumed by it.

In most reformed urban bureaucracies, large service-providing agencies operate relatively autonomously and independent of both executive and constituent politics. They are staffed almost exclusively by civil servants who are largely immune to the day-to-day political pressures of elected officials. Any basis for decision making must be implemented through these service bureaucracies. Agency personnel in reformed urban bureaucracies make decisions on the bases of historical precedent, convenience, demand, pressure, and professional norms. Presumably they trade off these multiple criteria, since they cannot maximize more than one at a time.

Several researchers (Levy et al. 1974; Lineberry 1977; Antunes and Plumlee 1977, pp. 313-312; Jones et al. 1978, pp. 332-368; Nivola 1978, pp. 59-81) have been able to explain unexpected findings in this context. With rare exception, however, strong empirical support has not been available. Rather, the explanation is born out of some combination of knowledge and informed hypotheses about how urban bureaucracies operate. In that sense the BDR hypothesis is a residual explanation. Nevertheless, it does explain how both the underclass and ecological explanations could be consistent with an analysis of a given service distribution, since they represent theories explaining *outcomes*, whereas the BDR theory explains the *process* by which these outcomes come about. The content of the rules themselves is a byproduct of a variety of motivating principles or models of how services ought to be distributed. Indeed, the rules may incorporate within them operating principles suggested by the underclass and ecological explanations.

The BDR, then, describes a process consistent with many different outcomes. The real challenge to students of urban-service distributions will be to develop models that identify and explain the content of the rules themselves. This task, however, may be far more onerous than any of the intellectual problems yet identified in the service-distribution literature.

Identifying the determinants of an agency's BDRs would require a complicated investigation of the historical context of past decisions. Both actors and rules change over time. Past decisions impose constraints on present decisions. For example, a historical decision rule granting capital expenditures to favored groups may result in an inequitable configuration of police precincts throughout the city. The existence of a fixed plant location as a result of previous organizational processes and actors imposes constraints on the rules of new organizations and actors. Decision making becomes marginal—the superimposition of new rules on old ones. The resulting outcomes are therefore the stepchildren of a multiplicity of actors and decisions over time. The resulting distributions may very well have been produced by pure rules or even single rules, which, however, have been superimposed through a historical process. The result is a very complex pattern of outcomes.

The problem for the researcher lies in having to infer what the rules must have been to have created an existing distribution pattern. These inferences are likely to be ad hoc. The research required to verify the identification of the rules would likely make even the most eager researcher shrink from the task. Without such research, however, the causal process that created rule superimposition would never be uncovered, and the explanation of the observed pattern would be *unnecessarily* ad hoc.

Thus, although the BDR model does not help identify the rules that have resulted in existing distributions, it does fulfill the more modest role of suggesting the processes that explain varying and inconsistent results. It has the added feature of identifying the appropriate political responses by public officials when the "facts" indicate unacceptable distribution patterns. A BDR explanation of existing distributions, whether unanticipated or not, suggests that bureaucratic reform lies at the heart of service-distribution problems. Bureaucracies would have to be altered and internal incentive structures changed in order to effect different outcomes.

City bureaucracies are, however, extremely resistant to change. Bureaucrats are insulated from political accountability through the civil service, and public bureaucracies seem to retain an internal logic of their own. Although it is theoretically possible to change the manner in which bureaucratic organizations function, in practice, policies that rely on that kind of change for their success are usually ineffective.

What route, then, should a public official take in response to growing discontent of organized public interests with service distributions? Recent revisions of the New York City Charter (described earlier) are designed to address just these issues. These revisions mandate four programs relevant to the distribution of public services; coterminality (of neighborhoods and service districts), management decentralization, geographic-based budgeting, and agency service statements. Based on the view that highly centralized public bureaucracies are unresponsive and inefficient, the mandated revisions seek to involve neighborhoods directly in service allocation and make public-service bureaucracies accountable to them for their allocation decisions.

Five years after the revised charter was adopted, virtually all mandated services have completed coterminality of service districts. There are fifty-nine community boards, each of which has a direct manager who participates regularly in meetings with municipal-service people (on the District Service Cabinet) to communicate needs and voice complaints. In addition, by January 1981 geographic-based budgeting is scheduled to be achieved.

The reforms in New York implicitly accept the appropriateness of the BDR model. Specifically, the charter revisions seek to address the service-delivery problems that stem from highly centralized and insulated bureaucracies. Whether current allocations are the result of an intentional process reflecting some rational assessment of needs or merely the unintentional byproducts of the application of a multiplicity of bureaucratic decision rules, mandated programs under the charter seek to make bureaucrats accountable.

Altering internal bureaucratic incentives and changing the internal logic of an organization are difficult goals. Nevertheless, geographical budgeting will require that agency heads develop detailed operational indicators of service allocations through the Agency Service Statements. They will be required to justify egregious differentials. In order for this to be done, decision rules, or at least a needs-based allocation formula, must be made explicit. Once the determinations of allocations are specific, they will be opened to public scrutiny. Competing notions of need will then enter the political process since the city council must vote on the city budget. Making decision rules explicit will, therefore, make their content a matter of debate. This will tend to minimize the possibility of blatantly discriminatory criteria or plainly inadequate outcomes.

Charter Revisions and the Future of Service
Delivery in New York

Two questions suggest themselves in an assessment of the impact on services of management decentralization and the reorganization of service-delivery mechanisms in New York City. (1) Will service bureaucracies respond at the local level by delegating decision-making authority to district supervisors? (2) Will communities mobilize sufficiently to apply pressure to nudge recalcitrant agencies? Few data are available so far, but difficulties may already be evident. Two preliminary reviews of management decentralization have been conducted, for the Department of Parks and Recreation and for the Bureau of Highway Operations.[3] The findings, though somewhat agency specific, do suggest more generic problems in altering centralized decision making and, thus, extant BDRs. Some of these difficulties stem from the severe fiscal constraints imposed by the city's efforts to close the budget gap, others from the unwillingness or inability of agencies to provide resources and information to local district service administrators. A last category may be attributed to the lack of training and competence of local supervisors to make allocation decisions.

A brief review of the findings of the task-force review of the Bureau of Highway Operations will serve to highlight the serious impediments that must be overcome if neighborhood service-delivery outcomes are to be altered. The task force found, for example, that although a district foreman assigned to a neighborhood had discretion in the allocation of work crews to perform minor repairs within the district, he had little to do with developing a comprehensive street-maintenance policy in the district. Any discretion over the volume of repair materials he received, or decisions about resurfacing or large-scale wear-and-tear functions, remain within the purview of a borough superintendent or the central office. This was also true for decisions about which streets should be reconstructed. District foremen, therefore, saw themselves as nothing more than glorified gang foremen with few significant responsibilities necessary for altering the condition of streets within their districts.

The failure to achieve meaningful decentralization of authority was exacerbated by the city's fiscal condition, which has resulted in attrition of the work force and a continuing deterioration in the condition and level of repair of needed equipment. District foremen described a crisis atmosphere that led to frustration and a sense of powerlessness. Borough Operations officers were quoted as saying that district community boards within their jurisdictions clamored for their fair or equal share of material allocations, (for example, of asphalt) and that the easiest way to respond has been to allocate equally regardless of need.

Exacerbating the district foreman's lack of managerial status in responding to community needs is the burden of clerical responsibilities. Clerical support is inadequate, and highway repairmen often staff the district office and function as clerks. Trained manpower is therefore not used in maintenance activities because of resource constraints. Additional impediments to successful implementation of management decentralization were reported to be the lack of information systems necessary to apprise local district foremen of activities in their districts that are centrally planned. This puts foremen in difficult situations

with community boards that question their status since the board often has
more information on planned projects through direct contact with the central
office than do the district foremen.

These examples illustrate constraints imposed by the department itself
because of its historic centralized operating structure. Interviews with members of the Community Board Assistance Unit indicate that, not surprisingly,
central management within most service bureaucracies have been reluctant to
delegate decision-making authority and has been uncomfortable with the concept of management decentralization. A combination of limited commitment by
operating managers in many agencies and severely constrained resources has
resulted in limited impact. The results of both task-force studies suggest that
district service administrators are not adequately trained for management
authority and also lack from their supervisors to assume such authority. Only
the Sanitation Department had contracted with the city's management-training
institute to train their local service administrators for their new management
function.[4]

Constraints on management decentralization also are due to the inherent
complexities of many agency activities. Not all services are easily packageable
and allocated as discrete units on a neighborhood basis. Streets and facilities
beneath the streets, for example, cross neighborhood boundaries. Central coordination of activities by multiple agencies to open and use the streets and
facilities below them must be coordinated and planned to minimize disruption
and costs. An extensive coordinating network is needed to mediate disputes
over claims by different agencies and jurisdictions over the tearing up and resurfacing of streets. Central coordination is therefore crucial. Many similar
circumstances of the need for centralized operation are common to other city
service agencies. However, the extent of the failure to delegate decision-making
authority adequately to local service administrators seems fraught with deeper
and more endemic bureaucratic logic.

The model for charter revision was the Office of Neighborhood Government
Experiment, which was implemented on a limited scale in eight districts in 1972.
An evaluation of this district-service experiment resulted in findings that, inter-
preted pessimistically, indicated:

> (1) It is extremely difficult to get centralized departments to delegate
> more authority to their local administrators to permit them to coor-
> dinate activities in dealing with local problems. . . . (2) It is not possible
> to improve service delivery by setting up a powerless district manager
> and cabinet. A few successful projects don't indicate an overall poten-
> tial. . . . (3) The administrative decentralization did not improve the
> accessibility of city agencies to the public. The improved responsive-
> ness of city agencies experienced by some of those who did make
> contact with them . . . involved only 2% of the adult population. . . .
> [Barton et al. 1977, pp. 253–254]

The unimpressive results of the experiment were explained by idiosyncratic circumstances, such as a feud between the mayor and the city council and inadequacy of resources. But the theoretical literature and empirical evaluations show that massive bureaucratic reform is unlikely to occur except under very unusual circumstances (Weiss 1980). The question here is what the role of structural reform of bureaucratic decision making will be in altering the distribution of city services. The role of executive and community political support is clearly important. New York Mayor Koch has abandoned active political pursuit of implementation and monitoring of charter compliance as a priority.[5] Few agency commissioners are committed to management decentralization, and communities have not yet mobilized to apply significant pressure.

Although proponents of the charter revisions argued that instituting Community Boards and District Service Cabinets would bring government closer to the people and make bureaucracies responsive to communities, evidence of such significant impact is not available. It is more likely to be the mandated budget-reporting changes that will serve to enhance the bargaining interests of neighborhoods. Early reports on decentralization experiments indicate unimpressive results in altering any fundamental bureaucratic relationships (Barton et al. 1977; Yates 1974). Organized public interests, however, can for the first time enter the debate on decision rules once agency heads are required to justify them.[6]

Notes

1. The original research was funded by the U.S. Department of Housing and Urban Development, and the results were originally reported in Mary Bryna Sanger, "Public Services: An Investigation of Intracity Distribution Patterns" (Ph.D. dissertation, Brandeis University, 1976).

2. Coterminality is virtually completed for most mandated services. The police department has received an extension and does not expect to be fully coterminous until 1982. The fire department has been exempted from compliance.

3. An Internal Task Force on Management Decentralization was put together. It included representatives from the Community Board Assistance Unit (CBAU) in the mayor's office, the mayor's Office of Management and Budget, the mayor's Office of Operations, the Department of Transportation, and the Department of Parks and Recreation. The results reported here are from draft documents of the final reports. They have not been published, and the findings may ultimately differ from those reported here.

4. The Urban Academy is a nonprofit institute with an exclusive contract with the City of New York for management training of personnel.

5. One of the victims of recent budget cutbacks was the CBAU, which had been located in the mayor's office.

6. Not all observers view this as a positive development. An examination of fiscal politics indicates that the prospects of decentralization are less rosy than generally believed. Extensive decentralization is likely to bring under scrutiny allocation decisions that are currently made by "non-decision making." A gain in rationality therefore is questionable, given the politicization and district self-serving that will probably develop around these issues. Moreover, a reduction of redistributive services and, contrary to common expectations, an increased polarization in the city are also likely consequences of widespread decentralization (Sunshine 1974, pp. 273-299).

References

Antunes, G., and Plumlee, J. 1977. "The Distribution of an Urban Public Service: Ethnicity, Socioeconomic Status and Bureaucracy as Determinants of the Quality of Neighborhood Streets." *Urban Affairs Quarterly* 12:312-332.

Barton, A., et al. 1977. *Decentralizing City Government: An Evaluation of the New York City District Manager Experiment.* Lexington, Mass.: Lexington Books, D.C. Heath and Company.

Jones, B., et al. 1978. "Service Delivery Rules and the Distribution of Local Government Services: Three Detroit Bureaucracies." *Journal of Politics* 40:332-368.

Levy, E., et al. 1974. *Urban Outcomes: Schools, Streets and Libraries.* Berkeley: University of California Press.

Lindsay, J. 1970. "A Plan for Neighborhood Government for New York City." New York: Office of the Mayor.

Lineberry, R. 1977. *Equality and Public Policy.* Beverly Hills, Calif.: Sage Publications.

Marquez, C. 1971. "Municipal Expenditures by Neighborhood." Report prepared for the City Administrator's Office, City of New York.

Mladenka, K., and Hill, K. 1978. "The Distribution of Urban Police Services." *Journal of Politics* 40:112-133.

Nivola, P. 1978. "Distributing a Municipal Service: A Case Study of Housing Inspection." *Journal of Politics* 40:58-81.

Nordlinger, E. 1972. *Decentralizing the City. A Study of Boston's Little City Halls.* Cambridge, Mass.: MCI Press.

Rich, R. 1979. "Distribution of Services: Studying the Product of Urban Policy Making." In D. Marshall, ed., *Urban Policy Making.* Beverly Hills, Calif.: Sage Publications.

Shalala, D., and Merget, A. 1974. "Decentralization Plans." In T. Murphy and C. Warren, eds., *Organizing Public Services in Metropolitan America,* pp. 153-178. Lexington, Mass.: Lexington Books, D.C. Heath and Company.

Sunshine, J. 1974. "Decentralization: Fiscal Chimera or Budgetary Boom?" In W. Hawley and D. Rogers, eds. *Improving the Quality of Urban Management.* Beverly Hills, Calif.: Sage Publications.

Weiss, C. 1980. "Efforts at Bureaucratic Reform: What Have We Learned?" In C. Weiss and A. Barton, eds. *Making Bureaucracies Work,* pp. 7–26. Beverly Hills, Calif.: Sage Publications.

Weiss, C., and Barton, A., eds. 1980. *Making Bureaucracies Work.* Beverly Hills, Calif.: Sage Publications.

Yates, D. 1974. *Neighborhood Democracy.* Lexington, Mass.: Lexington Books, D.C. Heath and Company.

Yin, R., and Yates, D. 1975. *Street-Level Governments: Assessing Decentralization and Urban Systems.* Lexington, Mass.: Lexington Books, D.C. Heath and Company.

4 Bureaucratic Environments, Efficiency, and Equity in Urban-Service-Delivery Systems

Joseph P. Viteritti

The study of urban services has generally proceeded along two distinct paths, which have rarely crossed. As one reviewer of the literature has pointed out, there are two common approaches to the study of municipal services: an economic approach, which concentrates on the efficiency and productivity of local delivery systems, and a "more recent political approach [that] focuses on the distribution of services to identifiable demographic groups and asks who gains and who loses as a consequence of delivery practices" (Goldenberg 1979). Despite the fact that a more integrated approach is still in an early stage of development, the literature on urban-service distribution is substantial enough that it is possible to discern some patterns in its results. These patterns suggest that bureaucratic variables have a more significant impact on service distribution than do political variables, and that the outcome of the distributive process is, on balance, fair or at least nondiscriminatory with respect to the allocations made among different social groups (Jones 1980; Lineberry 1977; Levy, Meltsner, and Wildavsky 1974; Antunes and Plumlee 1977; Antunes and Mladenka 1976).

It may be that general statements such as these tell us less of what we know about bureaucratic decision making than of what we think about the political process as a whole. Such statements carry the assumption that bureaucratic decision making is something quite distinct from political decision making and that the former is more likely than the latter to result in equitable outcomes. It brings to mind the traditional analytical distinction between politics and administration that was once popular within the discipline of political science. Those who believed in the politics-administration dichotomy perceived career civil servants who worked in the bureaucracy as neutral participants in the governmental process who were to limit their personal judgments to matters concerned with administrative technique. All such judgments were to be made according to the criteria of operational efficiency. The current research literature tells us, however, that such technical administrative decisions have a significant impact in determining the more political question of who gets what services.

My own research on the subject is in basic agreement with the general findings that have been cited (Viteritti 1973, 1979). It suggests that bureaucratic institutions do play an important role in determining who gets what at the local level and that there is an aspect of administrative decision making that is distinct from the ordinary political process. It also proposes that when these institutions act apart from the influence of local political forces, the outcomes of the decisions are efficient from a managerial perspective and equitable with regard to service distributions. However, lest these general conclusions become part of an emerging conventional wisdom on the subject, I would like to issue a warning that we be careful not to overstate the case for the politics-administration dichotomy.

Bureaucracy is only part of a total institutional arrangement that shapes our governmental process. Its capacity to provide public goods and services in a fair and equitable manner is dependent on a set of circumstances that is produced not only by an internal dynamic that is indigenous to administrative institutions, but also by the interaction of these institutions with the external political environment. Thus the key issue in the study of urban-service distributions is not whether it is political or bureaucratic variables that decide the outcomes. Instead, the course of inquiry must seek to determine those aspects of the distributive process decided by political factors, those aspects decided by administrative factors, and why this distinction matters. It must end with the definition of a set of internal and external environmental conditions under which bureaucratic institutions are able to make distributive decisions that advance efficiency and equity. These are the issues I intend to address in this chapter.

Before this line of discussion proceeds, however, it is essential to examine the assumptions implicit in the questions themselves. To begin with, we have assumed that there is a tension between government decisions that are political and social outcomes that are equitable. If such a tension really does exist, then it becomes more relevant to discuss those characteristics that supposedly distinguish political decisions from administrative or bureaucratic ones. If the criterion of efficiency is the distinguishing feature of bureaucratic decisions, as has been suggested, then we must clarify how administrative efficiency is related to social equity.

Why Politics Tends to Be Inequitable

By *equity* I mean a distribution of goods and services allocated among individuals or groups on the basis of social need. This definition is significantly different from a strict egalitarian one, which would require the same distribution of goods and services to all people.[1] It is more concerned with giving individuals who are not of equal social status an equal opportunity for social advancement. In this sense the definition of equity that I have chosen places the state in a compensatory role. It calls for a distributive process that favors the poor. This standard of equity is quite consistent with the social values commonly espoused in a liberal democratic state. However, both history and logic tell us that the criteria that are used to define these social principles are not the same criteria by which the political process works. Thus not only is there a tension between the two, but they are in fact antithetical.

Political decision making is a process that operates in response to the forces of influence and power. The poor, who would be the key beneficiaries of the distributive process that has been advocated, do not enjoy significant levels of power or influence. Several decades of political-science research have shown us that the poor, in general, do not participate in public life and do not possess the social requisites for successful political participation; therefore, they are unlikely to assume an active or meaningful role in the political process for some time to come (see Lane 1959; Milbrath and Goel 1977; Matthews and Prothro 1967). Perhaps the most persuasive evidence along these lines has been the failure of the national "war on poverty" to bring about the "maximum feasible participation" of the poor in local community-action efforts during the 1960s. Despite all attempts to the contrary, it was uncommon for more than 5 percent of the eligible population to turn out to vote in local poverty-program elections (Levitan 1969; Moynihan 1969). Moreover, there is little reason to believe that any semblance of political success the program might have enjoyed was adequate to alter the power structure of our central cities significantly. These prospects for the politicization of the poor would be less discouraging if political factors did not have such an important impact on the distributive process. However, contrary to what some of the current research on the subject tells us, politics does play an important role in determining who gets what at the local level.

The Dual Level of Distributive Decisions:
Why Politics Is Important

The distributive process in local government is carried out on two distinct levels. One concerns the distribution of public resources *among different types of service functions*; the other concerns the distribution of public resources *within particular service functions* (Rich 1979). The most notable distinction between these two levels of decision making involves the public officials who make the decisions. Distributions within particular services are usually decided on by administrators in the bureaucracy. Distribution of resources among different services, however, is usually determined in the legislative branch with the advice of the chief executive. The point is that the latter kind of decision tends to be made by elected officials and for this reason can usually be expected to favor those individuals or groups who have the means to influence elections. Such means might include voting power, organizational capability, and financial resources. Ultimately, then, decisions that determine the allocation of resources among services tend to be susceptible to political influence.

The reason that distributions among functions are significant from the perspective of the equity issue is straightforward. Although most local services are available to most people, certain population groups use certain kinds of services more than others do. In other words, many local government agencies, because of the kinds of functions they perform, serve a very limited clientele. Some agencies serve the poor, others address the needs of the middle class, and still others serve both. Those agencies that provide social, compensatory, and certain kinds of developmental services tend to accommodate a predominantly poor clientele. These services include health (Benson and Lund 1961), public housing, and welfare programs. Middle-class citizens tend to make less use of such services, either because they have no need for them (as with welfare) or because they enjoy the economic option of purchasing them in the private market (as with health and housing). Instead, the middle class tends to show a preference for libraries and certain kinds of recreational or cultural services.[2]

The remaining local services make up a third, perhaps larger category of functions. These are the kinds of services that are needed, wanted, and utilized by a more general population. They comprise essential local functions including protective services (police and fire); general maintenance services (sanitation, roads, and streets); and to some extent education. It is in this third category that bureaucracy plays a significant role in determining the allocation of services among various population groups. Thus, although the bureaucratic role in the distributive process is an important one, it works within clearly defined boundaries that are set within the context of the overall governmental structure.

The Internal Environment: How Bureaucracy Differs from Politics

The politics-administration dichotomy referred to previously is representative of a basic ideal after which our bureaucratic institutions have been designed. The principles on which the bureaucracy is based distinguish it from other government institutions. The concept had its origins in the nineteenth-century reform movement against corruption in local government. Advocates of reform sought to reduce the influence of local clubs through the creation of a career civil service in which administrative officials would be selected on the basis of merit and be granted life tenure. The merit system was designed to replace cronyism with competence as a standard for official recruitment. Life tenure was meant to provide administrative officials with protection from the forces of politics and the control of politicians. Thus the bureaucratic model that grew out of the nineteenth-century reform movement was not just apolitical in nature—it was antipolitical. Not only was it part of a campaign to abolish corruption in politics, but it was also an attempt to eliminate influence as a guiding principle of administrative decision making. In place of influence, the reformers would introduce a new criterion of administrative performance. That criterion was efficiency.

Although the realities of history would cause one to revise the structure and process inherent in this century-old model of bureaucracy, the principles underlying its origins are relevant to today's institutions. Our public bureaucracy is still primarily composed of a career civil service. Although the tools of scientific management have been modified to adapt to a changing technology and a growing sensitivity to the individual human needs of personnel, efficiency remains a key criterion of administrative decision making. Its prominence has been manifest in a variety of managerial forms such as systems analysis, program budgeting, management by objectives, the productivity movement, and zero-based budgeting. All these innovations have been created in order to rationalize the administrative process so that the maximum level of service can be derived from the minimal expenditure of resources. As the fiscal crisis that has troubled our inner cities continues to grow in severity, the underlying ethos common to these various approaches, that of efficiency, will remain a central factor in urban government.

Two significant questions remain to be settled. Granted that a civil-service system has been implemented, has the public bureaucracy been sufficiently depoliticized to allow administrative decision making to proceed according to strict standards of efficiency? If a concern for efficiency truly does dominate this process, how does it relate to equity? Let us consider these questions in reverse order.

Why Efficiency and Equity are Related

An administrative system is said to be *efficient* when it produces the maximum level of output for the minimum expenditure of resources. Such administrative resources might include dollars, personnel, materials, or equipment—all of which are easily measurable. In a local-government bureaucracy, output usually refers to the level of services provided to the public. Since these services do not represent a tangible product, as might be the case in a manufacturing firm, agency output (and, therefore, efficiency) is often difficult to measure (see Ross and Burkhead 1975; Hatry 1972; Balk 1978). For example, one might measure the output of a police patrol function in a number of ways, none of which is totally adequate—man-hours of patrol, miles of street patrolled, number of arrests made by the patrol force.

In many instances, management personnel in an agency use output indicators as only a partial measure of performance, giving attention also to the outcome or effectiveness of the service function (see Hatry et al. 1977). An effectiveness indicator measures the impact a particular service has on the environment in which it is provided. Police officials may, for example, measure the effectiveness of a patrol function by its impact on the reported crime rate in a given area. It is this kind of indicator, which ultimately measures the quality of life in a community, that the public usually cares most about.

All the preceding types of indicators (output, efficiency, effectiveness) represent distinct levels of measurement in an administrative process designed to convert public resources into public services. When one considers the delivery of these services from a distributive perspective, the analysis may be done on yet another dimension, that of *resource availability*. It can be said that distributions are measurable not only by the level of service provided to or consumed by a community but also by the quantity and quality of resources made available. For example, whereas the level of fire service made available to a population group may be measured by the number of fires extinguished over a period of time, it may also be measured by the number of fire companies located within a given area.

In terms of sound management practice, an optimal distribution of resources is one that would lead to an efficient and effective delivery of services. Such a distribution would not only result in the maximum level of service, but would also cause these services to have the desired impact on the environment in which they are provided. In terms of the more normative and ethical concerns of government, an optimal distribution of resources is one that would result in a fair and equitable distribution of services to the general community. The point is that the pattern of resource distribution that produces an efficient and effective delivery of services may be similar to that which satisfies the conditions of equity (see Rich 1977).

A key to good management at the local level is to ensure that public resources and services are allocated or made available to different communities on the basis of service need. *Service need* here does not refer to the service preferences that are shown by different communities for particular service functions. As already noted in a previous section, allocations of that sort are more relevant to a decision-making process that occurs outside the bureaucracy. Nor does *need* refer to the kinds of service demands that become apparent when particular community or client groups exert political pressure on an agency to obtain more service, a process that will be discussed in a later section. The term *service need* here means a set of unequal social conditions requiring that, within the context of essential public services, some communities get more than others in order to be able to maintain an acceptable quality of life for all.

The present definition of service need is related to the notion of equity that has been advanced previously. However, it is also related to managerial concerns for efficiency and effectiveness. The point here is that a distribution of goods and services among communities that is not consistent with their particular social needs is not only inequitable but also *managerially indefensible*. This point can be illustrated with the case of fire services. To have an equal distribution of fire companies around a city is inefficient because it creates a situation in low-incidence areas in which agency resources (personnel and equipment) may lie idle and not be fully utilized. It is ineffective because it creates a situation in high-incidence areas in which personnel and equipment may not be available to respond to alarms, thereby threatening the safety of such communities.

The technology of urban-service-delivery systems today gives agency managers a variety of sophisticated means of measuring the relative service needs of the communities they serve (see Viteritti 1979). The police use a hazard rating system; fire departments use incidence rates; a sanitation department might use a street-cleanliness rating; and a school system may use achievement scores. These techniques or indicators for measuring service need are part of the growing technology of service distributions used in municipal government.

One of the most immediate and apparent outcomes of this approach in local delivery systems is that it generates an allocation of goods and services that tends to favor the poor, since the poor suffer from the highest rates of crime, arson, illiteracy, and so on. It shows in a very direct sense the connection between efficiency and equity and in a more general sense the relationship between sound management and social justice. However, if one accepts this line of thinking, it has a more significant, though perhaps less apparent, implication. It means that those same social characteristics that tend to hinder the poor in a distributive process governed by politics can work to the advantage of the poor in a decision-making environment based on sound management.

How Bureaucracy Can Be Political

Critics of the classical model of bureaucracy have questioned its validity and feasibility from two perspectives. From an internal-organizational perspective, they have found the model too mechanical. They argue that the model does not consider the human element within an organization, which may modify its capacity to do business in a systematic and efficient way. From an external perspective they have criticized the model for its failure to recognize the influence outside interest or client groups may have on policymaking and how such influence may hinder efficiency or effectiveness.

Both types of criticism are legitimate. Students of human relations have certainly demonstrated the need to integrate individuals into an organization so that the goals of the organization become the goals of its workers (Argyris 1957, 1964). In order to do this, management must provide incentives for cooperation and compliance so that the work force becomes a positive factor in administrative operations. As public employees have moved toward unionization, this element of the internal dynamic has become less a human-relations issue and more a political one. Organized workers have a stronger capacity to make their expectations known to management, to negotiate their terms, and to disrupt the functioning of an agency when they are not satisfied with the outcome of collective bargaining.

There is also an extensive literature in political science documenting the fact that public agencies sometimes become the instrument of influential client groups (Wildavsky 1964; Rourke 1969; Selznick 1949). This occurs because governmental bureaucracies are often dependent on their clientele for political support, particularly within the budgetary process. Thus public agencies have been known to exchange their managerial independence for the kind of support they need to maintain their viability. Such exchanges are difficult to reconcile with the notion of an apolitical professional bureaucracy.

In an effort to resolve the conflict between the ideals represented in the classical model and the realities of political and organizational life, social scientists such as Herbert Simon (1945) have revised the classical model. The neoclassical model that has emerged is still based on the notion that efficiency is the major criterion of performance in an administrative setting. However, along with this basic standard of operation there is the recognition that there are limits to the degree of rationality and efficiency achievable within a bureaucratic structure. These limits are determined to some extent by a managerial responsibility to be sensitive to the individual and collective needs of agency personnel and to the service demands of a public clientele. In the end, therefore, the role of the agency leader is to maintain a proper balance so that the organization can function efficiently and effectively. Existing research on the subject leaves little doubt that some leaders of local-government bureaucracies have been more successful at striking the proper balance than have others. Many have failed, and some may not even have tried. However, a full understanding of this subject requires the definition of the set of internal and external conditions that make the desired outcome most probable.

The Internal Conditions of Optimal Performance

The basic precondition that must exist before a government bureaucracy can operate in an efficient (and thereby equitable) manner is a simple one: a general institutional *willingness* to do so. This willingness must appear on two levels. First, it must emerge from a commitment on the part of the agency leadership. Second, it must be supported by the remaining members of the organization. The commitment of agency leadership to manage an organization efficiently is the function of a number of variables, including the personality and training of the agency head, the orientation of the chief executive who appoints that individual, and the history and culture of the organization itself. It is safe to say that, given the choice between managing an agency poorly or managing it well, most public executives would choose the latter.

The circumstances that engender widespread organizational support for sound management practice are usually more elusive. It is not that public employees below the executive rank do not want to do a good job, but rather that there is sometimes a tension between the individual needs of workers and the demand for organizational efficiency. Efficiency often dictates harder work, less generous pay increases, sparser fringe benefits, and sometimes the loss of job security. It should not be surprising, therefore, that such requirements often meet with resistance from individual workers and their union representatives.

Contrary to the general pattern, however, those administrative measures taken by management in order to bring about a more efficient allocation of agency resources do not generate a negative response from the work force. In fact, in my own research on the subject, such measures generally receive support from workers and their organized representatives in the unions (Viteritti 1979). This occurs because the managerial demand to allocate resources according to service needs is consistent with the collective-bargaining demand to equalize work loads among employees. Thus in New York, for example, a reallocation strategy that resulted in the redeployment of fire companies throughout the city had its origins in a union demand to balance departmental work loads by sending more personnel and equipment to high-incidence areas such as the South Bronx. This kind of behavior is not unique. What it tells us is that there is a connection, albeit an indirect one, between worker equity and service equity, and that this connection enhances an organizational capacity to do business efficiently.

Once an organizational commitment exists on all levels to allocate resources efficiently, the internal propensity of an agency to do so becomes a function of its own technical competence—that is, the level of sophistication it has achieved for identifying and measuring the relative service needs of a diverse community. This technical capacity and the willingness to apply it are representative of a developing, if not general, organization climate in public agencies that is being fostered by a trend toward rising professionalism, the advances of technology, and the requirements imposed by fiscal constraints.

The External Conditions of Optimal Performance

Once the internal conditions of optimal performance exist, the feasibility of its actual realization is determined in the external political environment. The fact remains that the public bureaucracy is part of a political system that has been known to discriminate against the poor. It is a system in which agency budgets are determined by elected legislative officials, in which agency heads are appointed by elected chief executives, in which politically powerful interest groups have been known to control the agencies that are supposed to serve or regulate them. How, one might ask, can such agencies, even under the standards of sound management practice, be expected to produce an allocation of goods and services that favors the poor?

An informed response to this question requires a closer look at the general pattern of empirical evidence on the various kinds of local services. The initial discussion of this variety of functions distinguished between those services that are consumed by a limited clientele and those that are responsive to the demands of a more general public. Since distributions of the former type are more relevant to a process that occurs outside the bureaucracy, it is the latter that are of concern here. I have included within the general category such services as police, fire, sanitation, street construction and maintenance, and (to a large though diminishing extent) education.

Let us now look at the research findings on service distribution of each of the functions in the general category. Since education was included in this category with some qualification, I will begin with education and explain my reservations. Although public education has traditionally been a local service that is utilized by a broad constituency, urban education is becoming more and more the bailiwick of the poor. There are many reasons for this, including school-integration efforts, white flight to the suburbs, and the declining quality of inner-city schools. The birth of such developments as the voucher movement, tax credits, and the increase in private schools—all peculiarly middle-class phenomena—indicates a continuing trend toward making urban education a poor people's service. In this sense, the inclusion of education in the general category is somewhat inappropriate. From an analytical perspective it is also difficult to compare resource distributions in education with those of the other services mentioned because a larger portion of educational support comes from nonlocal sources, particularly from state legislatures. Perhaps the legislative role in this distributional process, coupled with the homogeneity and shrinkage of the client population in urban schools, begins to explain why central-city school systems have been the victim of unfair school-finance formulas (see Wise 1969; Carrol 1979).

A look at the evidence on resource and service distribution within local school districts reveals some mixed patterns. In some cases the pattern appears to favor the poor, in others it favors the middle class, and in many the pattern is mixed or bimodal.[3] At the risk of overgeneralization, it can be said that a number of conflicting factors contribute to these mixed patterns: compensatory programs for the poor dictated by federal grants-in-aid, political pressure placed on local school boards for programs that cater to middle-class children, and an attempt by local school officials to respond to both kinds of demands simultaneously.

In the research literature with respect to other local services, the pattern is both more uniform and more telling. Of all these functions, the one that has generated the most substantial research is the police service. The evidence from this body of police research unambiguously reveals a distributional pattern that favors the poor (Mladenka and Hill 1977; Benson and Lund 1961; Lineberry 1977; Bollens 1961; Weicker 1971; Bloch 1974; Viteritti 1973, 1979). In most cases this pattern is attributed to internal rules of administrative procedure. In fact, police work has traditionally had one of the most sophisticated technologies for identifying the relative service needs of communities and deploying resources accordingly.

Although the research on fire services is less extensive than that on the police, it also reveals a consistent pattern. Local fire-department resources and services tend to be allocated on the basis of service needs, a criterion for allocative decisions that tends to favor the poor (Hirsch 1973; Viteritti 1979; Lineberry 1977). Research on sanitation services is scarcer. My own work on the subject, however, shows that in one large city (New York) resources and services are distributed on the basis of need. This pattern tends to favor the poorer areas of the city, in which street cleanliness ratings are lowest and population density highest (Viteritti 1979).

The last of the services in the client-general category mentioned here are those concerned with street construction and maintenance. Here the research findings are more ambiguous than for the three previous functions. They also point in a slightly different direction (Antunes and Plumlee 1977; Levy, Meltsner, and Wildavsky 1974). On the one hand, technical engineering standards are found to play a major role in influencing allocations toward an equal, if not equitable, distribution. On the other hand, a slight bias favoring the middle class is evident in these allocations and in the quality of streets. The reason generally given for this bias is a tendency on the part of the middle class to be more vocal and aggressive in demanding these kinds of services. The form this aggression takes varies from the kinds of demands that provoke a "squeaky-wheel" response to the kind of organized political action a business community launches in order to initiate new street construction.

When one examines the research on bureaucratic service distributions in its entirety, several general conclusions can be drawn. First, the evidence shows that some local agencies have a stronger proclivity than others to allocate their services in an efficient and equitable manner. To a large extent the pattern tends to correspond to service function. Second, those agencies most susceptible to political pressure seem to be least likely to realize the goals of efficiency and equity. Thus, although federal mandates have infused a compensatory element into local school-district budgets, the political sensitivity of school-board structures introduces a counterforce that favors the middle class. Likewise, in the area of road construction and maintenance, whatever middle-class bias does exist seems to be related to the role that political influence, or at least community pressure, plays in the process.

Finally, those agencies that have been found most successful in allocating their services efficiently and equitably (police, fire, sanitation) are those that have followed the more technical standards of decision making. This final point, when read in the context of the previous two, underscores a major theme that has been made throughout the course of this chapter: that bureaucratic decisions about service distributions are more likely to be efficient and equitable when they are made according to managerial rather than political criteria. By now this observation seems self-evident, but it begs a more significant question: what the circumstances are that permit executive officials in some types of service agencies to go about their business with fewer political constraints.

One characteristic shared by agencies of the three optimal performing types is that they all represent vital local services that are needed, wanted and used by the entire local population. Because they provide vital services that are essential to the safety, health, and welfare of a city, the political (and therefore financial) viability of these agencies is never brought into question. Their existence is part of a public mandate. Because they serve a general clientele, they do not rely on any one group for political support. For these reasons, agencies that provide police, fire, and sanitation services enjoy a more independent status in the governmental system, which permits them to administer their services with little or no political interference. This detachment from politics, when linked with an internal willingness and an technical capacity to do so, fosters an organizational climate that advances efficiency and equity in the distribution of services.

What We Know about Bureaucracy, Efficiency, and Equity

This chapter began with two basic assumptions. The first concerns a definition of equity that calls for an allocation of goods and services that favors the poor. The second concerns an understanding of politics as a process that discriminates against the poor. It was not my intention to prove either of these assumptions. The first represents a value judgment that one may or may not accept. The second is a function of a democratic system based on the principle of majority consent and at the same time responsive to the will of the influential. The validity of that assumption can be measured against a two-hundred-year history characterized by discrimination against minorities and the poor.

Together, these assumptions represent a basic tension that exists between the normative ideals of a democratic society and the way the political system actually works. The purpose of this chapter was to evaluate the role bureaucratic institutions might play in resolving that tension, particularly with regard to the distributive process in municipal government. That process has been described in terms of two dinstinct levels of decision making. One involves the allocation of public resources among different services; the other involves the allocation of public resources within particular services. The first level of decision is important with respect to the equity issue because of the client-specific nature of many local service functions. The second level is important because it defines the parameters of bureaucratic discretion in the distributive process.

The role of bureaucratic institutions in the distributive process is worthy of attention because under certain conditions these institutions operate according to a set of rules that are distinct from those that prevail in other government institutions. These rules may lead to an allocation of goods and services that favors the poor. I do not mean to suggest that individuals who work in bureaucratic institutions are more predisposed toward the principle of equity than individuals in any other branch of government. The equitable outcomes referred to here are merely a byproduct of a more basic managerial concern for efficiency.

For this reason the link between efficiency and equity is a crucial one. Neither do I mean to propose that once the allocation of services is made among different communities, such services will be of equal quality at the street level. The quality of street-level service depends on many variables, including the attitudes of personnel, the level of training within the agency, and the representativeness of the work force. These factors are certainly important ones, but they cannot be considered in a chapter of the present size and scope.

Finally, it should be stressed that it is not my intention to suggest that bureaucratic institutions can typically be expected to operate in an efficient and equitable manner. To the contrary, I have identified certain internal conditions that are necessary before an agency can be expected to reach such optimal levels of performance, including leadership commitment, employee compliance, and technical competence. These internal conditions must be complemented by an external environment that allows agency operations to remain relatively free of political interference. That external condition is most probable when the function of an agency is to provide a basic vital service to a broad-based clientele.

In conclusion, it must be said that the role of bureaucracy in the distribution of municipal services is both qualified and circumstantial. It is qualified because it is primarily concerned with distributions within a service rather than among services. It is circumstantial because it advances the cause of equity only when particular internal and external conditions exist. Nevertheless, the role of bureaucracy is important because under the conditions of optimal performance, those same social characteristics that work against the poor in the political process may work on their behalf in the administrative process. In other words, although the conditions of poverty tend to immobilize a group of people politically, they also tend to set the terms of service need in an administrative process governed by the standard of efficiency. This is no mean accomplishment, for it not only enlists bureaucracy in the cause of equity, but also contributes toward the modification of a basic dilemma of democratic government. That dilemma might be described in somewhat simplistic terms as a state of affairs in which "those who have, get; and those who have little, get little."

As the fiscal crisis that has embraced many U.S. cities becomes a more characteristic feature of urban life, the basic question of politics may change from the proverbial "who gets what?" to a more troubling "who gets less?" Given what has been said about the administrative process within bureaucratic institutions, one might hope that the new demand for economy in government will bring with it a more concentrated focus on efficiency. However, a major determinant of how the poor will fare within the new politics of retrenchment will be the kinds of decisions that are made at other levels of government concerning which service agencies will be required to absorb the most severe reductions. Given what has been said about the political process and its disinclination toward equity, there is little reason for optimism.

Notes

1. For a discussion of these concepts, see Tawney (1952); Flathman (1967); and Schaar (1967).

2. Those studies concerning library services include Benson and Lund (1961); Levy, Meltsner, and Wildavsky (1974); Martin (1969); and American Library Association (1963). Those concerning recreational or cultural services include Benson and Lund (1961) and Sexton (1963). It should also be noted that a substantial literature exists that shows a distribution in the use of park services that favors the poor. These include Lineberry (1977); Mladenka and Hill (1977); Gold (1973); and Fisk et al. (1974).

3. Those studies that show a bias toward the poor include Levy, Meltsner, and Wildavsky (1974); Lyon (1970); and Katzman (1968). Those favoring the middle class include Sexton (1961); Owen (1972); Berk and Hartman (1974); Burkhead, Fox, and Holland (1967); and Baron (1971). Those with mixed findings include Benson and Lund (1961); Mandel (1975); and Martyn (1965).

References

American Library Association. 1963. *Access to Libraries.* Chicago: American Library Association.

Antunes, G., and Mladenka, K. 1976. "The Politics of Local Services and Service Distributions." In L.H. Masotti and R.L. Lineberry, eds., *The New Urban Politics,* Chap. 7. Cambridge, Mass.: Ballinger.

Antunes, G., and Plumlee, J. 1977. "The Distribution of Urban Public Service." *Urban Affairs Quarterly* 4(March).

Argyris, C. 1957. *Personality and Organization.* New York: Harper and Row.
——. 1964. *Integrating the Individual and the Organization.* New York: Wiley.

Balk, W., ed. 1978. "Symposium on Productivity in Government." *Public Administration Review* 38(January-February).

Baron, H.M. 1971. "Race and Status in School Spending." *Journal of Human Resources* (Winter).

Benson, C., and Lund, P. 1961. *Neighborhood Distribution of Local Government Services.* Berkeley: University of California Press.

Berk, R.A., and Hartman, A. 1974. "Race and per Pupil Staffing Expenditures in Chicago Elementary Schools." Chicago: Center for Urban Affairs, Northwestern University.

Bloch, P.B. 1974. *Equality and the Distribution of Police Services.* Washington, D.C.: Urban Institute.

Bollens, J. 1961. *Exploring the Metropolitan Community.* Berkeley: University of California Press, chap. 14.

Burkhead, J.; Fox, T.D.; and Holland, J.W. 1967. *Input and Output in Large City High Schools.* Syracuse, N.Y.: Syracuse University Press.

Carrol, S.J. 1979. *The Search for Equity in School Finance.* Santa Monica, Calif.: Rand Corporation.

Fisk, D., et al. 1974. *Equality and the Distribution of Recreation Services.* Washington, D.C.: Urban Institute.

Flathman, R. 1967. "Equality and Generalization: A Formal Analysis." In J.R. Pennock and J.W. Chapman, eds., *Nomos IX: Equality.* New York: Atherton.

Gold, S.D. 1973. "The Distribution of Urban Government Services in Theory and Practice." *Public Finance Quarterly* 2(January).

Goldenberg, E.N. 1979. "Evaluating Municipal Service," *Public Administration Review* 39(January–February).

Hatry, H. 1972. "Issues in Productivity Measurement in Local Government." *Public Administration Review* 32(November–December).

Hatry, H., et al. 1977. *How Effective Are Your Community Services?* Washington, D.C.: Urban Institute.

Hirsch, W. 1973. *Urban Economic Analysis.* New York: McGraw-Hill.

Jones, B.D. 1980. *Service Delivery in the City.* New York: Longman.

Katzman, M.T. 1968. "Distribution and Production in a Big City Elementary School." *Yale Economic Essays* (Spring).

Lane, R. 1969. *Political Life.* Glencoe, Ill.: Free Press.

Levitan, S. 1969. *The Great Society's Poor Law.* Baltimore, Md.: Johns Hopkins University Press.

Levy, F.S., Meltsner, A.J.; and Wildavsky, A. 1974. *Urban Outcomes.* Berkeley: University of California, Press.

Lineberry, R.L. 1977. *Equality and Urban Policy.* Beverly Hills, Calif.: Sage Publications.

Lyon, D. 1970. "Capital Spending and the Neighborhoods of Philadelphia." *Business Review* (May).

Mandel, A.S. 1975. *Resource Distribution inside School Districts.* Lexington, Mass.: Lexington Books, D.C. Heath and Company.

Martin, L.A. 1969. *Library Response to Urban Change.* Chicago: American Library Association.

Martyn, K.A. 1965. *Report on Education to the Governor's Commission on the Los Angeles Riots.* Sacramento, Calif.: Office of the Governor.

Matthews, D., and Prothro, J. 1967. *Negroes and the New Southern Politics.* New York: Harcourt, Brace and World.

Milbrath, L., Goel, M.L. *Political Participation,* 2nd ed. Chicago: Rand McNally.

Mladenka, K.R., and Hill, K.Q. 1977. "The Distribution of Benefits in an Urban Environment." *Urban Affairs Quarterly* 13(September).

Moynihan, D.P. 1969. *Maximum Feasible Misunderstanding.* New York: Free Press.

Owen, J.D. 1972. "The Distribution of Educational Resources in Large Cities." *Journal of Human Resources* 7 (Winter).

Rich, R. 1977. "Equity and Institutional Design in Urban Service Delivery." *Urban Affairs Quarterly* 12(March).

——. 1979. "Neglected Issues in the Study of Urban Service Distributions: A Research Agenda." *Urban Studies* 16(June).

Ross, J.P., and Burkhead, J. 1974. *Productivity in the Local Government Sector.* Lexington Mass.: Lexington Books, D.C. Heath and Company.

Rourke, F.E. 1969. *Bureaucracy, Politics and Public Policy.* Boston: Little, Brown.

Schaar, J. 1967. "Equality of Opportunity and Beyond." In J.R. Pennock and J.W. Chapman, eds., *Nomos IX: Equality.* New York: Atherton.

Selznick, P. 1949. *TVA and the Grass Roots.* Berkeley: University of California Press.

Sexton, P. 1961. *Education and Income.* New York: Viking.

——. 1963. *Comparative Recreation Needs and Services in New York Neighborhoods.* New York: Community Council of Greater New York.

Simon, H. 1945. *Administrative Behavior.* New York: Collier-Macmillan.

Tawney, R.H. 1952. *Equality.* London: George Allen and Unwin.

Viteritti, J.P. 1973. *Police, Politics and Pluralism in New York City.* Beverly Hills, Calif.: Sage Publications.

——. 1979. *Bureaucracy and Social Justice.* Port Washington, N.Y.: Kennikat Press.

Weicker, J. 1971. "The Allocation of Police Protection by Income Class." *Urban Studies* (October).

Wildavsky, A. 1964. *The Politics of the Budgetary Process.* Boston: Little, Brown.

Wise, A. 1969. *Rich Schools, Poor Schools.* Berkeley: University of California Press.

5 Political Strategies and Public-Service Patterns: The Impact of the Black Civil-Rights Movement on Municipal-Service Distributions

James W. Button

Most research on the distribution of municipal services suggests that there is a good deal of racial and class equality and that where inequalities do exist, they are usually unpatterned, dispersed, and due to unknown factors (Antunes and Plumlee 1978; Lineberry 1977; and Rich 1979). For most blacks in smaller communities in the South, however, there has often been a great deal of in-equality in public services, at least until relatively recently (*Hawkins* v. *Shaw* 1971; Keech 1968; and Wirt 1970). The civil-rights movement of the 1960s and its political mobilization of blacks brought a direct challenge to systematic inequality in the provision of basic public services. Whether or not this political movement was successful in altering the distribution of such services for south-ern blacks remains an unanswered question.

The few studies that have been undertaken of the consequences of black political mobilization have tended to be extremely impressionistic, limited to just one or two cities, sorely outdated by recent changes in black participation in the South, or narrowly confined to voting as the sole indicator of political participation. In a study of Florida in 1955, for example, Hugh Price claimed that black voting in some cities seemed to have resulted in better police protec-tion and more public services such as paved streets, playgrounds, and civic centers. Reviewing some of the accomplishments of black elected officials in the 1970s in several southern cities, Campbell and Feagin (1975) concluded that such officials have provided their constituents with some benefits in the areas of employment, housing, health care, education, consumer protection, and police relations. Nevertheless, they contended that without federal and private financial support, these black officials would have been much less beneficial, especially in rural areas. In another study, Frederick Wirt (1970) investigated one predominantly black county in Mississippi in the late 1960s and found that black political participation there had meant more black police, more paved roads and street lights, less prejudiced media attention, and some psychological benefits.

However, not all observers have been this optimistic. In an overview of contemporary black politics, Hanes Walton (1972) maintained that many black elected officials in the rural, black-belt regions of the South lacked the economic means to improve conditions for their constituents. Walton contended that rural, small-town black officials were overburdened with such problems as lack of industry, low tax rolls, and uncooperative whites. Similarly, Charles Bullock's (1975) study of southern black officials has indicated that many of them reside in the poorest counties in their respective states and that, although redistributive public programs are helpful, they still leave the poor counties disadvantaged since these counties have the greatest needs.

The most serious weakness in all these studies is the noticeable lack of empirical evidence to support basic contentions. Only William Keech (1968) has attempted to investigate systematically the benefits to be derived from black voting. Looking at two southern cities (Durham, North Carolina, and Tuskegee, Alabama) both longitudinally and in depth, Keech compared concomitant variations in black participation (mainly voting) with public- and private- (nongovernmental) sector payoffs. He reported that increases in black voting seemed to bring about some progress in the public sector for blacks (better streets, water and sewage systems, and recreation facilities) but did not effect any significant changes in the private sector, especially in the important areas of housing and employment.

Yet Keech's study also has several major limitations. His sample of cities is much too limited to have theoretical implications beyond the two cities involved. He investigated only black voting, neglecting other political variables, such as court litigation, demonstrations, and federal intervention, that may have had important effects on policy. In addition, because the study occurred before or during the period of greatest change in black political participation in the South, it could not have captured policy changes that may have taken place in the late 1960s and early 1970s. Finally, Keech did not measure his dependent variables (public- and private-sector benefits) with much precision.

The purpose of this study is to investigate in six southern cities the impact of the black civil-rights movement on the distribution of two basic services: streets and police protection. The study is unique in the service-distribution literature for several reasons: it focuses on more than one city and on smaller cities (less than 50,000 in population); it explores a variety of political variables and the effect of each on more than one service area; and it takes a longitudinal approach, covering almost a twenty-year period. Finally, the study combines both objective and subjective indicators of public-service distribution and attempts to link these indicators with various political factors.

Methodology

The state of Florida contains in microcosm the broad range of political environments in which blacks are found throughout the South. For example, the northern parts of the state are representative of the rural, agricultural Old South, whereas the southeastern segment is typical of the urbanized and sub-urbanized, fast-growing, relatively affluent New South. As in other parts of the South, black voter registration in Florida increased most rapidly during the early and mid-1960s, rising from 38.9 percent of age-eligible blacks in 1960 to 63.8 percent by late 1964. Moreover, the mounting number of black elected officials in Florida has paralleled developments in other southern states, increasing from less than half a dozen in 1965 to ninety-one in 1978. Thus Florida provides a clearly definable political unit, one reasonably typical of the South, within which to examine questions pertinent to the impact of increasing black political participation.

Within Florida, six communities—Crestview, Gretna, Lake City, Daytona Beach, Titusville, and Riviera Beach—were selected for longitudinal investigation of changes in municipal-service delivery and the effects of certain political variables. These cities were studied over an eighteen-year period (1960-1977) during which black political participation increased from almost none at the outset to a much greater level of participation. The primary objective was to explore the relationship between these changes in black political participation and public-service distributions.

By investigating more than one community, it was possible to compare the effects of demographic differences in black political strength among cities. Keech (1968) concluded that the size of the voting minority in a community affects resulting gains. His analysis suggests that there is a linear relationship between the size of the black electorate and black political gains until a threshold point of white fear and resistance is met. At this point, when the electorate is between 30 and 50 percent black, white opposition is greatest. When the black electorate moves beyond 50 percent of the voters, a linear relationship occurs once again as a black majority is able to overcome any white resistance. Therefore, the six communities were selected along a continuum of black electoral size ranging from relatively small (approximately 5 to 20 percent of the community's total voting population) to relatively large (more than 50 percent of the voting public).

The communities were also selected to control for other variables that may significantly affect the consequences of black political participation. Socio-economic status, political culture, and level of urbanization are all important community characteristics that vary to some degree over the six cities. These controls are, of course, imperfect since they do not allow for the variation of only one independent variable at a time. This limitation makes it difficult to ascertain the independent effects of any single community characteristic. Nevertheless, by investigating each city over time and by comparing developmental sequences from one city to another, it is possible to reach some conclusions about the singular effects of each independent variable. Table 5-1 depicts the types and characteristics of communities selected.

Table 5-1
Typology of Communities

City Characteristics		Old South	New South
		Crestview	Titusville
Low percentage black (10–29%)	Population (1976)	8,481	32,291
	Percentage population change (1960–1970)	6.5	376.1
	Percentage black (1970)	17.8	9.0
	Per capita income (1975)	$3,395	$4,510
		Lake City	Daytona Beach
Medium percentage black (30–50%)	Population (1976)	10,648	49,013
	Percentage population change (1960–1970)	11.7	21.2
	Percentage black (1970)	31.5	31.3
	Per capita income (1975)	$4,233	$4,191
		Gretna	Riviera Beach
High percentage black (over 50%)	Population (1976)	1,105	27,656
	Percentage population change (1960–1970)	36.5	64.0
	Percentage black (1970)	80.0	55.6
	Per capita income (1975)	$2,085	$4,012

Note: Data on population and per capita income are Bureau of the Census estimates reported in Department of the Treasury, Office of Revenue Sharing, *Initial State and Local Data Elements, Entitlement Period 10* (1978), pp. 32–36. Other demographic data are 1970 U.S. census information.

The dependent variables in this study consist of changes in two municipal services: street paving and police protection. These services are not only two of the most important services that almost all communities provide, but also have often been the focus of allegations of inequality from many southern blacks. In addition, these two services represent different kinds of municipal services. Streets are regarded as primarily capital intensive, whereas law enforcement is considered essentially human or labor intensive. I hypothesize that black political participation will bring about a more equal distribution of street paving than of police protection (Keech 1968; Matthews and Prothro 1966).

In terms of measurement of dependent variables, there are severe difficulties in securing comparable service-output indicators over time and across communities (Lineberry and Welch 1974). Thus this investigation relies primarily on quantitative (not qualitative) indicators, such as the proportion of streets paved and the proportion of blacks on the police force. Particularly in the case of police protection, however, other more qualitative indicators, when available, will also be utilized. These include police patrolling patterns, the existence of programs to enhance police-community relations, and reported allegations of police brutality against blacks.

In addition to longitudinal and comparative emphases that enhance the reliability of making inferences, this investigation uses multiple modes of analysis to corroborate the findings of any single indicator. These sources include a thorough search of available public records and interviews with a sample of departmental personnel in order to chart service-level changes over time; lengthy interviews with a total of fifty-eight white and fifty-two black knowledgeable community members in order to tap their retrospective perceptions concerning service distributions and the influence of black participation; and a careful reading of local and regional newspapers from 1960 through 1977. The 110 community knowledgeables interviewed were public and private citizens who were familiar with politics and race relations in each community over a period of at least ten or fifteen years (average length of residence was twenty-seven years). Names were gathered initially from newspapers, public officials, and prominent private citizens about knowledgeable community residents. Before an individual was interviewed, however, he or she had to be nominated by at least two other persons. At the end of each interview respondents were asked to nominate other community knowledgeables. This "reputational approach" generated a substantial number of names of white and black citizens; yet only those mentioned at least twice were contacted for interviews. More than 80 percent of those contacted were actually interviewed in each city.

Results: Street Paving

City residents tend to rank road conditions and maintenance high on their lists of municipal priorities (Antunes and Plumlee 1978; Hansen 1975). In a survey of citizens in ten major U.S. cities, Fowler (1974) found that blacks placed street conditions fourth in priority out of a list of ten service areas and that blacks were much more concerned than whites about service improvements in both streets and other services.

In this study, knowledgeable citizens of both races listed poor roads as the second most serious problem their community has faced over the last ten to fifteen years. Moreover, in a list of seven municipal services, they ranked streets first in terms of inequality in service effectiveness between white and black subcommunities over the last fifteen years. To what extent is this perception accurate, to what degree have roads improved for both blacks and whites, and what role have various political variables played in these service changes?

Street paving is an excellent and easily attainable quantitative indicator of street services, and table 5-2 summarizes the data on street paving in both black and white areas for each of the six cities between 1960 and 1976-1977. These results indicate that the proportion of streets paved in the black

Table 5-2
Street Paving in Black and White Subcommunities in Six Florida Cities,
1960-1977

Communities	Percentages of Blacks and Whites (1960)		Percentages of Blacks and Whites (1976-1977)[a]		Percentage Absolute Change[b]		Percentage Relative Change[c]
	Black	White	Black	White	Black	White	
Crestview	12	38	39	58	27	20	−7
Lake City	10	50	35	97	25	47	+22
Gretna	0	20	25	35	25	15	−10
Titusville	10	92	72	98	62	6	−56
Daytona Beach	50	97	97	99	47	2	−45
Riviera Beach	37	85	96	100	59	15	−44

Note: Data on street paving in 1960 were not available in official public records. Therefore, the 1960 figures for each city were estimates based on newspaper reports, interviews with departmental officials who were in office in 1960, and later public records. Data for 1976-1977 were secured from departmental records, federal grant applications, and windshield surveys.

[a]Data on street paving in Lake City, Titusville, and Riviera Beach were gathered in 1976; data for Crestview, Daytona Beach, and Gretna were retrieved in 1977.

[b]The percentage of absolute change is computed by subtracting the percentage of streets paved in 1960 from the 1976-1977 percentage.

[c]The percentage of relative change is derived by subtracting the absolute service-change figure for the black subcommunity from the comparable figure for the white subcommunity. A negative change indicates that differences between black and white street paving are declining; that is, the gap in service delivery is getting smaller.

subcommunities was very low in 1960 (the average was 20 percent) but that the proportion had improved in all cities by 1976-1977 (when the average was 61 percent). The average proportion of streets paved in white areas in 1960 was estimated at 64 percent, and this increased in all cities to an average of 81 percent by 1976-1977. Thus the level of paving in most black areas by 1976-1977 was about the same as it had been for most white areas in 1960. In terms of absolute changes over this period, it is clear that street paving occurred more frequently (proportionately) in black than in white subcommunities (with the single exception of Lake City, where the reverse occurred). Hence the relative-change figures, which compare absolute change rates for blacks and whites, indicate that the gaps in street paving between black and white areas have narrowed in five of the six communities.

The results in table 5-2 also show some differences according to type of city. Clearly the rates of absolute change in street paving for blacks, as well as relative change rates, are much greater in the New South cities (Titusville,

Daytona Beach, and Riviera Beach) than in the Old South cities (Crestview, Lake City, and Gretna). Part of this difference may be due to the fact that in the more affluent New South cities a high proportion of streets in the white areas had already been paved by 1960, so that greater paving resources could henceforth be more easily allocated to the black areas without detracting from the white areas. In the poorer Old South cities, however, the average proportion of white streets paved in 1960 was only 36 percent, and the rates of absolute change were about the same for both black and white areas (with the exception again of Lake City).

In terms of variations among cities in proportion of blacks in the population, there are only moderate differences in rates of street paving. In support of Keech's hypothesis, the medium-proportion black cities (Lake City and Daytona Beach), where whites may feel most threatened, show somewhat lower absolute and relative change rates for blacks than do either the low- or high-proportion black cities. Yet contrary to Keech, absolute and relative changes in street paving were no greater in the two majority-black cities (Riviera Beach and Gretna) than in the two cities with relatively small black proportions (Crestview and Titusville).

In addition to these objective indicators for streets, community knowledge-ables in each city evaluated street-service effectiveness for both blacks and whites for 1960 and again for 1976–1977 on a three-point ordinal scale (1 = not effective; 2 = somewhat effective; and 3 = very effective). These perceptual data for each community closely approximated the objective data on street paving (Button and Scher 1979). In order to explore the influence of political variables on changes in street services, knowledgeable citizens were asked to rate the effectiveness of nine general political strategies by which blacks have attempted to influence changes in cities during the civil-rights movement and after. This rating system consisted of a five-point ordinal scale with 1 representing least effective and 5 representing most effective. The political variables were as follows: voting, petitioning, attending public meetings, protesting, rioting, taking court action, applying outside pressure from state or federal governments, having blacks in public office, and securing federal grants. These evaluations of various political strategies were then correlated (Kendall's Tau B) with the perceived changes (both absolute and relative) in black street services.

The results show few political variables even moderately correlated with either absolute or relative perceived changes in black streets. In fact, only voting and having blacks in public office are correlated at moderate levels with absolute (.16 and .21, respectively) and relative (.24 and .22, respectively) black service changes over all cities. These moderate correlations hold up for all community groupings except, as would be expected, in cities with a low percentage of blacks. In these two cities (Crestview and Titusville) blacks made up no more than 15 percent of registered voters at any time, and only Crestview was able to elect (in 1968) a single black councilman.

As might also be expected, and as Keech had suggested, voting is highly correlated with both perceived absolute (.48) and relative (.46) street-service changes in the majority-black communities (Gretna and Riviera Beach). Correlations are also high (.42 and .35, respectively) for the political strategy of attending public meetings. In both communities, blacks achieved a majority of registered voters by the early 1970s and shortly thereafter elected black majorities to the city councils. Blacks were thus able to reorder street-service priorities, and the proportion of street paving in black areas increased markedly by the mid-1970s. In addition, black groups, including neighborhood and formalized interest groups like the National Association for the Advancement of Colored People (NAACP), voiced demands for improved streets at various public meetings.

Somewhat surprising were the low correlations between the securing of federal grants and perceived changes in streets. Only the low- and medium-proportion black communities showed even moderate correlations between absolute changes and federal grants (.21 and .18, respectively). It may be that these low correlations are attributable to the fact that use of federal dollars for street paving is a relatively recent development in most of these communities. At any rate, other sources of data, including interviews with public officials, public records, and newspaper reports, all strongly suggest the importance of federal funds in financing recent street paving in black areas. For example, between 1973 and 1977 all communities obtained Community Development Block Grants targeted primarily for the black areas and with substantial proportions of the funds earmarked for street paving and drainage. Moreover, since 1974 four of the six cities allocated portions of federal revenue-sharing monies for street paving in black sections.

Federal funds seemed especially important in light of three factors prevalent in most of the communities:

1. Private developers had paved streets and included that in the costs of many white housing developments, but practically no such private development took place in black areas.
2. Street-assessment plans, whereby property owners are assessed a portion of the costs of paving their streets, were rarely successful in black areas because most blacks could not afford such charges.
3. A number of public officials and knowledgeable citizens expressed the beliefs that blacks are relatively poor and therefore they do not pay their fair share of local taxes and thus should not receive city services in proportion to their numbers.

Other political strategies often employed by urban blacks as a means of expressing grievances and sometimes influencing municipal policy are protesting and rioting (Eisinger 1976; Schumaker 1975; and Welch 1975). Community knowledgeables' evaluations of these strategies for the six cities showed generally very low correlations with changes in black street services. However, in the case of rioting in Old South, low- and medium-proportion black communities, the correlations are moderate but *negative* for both perceived absolute and relative service changes. The actual number of reported riots in these particular communities was low, and the expressed grievances of rioters rarely concerned street services. Nonetheless, these negative correlations suggest that, in conservative Old South cities and in communities where blacks are clearly a minority, rioting may decrease political support and thus serve to impede service improvements.

Results: Police Protection

The police function is one of the largest single service expenditures in most city budgets, and the police officer is also a significant symbol of political authority for many citizens. Yet most blacks express a higher level of dissatisfaction with police services than most whites, although the evidence on whether the police actually discriminate against black neighborhoods is mixed (National Advisory Commission on Civil Disorders [Kerner Commission] 1968; Lineberry 1977; Mladenka and Hill 1978). This black dissatisfaction with the police usually takes several forms, including complaints of police brutality, discriminatory police employment and promotion practices, and lack of adequate police protection.

In the six cities studied here, most community knowledgeables ranked police protection third in a list of seven municipal services in terms of inequality in service effectiveness over the previous fifteen years. More objective indicators also depict clear discrimination against blacks in the provision of police services in the early 1960s and show only moderate improvement by 1976–1977. (table 5-3). The lone exception is predominantly black Gretna, which employed five blacks in an eight-man department in 1977, but this community did not even have its own police force until that year. Surprisingly, the proportional changes in black police are somewhat greater in Old South than in New South communities. The New South cities had relatively high qualification requirements for police, especially in the area of formal education; this, plus the keen competition for well-qualified blacks from the growing private sector, made it difficult to recruit and retain black police. As expected, the majority-black communities had considerably higher proportions of black police than other communities by the later 1970s, but not even these cities were able to reorder priorities so as to achieve proportional equality for blacks in their police departments.

In terms of promotions and supervisory positions for black police, the changes since 1960 have been even more modest. No black policeman was ranked above patrolman in 1960 in any of the six communities. By 1976–1977 only Riviera Beach, with a black police chief and two black captains since 1971, had any blacks above the rank of sergeant; and only Daytona Beach and Lake

Table 5-3
Black Police in Six Florida Cities, 1960-1977

	Ratios and Percentages of Black Police				
	1960		1976-1977[a]		Percentage Change, 1960-1977
Communities	Ratio	Percentage	Ratio	Percentage	
Crestview	(0/9)	0	(2/12)	17	+17
Lake City	(2/16)	13	(6/32)	19	+6
Gretna	_b	0	(5/8)	63	+63
Titusville	(1/14)	7	(1/43)	2	−5
Daytona Beach	(6/78)	8	(10/154)	7	−1
Riviera Beach	(5/23)	22	(18/67)	27	+5

Note: Data on numbers and proportions of blacks on police forces in 1960 were not available in official public records. Therefore, the 1960 figures for each city were estimates based on newspaper reports, interviews with departmental officials who were in office in 1960, and later public records. Data for 1976-1977 were secured from departmental records.

[a]Data on black police in Lake City, Titusville, and Riviera Beach were gathered in 1976; data for Crestview, Daytona Beach, and Gretna were retrieved in 1977.

[b]Gretna had no police force in 1960. Its police protection was provided by the county sheriff's department, which employed three or four deputies but no blacks in 1960.

City had black sergeants. Crestview, Titusville, and Lake City each had a black policeman who had been on the force for ten or more years, and each had been passed over several times for promotion. Much of this was due to the fear, expressed by both black and white police, of having a black supervise whites. Indeed, only in Riviera Beach do some black officers supervise white police.

Low proportions and low rankings of black police do not necessarily mean poorer police protection for minority neighborhoods. Perhaps a better indicator of quality of police service is the distribution of police-patrol manpower within a city (Bloch 1974; Mladenka and Hill 1978). In 1960 evidence suggests that only black police routinely patrolled black neighborhoods in each of the communities, that they could arrest only black citizens and not whites, and that white police would usually respond only reactively (if at all) to demands or reported crimes in black areas. With the low proportion of black police relative to the proportion black in each community's population, it is clear that the minority sections were underpatrolled compared with most white areas.

Nevertheless, by the late 1960s and certainly by the early 1970s, white officers were routinely patrolling some black neighborhoods, patrols were often integrated, and black police were increasingly allowed to arrest white citizens. These trends were especially apparent in New South cities. Thus Titusville and Riviera Beach began to increase police patrols in high-crime black neighborhoods, whereas the only cities to develop police-community-relations programs were

Titusville and Daytona Beach. By the mid-1970s reported incidents of alleged police brutality toward blacks had declined in almost all communities.

Which political factors help to account for these moderate changes in police protection? One indication is the correlates of community knowledgeables' evaluations of changes in police service and evaluations of various political strategies. As in the case of street services, the informed citizens' perceptions of changes in police services correspond closely to the objective output indicators. The results of correlation analysis, however, are quite different here than they were in the case of street services. First, the conventional electoral strategies of voting and having blacks in public office are less highly correlated with both perceived absolute (.09 and .12, respectively) and relative (.01 and .25, respectively) police-service changes. Only the variable blacks in office is moderately correlated with perceived improvements in police protection in New South and majority-black communities. In a previous study of Florida communities, Clubok, DeGrove, and Farris (1964) suggested that the black vote is often manipulated by white elites, especially in Old South cities. Keech (1968) also found that black electoral politics had little impact on changing police services, except possibly to reduce police brutality to some extent.

Second, unlike the case of street improvements, attending public meetings is a variable that is moderately correlated (.24) with perceived absolute police-service changes, especially in Old South (.37), medium-proportion black (.22), and majority-black (.40) communities. Black political groups often used public meetings as a strategic means of articulating demands for more black police and less police brutality. In addition, in three communities biracial or human-relations organizations also served to voice black concerns, particularly about the police.

Third, although federal grants were important in improving streets for blacks, such grants had little to do with changing police services. The correlations with perceived absolute and relative changes in police protection for blacks are very low (-.01 and -.05, respectively). Moreover, other indicators reaffirm this finding. Only Lake City (through the county sheriff) recieved any federal riot-control money (a $5,000 grant), and only Gretna used relatively large proportions of its federal revenue sharing and Comprehensive Employment and Training Act (CETA) funds for its police force. Perhaps the most significant federal influence was an Office of Revenue Sharing investigation and ultimate finding in 1977 that Daytona Beach was racially discriminating in its hiring practices, especially in its public-safety department. In order not to lose federal funds, the city revised its hiring practices; more black police have since been hired and promoted.

Finally, unlike the case of street services, protesting and even rioting by blacks has tended to bring about improvements in police services. The evaluations of knowledgeable citizens suggest this, as protesting is moderately correlated with absolute changes in police protection in Old South (.20), low-proportion black (.23), and majority-black (.29) communities. Rioting, too, is moderately associated with perceived relative changes in police protection in Old South (.28) and majority-black (.39) cities. Other data lend even stronger support to this proposition. All six communities had at least one black protest, and four had riots, in which criticisms of the police were major reported grievances. In every situation except one (a minor protest in Crestview), black protesting and rioting were followed by at least some reported changes in police services to meet black demands. This was particularly true in the case of riots, as police brutality or lack of black police were stated grievances in every major collective outburst; more black police were hired, patrolling patterns changed, or a police chief dismissed in the near aftermaths of each of these disturbances.

Conclusion

This longitudinal study of six Florida communities documents the degree of inequality in the distribution of two municipal services and begins to link changes in service distribution with various political factors. In 1960 street paving and police services were clearly distributed unequally in each of these communities, with blacks receiving substantially less than whites. By 1976–1977, these municipal services, especially street paving, were distributed more equally; but blacks had still not caught up with most whites in any of these communities.

Nevertheless, blacks made the greatest gains in New South (except for proportion of black police) and majority-black cities. The relatively affluent, growing New South communities usually lack the cultural and legal traditions of discrimination against blacks that are still prevalent in Old South municipalities. In addition, where blacks form a majority of the voting population, as in Gretna and Riviera Beach by the early 1970s, they are able to redistribute basic public services. Yet as blacks increase their proportion of the voting population but still constitute less than a majority, they do not necessarily secure a much more equal share of basic services. Thus street- and police-service changes for blacks in Daytona Beach and Lake City were about the same as similar changes in Titusville and Crestview. This finding lends support to Keech's contention that there is a middle range of black proportion of the population at which whites feel most threatened and will resist black service demands.

In terms of the role of political variables, these factors seem to be only moderately important in explaining either absolute or relative changes in the distribution of services for blacks. It may be that this study has not tapped the most important political variables or that they have not been measured adequately. Or it may be, as indicated by other studies, that bureaucratic decision rules or socioeconomic factors are most important in explaining the delivery patterns of municipal services (Antunes and Mladenka 1976; Jones 1980; Lineberry 1977).

However, this study does indicate that certain political variables are more effective than others in changing the distribution of services, and that the importance of political factors varies depending on the kind of municipal service and type of community. Conventional strategies like voting, electing blacks to office, and securing federal grants were the most effective political variables in improving street services for blacks. Yet these conventional strategies were not very effective in altering black police services; here, black political organizations, voicing demands at public meetings, protesting, and rioting were evaluated as much more important. This indicates that conventional political strategies and federal grants work well when service changes require simply a reallocation of money, but that more unconventional strategies may be necessary when a service redistribution requires more extensive policy changes. In terms of type of community, it seems that in New South cities, where politics is relatively pluralistic, and in majority-black communities, where blacks have gained political control, a variety of either conventional or unconventional political factors is effective. In Old South and in low-proportion-black communities, however, where political systems are relatively closed and blacks have little control, unconventional strategies may have a negative impact, and outside support in the form of federal grants is important.

Although it is difficult to generalize beyond these six communities, the results of this study at least suggest that in smaller cities in the South there has been a great deal of racial inequality in the distribution of municipal services. These service inequalities have been reduced substantially in the last two decades; yet racial differences in service distributions still exist, especially in police protection. Little research has been done on the influence of political variables in the distribution of public services, and this study suggests that political factors are only moderately significant. Yet these findings challenge the results of previous studies that have concluded that there are few racial inequalities in municipal services and that political variables are not important.

References

Antunes, G., and Mladenka, K. 1976. "The Politics of Local Services and Service Distribution." In L.H. Masotti and R.L. Lineberry, eds., *The New Urban Politics,* pp. 147–169. Cambridge, Mass.: Ballinger.

Antunes, G.E., and Plumlee, J.P. 1978. "Ethnicity, Socioeconomic Status, and Bureaucracy as Determinants of the Quality of Neighborhood Streets." In R.L. Lineberry, ed., *The Politics and Economics of Urban Services,* pp. 51–70. Beverly Hills, Calif.: Sage Publications.

Bloch, P.B. 1974. *Equality of Distribution of Police Services: A Case Study of Washington, D.C.* Washington D.C.: Urban Institute.

Bullock, C.S. 1975. "The Election of Blacks in the South: Preconditions and Consequences." *American Journal of Political Science* 19:727–740.

Button, J., and Scher, R. 1979. "Impact of the Civil Rights Movement: Perceptions of Black Municipal Service Changes." *Social Science Quarterly* 60:497–510.

Campbell, D., and Feagin, J.R. 1975. "Black Politics in the South: A Descriptive Analysis." *Journal of Politics* 37:129–162.

Clubok, A.B.; DeGrove, J.M.; and Farris, C.D. 1964. "The Manipulated Negro Vote: Some Pre-Conditions and Consequences." *Journal of Politics* 26:112–129.

Eisinger, P.K. 1976. *Patterns of Interracial Politics: Conflict and Cooperation in the City.* New York: Academic Press.

Fowler, F.J. 1974. *Citizen Attitudes toward Local Government, Services, and Taxes.* Cambridge, Mass.: Ballinger.

Hansen, S.B. 1975. "Participation, Political Structure, and Concurrence." *American Political Science Review* 69:1181–1199.

Hawkins v. *Shaw.* 1971. 437 F. 2d 1286, 1287 (5th Circuit).

Jones, B.D. 1980. *Service Delivery in the City.* New York: Longmon.

Keech, W.R. 1968. *The Impact of Negro Voting: The Role of the Vote in the Quest for Equality.* Chicago: Rand McNally.

Lineberry, R.L. 1977. *Equality and Urban Policy: The Distribution of Municipal Public Services.* Beverly Hills, Calif.: Sage Publications.

Lineberry, R.L., and Welch, R.E. 1974. "Who Gets What: Measuring the Distribution of Urban Services." *Social Science Quarterly* 54:700–712.

Matthews, D.R., and Prothro, J.W. 1966. *Negroes and the New Southern Politics.* New York: Harcourt, Brace and World.

Mladenka, K.R., and Hill, K.Q. 1978. "The Distribution of Urban Police Services." *Journal of Politics* 40:112–133.

National Advisory Commission on Civil Disorders (Kerner Commission). 1968. *Report.* Washington, D.C.: U.S. Government Printing Office.

Price, H.D. 1955. "The Negro and Florida Politics, 1944–1954." *Journal of Politics* 17:198–220.

Rich, R.C. 1979. "Neglected Issues in the Study of Urban Service Distributions: A Research Agenda." *Urban Studies* 16:143–156.

Schumaker, P.D. 1975. "Policy Responsiveness to Protest-Group Demands." *Journal of Politics* 37:488–521.

Walton, H. 1972. *Black Politics: A Theoretical and Structural Analysis.* Philadelphia: Lippincott.

Welch, S. 1975. "The Impact of Urban Riots on Urban Expenditures." *American Journal of Political Science* 19:741–760.

Wirt, F. 1970. *Politics of Southern Equality: Law and Social Change in a Mississippi County.* Chicago: Aldine.

The Effects of Exclusionary Zoning and Residential Segregation on Urban-Service Distributions

Russell S. Harrison

Much recent policy research into the equity of service distributions has focused on intrajurisdictional differences among neighborhoods within specific municipalities. One reason for this concern was a series of federal court rulings in *Hawkins* v. *Town of Shaw* (1972) and its progeny, which focused attention on intrajurisdictional differences in neighborhood services (Lineberry 1974). Other intrajurisdictional research into service distributions has been encouraged by the Ford Foundation, by political activists who favor the idea of community control over local schools, by various federal aid programs that stress neighborhood benefits and neighborhood control over administrative decisions, and by municipal departments desiring to understand and improve administrative allocation decisions (Merget 1979; Rich 1979; Frederickson 1973; Altschuler 1970). As a result, sophisticated studies have begun to measure differences in public goods and services among neighborhoods in places as diverse as Berkeley and Oakland, California, in the West, and Houston, Washington, D.C., and New York in the East (Benson and Lund 1969; Levy and Meltsner 1974; Lineberry 1977; *Burner* v. *Washington* 1972; Block 1974; Fisk and Lancer 1974; *Beal* v. *Lindsay* 1972).

Even though the recent attention paid to intrajurisdictional differences in services is proper, it should not be allowed to obscure the need for continued attention to interjurisdictional differences. In particular, too little attention has been paid to the problem of service inequities among independent, autonomous local governments. Too often the concern for service equity has stopped at the city limits (Rich 1979, pp. 148-150).

Empirical analysis of interjurisdictional differences in public services and private resources should be pursued to clarify problems of exclusionary zoning and residential segregation in metropolitan areas. Exclusionary zoning and metropolitan residential segregation have been strongly condemned in a wide variety of recent state-court cases (National Committee against Discrimination in Housing and Urban Land Institute 1974; *Oakwood at Madison, Inc.* v. *Township of Madison* 1973, 1977; *Southern Burlington County NAACP* v. *Mt. Laurel* 1975; *Berger et al.* v. *New Jersey and the Borough of Mantoloking* 1976; *Urban League of Greater New Brunswick* v. *Cartaret* 1976; *Home Builders League of South Jersey, Inc.* v. *Township of Berlin* 1979; *Borough of Morris Plains* v. *Department of the Public Advocate* 1979). Research into causes and cures for these problems would therefore seem highly desirable. In particular, it would seem desirable to test the fiscal-zoning theory of metropolitan residential segregation, which predicts that defective patterns of local-government organization and finance lead to interjurisdictional differences in private resources and public services.

The Fiscal-Zoning Theory

In this chapter I will attempt to integrate the scattered fiscal-zoning arguments into a relatively coherent empirical theory, to explain how it relates to questions of urban-service distributions, and to present evidence that constitutes a preliminary test of that theory.

No one has spelled out precisely the total dimensions of the fiscal-zoning theory or those aspects that are particularly subject to empirical proof or disproof. However, it can generally be interpreted as implying the existence of positive relationships among fragmented structures of public finance and governmental organization in metropolitan areas, restrictive land-use laws, increased housing costs, interjurisdictional residential segregation, and fiscal inequality among local governments responsible for administering major local programs.

The existence of these relationships has been argued in several bodies of research. Research on equality in public-school finance, especially research inspired by state-court cases like *Serrano* v. *Priest* (1971), is one major source (Harrison 1976). Another major source for these arguments has been court litigation and related legal research attacking exclusionary zoning in urban housing markets (*Southern Burlington County NAACP* v. *Mt. Laurel* 1975; National Committee against Discrimination in Housing *1974; Sternlieb and* Listokin 1976; Babcock and Bosselman 1963, 1973; Williams and Norman 1970; Williams 1955, 1970; Willians and Wacks 1969; Sager 1970). Empirical research into causes and consequences for exclusionary zoning and residential segregation has also served to refine many of these ideas (Seidel 1978; Sagalyn and Sternlieb 1972; Hamilton 1973; Hamilton, Mills, and Puryear 1975; Hill 1974; Harrison 1976).

The simplified causal diagram in figure 6-1 represents a preliminary effort to synthesize some of the basic assumptions or arguments developed in this scattered literature. This diagram is also intended as a guide to future research. It attempts to predict some of the major policy antecedents for unequal private and public resources among local governments.

Such predictions can be evaluated not only in terms of their intuitive appeal, but also in terms of social-science measurement techniques. In fact, if these predictions are not formally tested and documented with reliable data, then the fiscal-zoning theory must be viewed much more as a thesis, or collection of theses, than as a reliable theory. As it now stands, the fiscal-zoning theory is

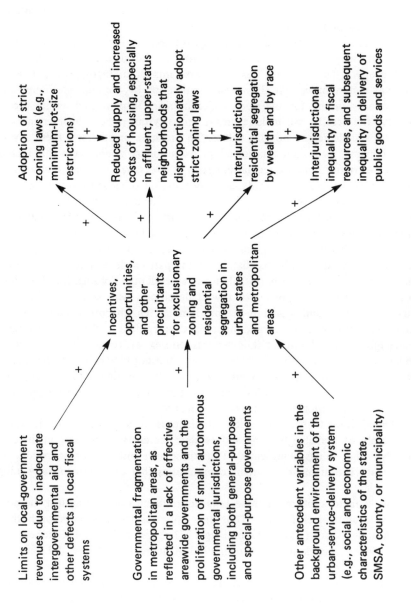

Figure 6–1. Simplified Causal Diagram of the Fiscal-Zoning Theory

highly controversial not simply because it has been used to challenge practices such as exclusionary zoning that are common to many local communities in urban areas, and not simply because it challenges alternative theoretical models of metropolitan life, but also because the process of empirical documentation has not proceeded very far.

To clarify the empirical and normative implications of the fiscal-zoning theory, it can be usefully interpreted as follows. Local-government reliance on local property-tax revenues has a perverse impact in metropolitan areas: it punishes communities that allow easy immigration by the poor and minorities. If low-cost housing for the poor and minorities is permitted within a community, the results will include higher property-tax rates, a lower quality of services, and decreased housing values. To preclude or minimize these adverse fiscal impacts, local communities adopt exclusionary zoning laws that include overtly restrictive land-use regulations such as excessive minimum requirements for lot sizes, setbacks, side yards, and floor areas. Exclusionary zoning laws also include more covert practices such as growth controls, failure to zone for multi-family rental housing, and bans on trailer courts. All these practices reduce the supply of housing affordable by low- and moderate-income families.

Such exclusionary zoning practices are especially popular in certain affluent, predominantly white suburbs that lie in the path of development and contain vast tracts of land eminently suitable for new residential housing. Local residents exercise their land-use powers to thwart developers who would build housing suitable for low- and moderate-income families. On the other hand, they encourage selective commercial and industrial development that maximizes ratables but requires only limited public services. Stores, office buildings, and white-collar workers are welcomed in these suburbs, but not blue collars or black faces. Thus residents can continue to enjoy low tax rates or high public expenditures per family and per student, along with the other amenities possible in an upper-status, socially homogeneous enclave of privilege.

Once adopted, strict zoning laws and land-use regulations effectively restrict the supply of available housing and escalate the costs for housing in the community, other things being equal. Thus these laws and regulations exclude the poor from the affluent suburban communities that disproportionately adopt them.

In de facto application these laws discriminate not only against the poor, but also against black families. Thus they cause residential segregation both by wealth and by race (Alol and Goldberg 1971; Sager 1970; Alol, Goldberg, and White 1969; Babcock and Bosselman 1963; Williams 1955; Kirby, deLeeuw, and Silverman 1972).

There are various reasons that blacks suffer disproportionately from exclusionary zoning laws and increased housing costs. In general, blacks have lower average wages and less stable incomes than do whites. Moreover, they disproportionately lack the equity accrued from previous home ownership. Of those blacks who do own houses, many are located in center-city slum neighborhoods in which house values may actually decline over time relative to average house values in the overall metropolitan area. Thus blacks in particular cannot afford to relocate in suburbs with zoning regulations that restrict they supply of low-cost housing.

As a result of the unequal impact of exclusionary zoning laws, residential segregation is preserved and promoted in the metropolitan area, to the disadvantage of the poor in general and of blacks in particular. To the extent that exclusionary zoning exaggerates economic segregation, it increases fiscal disparities among local jurisdictions because the taxable resources among metropolitan communities become more inequitably distributed. To the extent that exclusionary zoning exaggerates racial segregation among metropolitan communities, it encourages white flight from the center city as a response to school integration and to other sources of stress for conservative white families. Thus a cycle of center-city deterioration and decline is promoted, with subsequent impairment of the ability of the center-city government to provide needed goods and services to its citizens. Similar distortions apply not simply to the center-city ghetto, but also to the older, poorer, blacker suburbs in the urban fringe. The result is fiscal imbalance and unequal services throughout the entire metropolitan area.

To reduce the fiscal incentives that lead to these results, reforms are needed. Increased federal and state aid are obvious possibilities. To the extent that local citizens are not dependent strictly on local funds to finance local programs, they have fewer incentives for fiscal zoning. To reduce the opportunities for fiscal zoning, governmental consolidation is required. This can be accomplished by giving the county government a larger role in providing goods and services, by restricting the incorporation of small suburban enclaves with unbridled land-use powers, or by establishing metropolitan governments with centralized fiscal and zoning responsibilities (Rich 1977).

How valid is this theory of fiscal zoning? A few experts on land use and urban finances accept one or more tenets of the fiscal-zoning theory, or at least the general notions that zoning laws affect where and how people live and that fiscal considerations affect what zoning laws are adopted (for example, Netzer 1974; Seidel 1978; U.S. National Commission on Urban Problems 1968; Sternlieb and Listokin 1976); but many experts have attacked major empirical predictions of the fiscal-zoning theory. For example, several authors deny that exclusionary zoning laws have any independent effect on housing prices or residents' incomes. Thus land-use laws or "fiscal zoning" cannot fairly be cited as a cause of residential segregation or of differences in public services observable in most metropolitan areas (Orr 1975, pp. 74–75; Rose 1979).

Some other researchers argue that the role of fiscal variables in shaping residential segregation patterns is so limited as to invalidate the whole fiscal-zoning theory. They might concede that governmental fragmentation increases opportunities for exclusionary zoning and residential segregation. But they do not concede that intergovernmental-aid variables or local fiscal policies significantly increase or decrease incentives for governmental fragmentation, exclusionary zoning, and metropolitan residential segregation (Branfman, Cohen, and Trubeck 1973; Windsor and James 1975; Windsor 1979).

Still other researchers reject any notion that governmental consolidation can improve the equity of service distributions in metropolitan areas. They deny that attempts at governmental consolidation have any real possibility of success. Even if they allow for the possibility of consolidation, they deny that governmental fragmentation is a significant source of metropolitan residential segregation. Even if governmental fragmentation might lead to residential segregation and cause inequality in the distribution of private resources, they deny that governmental fragmentation has any serious adverse or inequitable impacts on the distribution of public resources. From their point of view, the private-market system of fiercely competing autonomous producers of private goods and services is the optimal model for the public sector to follow (Bish 1971; Ostrom 1972; Schaefer 1975; Neiman 1976; cf. Hill 1976).

Who is right? Do defective patterns of local-government finance and organization lead to exclusionary zoning, residential segregation, and inequality in public services? On one side of the issue stand the proponents of the fiscal-zoning model, who are generally advocates of metropolitan reform by governmental consolidation and fiscal centralization. On the other side stand many advocates of a public-choice model of metropolitan decision making, who generally defend the polycentric status quo. Which position best describes urban realities nationwide?

Unfortunately, no definitive answers are available. In part, the lack of consensus occurs because the proponents and opponents of the fiscal-zoning model define equity and fairness differently or focus on different consequences of governmental organization. However, there is not even consensus in the public-policy literature about major causes and cures for metropolitan segregation and inequality in public expenditures among different metropolitan communities. Even though research techniques are available that could provide reliable empirical answers, there is still confusion about policy antecedents for differences in private or public resources among metropolitan communities.

A major reason is simply that few policy researchers have made the effort necessary to collect and compute indexes of residential segregation or fiscal inequality among the many local governments in various metropolitan areas. Still fewer have attempted to connect residential segregation or fiscal inequality with their policy antecedents. Those who have made such attempts have often been content with incomplete data. They analyzed data only for communities within one metropolitan area within one state, or focused only a few communities within each metropolitan area they studied, or examined only a small nonrandom sample of metropolitan areas that excludes major regions (Orr 1975;

Branfman, Cohen, and Trubeck 1973). Thus empirical answers based on comprehensive data are sadly lacking.

Empirical Research

This chapter reports three sets of relevant evidence that seem useful for clarifying some of the more controversial predictions of the fiscal-zoning theory. One sample contains data on zoning laws and house prices for municipalities throughout an entire state. Another sample contains data on housing laws and residential segregation by race for every county within a state. A third sample contains data on fiscal and structural antecedents for residential segregation and fiscal inequality among local governments for major metropolitan areas throughout the United States. Even though these data sources cannot conclusively answer all the complex issues raised by the fiscal-zoning theory, they can at least illustrate data sources useful for testing many of those issues.

Of course, there are many analytical methods useful for testing complex policy theories. However, one particularly useful method is to translate verbal predictions into mathematical predictions of positive and negative relationships, and then to measure actual empirical relationships with multivariate regression or correlation analysis of cross-sectional data. This basic approach will be followed in this analysis.

One highly controversial prediction of the fiscal-zoning theory is that exclusionary zoning laws increase the costs of housing in local municipalities that adopt such laws, even taking into account socioeconomic antecedents that may affect both local zoning laws and local housing patterns.

To test this prediction, one must select a local zoning law as the independent variable. Minimum-lot-size restrictions seem a highly appropriate choice, since they have served as the focal point of much exclusionary-zoning litigation (*National Land and Investment Company* v. *Kohn* 1965; *In Re Appeal of Kit-Mar Builders, Inc.* 1970). One must select as the dependent variable a representative index of housing costs, such as the median value of a single-family, owner-occupied house in each municipality.

In addition, one must take into account that various background characteristics of each community may affect both the adoption of zoning laws and the costs of housing. These effects must be controlled to avoid spurious relationships. Potential sources of spurious relationships include variables such as the area, size, density, racial composition, and average family income both for a local community and for the overall area in which the community is located. To control for these potential sources of spurious relationships, partial correlations must be computed to measure the linkage between zoning laws and housing prices.

It is very difficult to collect information on zoning laws, housing prices, and background characteristics for a comprehensive sample of municipalities.

However, I was able to obtain relevant information for almost all the municipalities in the state of New Jersey, except for certain places with less than 2,500
population and for certain townships for which complete information was not
available. The New Jersey sample seemed particularly useful because it covered
all sections of one of the most urban states in the nation and because many New
Jersey municipalities have used their zoning powers to adopt exclusionary zoning
laws. House prices are not yet available from the 1980 census of housing for
each New Jersey municipality. Thus I used 1970 house prices as the dependent
variable and correlated them with 1967 zoning laws, using available data. The
control variables were measured using both 1960 and 1970 data.

Table 6-1 reports the results from this study. Here exclusionary zoning laws
do seem correlated with increased housing costs. Specifically, where the minimum lot size required per residential building is higher, so is the average price
of housing in that community.

There are many ways to interpret this relationship. However, one reason
seems obvious. Stricter minimum-lot-size laws reduce the supply of building lots
per acre available for residential use. As the supply of housing decreases, the cost
per unit increases.

Table 6-1
**Correlations of Minimum-Lot-Size Laws in 1967 with Median Value of Owner-
Occupied, Single-Family Houses in 1970 for All New Jersey Municipalities with
Available Data**

Control Variables	Partial Correlation Coefficient	Degrees of Freedom	Significance Level
1. Local population density in 1960	.23	478	.001
2. County per capita income	.22	478	.001
3. County percentage black	.22	478	.001
4. Per capita local income	.22	478	.001
5. Local population size in 1960	.23	478	.001
6. Local population size in 1970	.23	478	.001
7. Local percentage black in 1960	.23	478	.001
8. Local percentage black in 1970	.23	478	.001
9. Local land area	.27	478	.001
10. All of the above	.18	470	.001

Sources: U.S. Bureau of Census, *Census of Housing, 1970; Census of Population, 1970;
Census of Population 1960* (Washington, D.C.: U.S. Government Printing Office, 70). New
Jersey Department of Community Affairs, *Zoning in New Jersey*. Trenton, N.J.: Depart-
ment of Community Affairs, State of New Jersey, ND.

This particular study includes controls for a variety of the prominent social- and economic-background characteristics of each local community and its larger county environment, both past and present. Nevertheless, all the results are statistically significant. Similar results might be expected for other possible indexes of house prices, other types of zoning laws, or other appropriate background variables. Overall, the use of additional independent variables can be expected to explain addition variation in housing costs. Further research on these lines would seem indicated.

Another controversial prediction of the fiscal-zoning theory, or at least the version of the fiscal-zoning theory presented in this analysis, focuses on the discriminatory racial impact of strict zoning laws. A positive relationships is predicted between exclusionary zoning laws and inequality in the distribution of housing opportunities for people of different races.

Many social scientists might concede that where zoning is more restrictive, there will be greater dispersion in the location of rich and poor families. However, it is much less obvious to many housing analysts that strict zoning laws might be related to dispersion and polarization in the location of white and black families, or to some other index of racial segregation. Thus it is interesting to measure the relationship between zoning laws and an index of residential segregation by race, again using data from New Jersey.

To measure racial segregation within a county, one can simply determine the coefficient of variation for the percentage black in each municipality of each county. Those counties with more dispersion in racial composition presumably have more residential segregation.

To measure racial segregation in New Jersey, I computed a coefficient of variation for th percentage black in each municipality in each county in both 1960 and 1970, and then computed the percentage increase in segregation over this ten-year period. Such an index takes into account that counties with high levels of segregation in the past may have high levels of segregation in the future, regardless of exclusionary zoning.

To measure exclusionary zoning, I developed a complicated index. For each county I first computed the average minimum lot size for each municipality, and then multiplied it by the average number of residential zones for each municipality. This more refined index takes into account a common practice of exclusionary municipalities: they allow small lots in at least one residential zone but impose much stricter requirements in other zones. In fact, a close reading of many zoning ordinances indicates that the strictness of minimum-lot-size requirements increases as a function of the number of total zones that are adopted. Therefore, I assume that where there are many zones within a community, most of the open land in the locality has even narrower restrictions than can be deduced from the absolute minimum adopted for the most lenient zone.

To control for potential sources of spurious relationships, I utilized three suppressor variables. According to the fiscal-zoning theory, where there is more intergovernmental aid, there may be less residential segregation, as well as fewer incentives for exclusionary zoning. Thus in order to isolate the linkage between zoning laws and racial segregation, one must control for intergovernmental aid— for example, as measured by the proportion of total local revenues in the county area that is financed by state and federal aid. Moreover, according to a broadly defined fiscal-zoning theory, one must also control for the degree of governmental fragmentation within an area. Namely, the larger the number of independent municipalities within a county area, the greater the opportunities for exclusionary zoning and the greater the probability of residential segregation. Further, a broadly defined fiscal-zoning theory allows for the possibility that various social and economic pressures may also precipitate both exclusionary zoning and residential segregation. For example, it has often been argued that areas with larger concentrations of minority groups will tend to display greater racial discrimination. Therefore, I will also control for the percentage of black and Hispanic persons in each county.

For these variables I was able to obtain data for all the 567 municipalities in New Jersey, matching 1967 laws against changes in racial segregation from 1960 to 1970. However, because the indexes of average minimum lot sizes and residential segregation were computed by county, I was allowed only 21 units of analysis, since there are only 21 counties in New Jersey.

With such a small number of cases, one cannot expect high levels of statistical significance. Moreover, when one measures partial relationships that include statistical controls for three other confounding variables, one loses further degrees of freedom. This also reduces observed levels of statistical significance. Thus the results in table 6–2 are impressive.

At least in this state, zoning laws *do* seem closely connected with patterns of racial imbalance in housing opportunities. Consistently higher rates of growth in racial segregation are found in those counties in which the average community imposes higher minimum-lot-size restrictions, and in which the typical community imposes a variety of residential zones, many with lot-size requirements far more stringent than those in the zone with the least restrictive minimum requirement. As increasingly severe lot-size regulations begin to cover more and more acres in an urban housing market, it becomes increasingly difficult for blacks and the poor to find housing opportunities in the same municipalities in which whites and the rich are concentrated.

Overall, these two tables illustrate how data on individual municipalities or counties within a given state can be utilized to evaluate the fiscal-zoning theory, not only in New Jersey, but also in other states. Indeed, much more research would seem desirable to explore further the highly controversial predictions of the fiscal-zoning theory that zoning laws can create serious distortions in urban housing markets.

Table 6–3 illustrates still another type of data source that can be used to evaluate the fiscal-zoning theory. Table 6–3 reports data obtained from a sample

Table 6–2
Correlations of Average Minimum-Lot-Size Regulations in 1967 for Each of New Jersey's Twenty-one Counties with Percentage Increase in Residential Segregation by Race from 1960 to 1970

	Correlation Coefficient	Number of Counties	Significant at .05 Level of Probability?
1. Bivariate correlation	.46	21 of 21	Yes
2. Partial correlation coefficient, controlling for			
a. percentage minority in county, both black and Hispanic	.49	21 of 21	Yes
b. percentage revenues raised by local governments in county from intergovernmental aid			
c. number of municipalities in each county			

Sources: U.S. Bureau of Census, *Census of Population, 1970; Census of Government, 1967* (Washington, D.C.: U.S. Government Printing Office, 70). New Jersey Department of Community Affairs, *Zoning in New Jersey*. Trenton, N.J.: Department of Community Affairs, State of New Jersey, ND.

Note: As measured by changes in the coefficient of variation for the percentage black in each municipality in each county.

of major metropolitan areas in the United States. Such data can be used to evaluate another highly controversial prediction by the fiscal-zoning theory. Namely, the table clarifies whether a fragmented system of local-government finance and structural organization leads to inequality in the distribution of both private resources and public resources in metropolitan areas.

The dependent variables are coefficients of variation that measure the dispersion of whites and blacks among municipalities in each metropolitan area, as well as the dispersion of per-student expenditures among the school systems of each metropolitan area. These coefficients of variation serve as useful operational indicators to measure residential segregation by race and fiscal inequality among local governments in each of the 100 largest Standard Metropolitan Statistical Areas (SMSAs) in the United States.

This research uses racial-segregation patterns in 1970 because detailed racial totals for every municipality in every metropolitan area are not yet available from the 1980 census of population. For symmetry, the dispersion of public-school expenditures is also measured for 1970. The intergovernmental-aid and governmental-fragmentation variables are measured using data from the 1967

Table 6–3

**Beta Coefficients Linking Intergovernmental Aid and Governmental
Fragmentation to Metropolitan Residential Segregation and Inequality in
Public-School Expenditures, in a Sample of Large SMSAs**

	Dependent Variables (1970 data = three year lag)	
	Metropolitan Residential Segregation by Race (Coefficient of Variation for Percentage Black in Each Municipality of Each SMSA)	Inequality in Public-School Finances (Coefficient of Variation for per Student Expenditures in Each School System of Each SMSA with Available Data)
Policy Antecedents (1967 data)		
1. Intergovernmental aid: state aid for education as proportion of local revenues	−.18	−.39
2. Governmental fragmentation:		
a. Number of governments per capita in SMSA	.35	–
b. Number of school systems in SMSA	–	.20

Source: Data were obtained from U.S. Bureau of Census, *Census of Population, 1970;
Census of Government, 1967* (Washington, D.C.: U.S. Government Printing Office, 1970);
and U.S. Office of Education, *Statistics of Local Public School Systems, Finance, 1969-1970*
(Washington, D.C.: U.S. Government Printing Office, 1972).

Notes: The sample covers the 100 largest SMSAs in the United States in 1970. The control
variables used in this analysis include either social and economic variables (such as percentage families with incomes of $10,000 or more, black income relative to white income,
the gini index of income concentration, population size, percentage urban, density, and
percentage black in the SMSA) or policy variables (such as local-property-tax use, property-
tax assessment ratios, and federal aid use in the SMSA). The measurement of these variables
and their correlations with residential segregation or fiscal inequality have been explored in
previous research see R.S. Harrison, *Equality in Public School Finance* (Lexington, Mass.:
Lexington Books, D.C. Heath and Company, 1976).

census of governments. The control variables include a variety of social, economic, and policy variables that previous research indicates are also correlated
with either residential segregation or fiscal inequality in metropolitan areas
(Harrison 1976, pp. 138–139, 181).

For this research, state aid is predicted to be an intergovernmental-revenue
variable that reduces incentives for exclusionary zoning and residential segregation in metropolitan areas, and reduces fiscal inequality among local-govern-
mental jurisdictions. In fact, where state aid is a larger proportion of local
expenditures on education, there is less metropolitan residential segregation by

race for this sample. Moreover, where there is more state aid, there is also less inequality in public-school finances.

Governmental fragmentation can be measured in many different ways, including measurement of the total number of governments in a metropolitan area or the number of specific jurisdictions, such as school systems, in the metropolitan area. Such indexes are positively correlated with patterns of residential segregation and fiscal inequality. Where there is a larger number of local governments in a metropolitan area, there is more residential segregation by race among the local governments in the metropolitan area. Moreover, where there is a larger number of school systems in metropolitan areas, there is greater inequality in expenditures among the school system in the metropolitan area.

Even with extensive controls, all these measured relationships are in the predicted directions. It would seem that *limited intergovernmental aid and excessive governmental fragmentation can create incentives and opportunities for residential segregation and fiscal inequality in metropolitan areas.* It would seem, further, that whatever policy antecedents increase the dispersion of private resources among local governments in metropolitan areas also increase the dispersion of public goods and services in metropolitan areas.

Implications for Research and Reform

Of course, such evidence as has been reported is far from complete. Alternative indicators for key independent and dependent variables need to be constructed, along with alternative control variables. Much further analysis is needed to explore in detail the relationship between the theoretical concepts in the fiscal-zoning theory and operational indicators such as those used in this limited research. Other limits on local government finances and other types of governmental fragmentation may generally increase residential segregation and fiscal inequality. Future research should study their effects on urban service distributions and the effects due to independent variables other than limits on local-givernment finances and governmental fragmentation. Empirical results from different samples need to be compared and contrasted.

Even before further research is done, however, policy scientists should consider carefully the implications of empirical findings that link limits on local-government finance, governmental fragmentation in metropolitan areas, interjurisdictional residential segregation, and inequality in the distribution of public goods and services in metropolitan areas.

Some policy scientists may be public-choice theorists who favor a polycentric model of metropolitan policymaking. Others may be advocates of metropolitan reform who espouse the values of governmental consolidation and centralization, both structural and fiscal. Regardless of their previous sympathies in the consolidation-fragmentation debate, policy scientists should consider carefully evidence that fiscal centralization and governmental consolidation may help balance interjurisdictional needs and services in metropolitan areas.

These findings should also be carefully considered by those concerned with the problem of inequality in public-school finance. In *Robinson* v. *Cahill* (1973), *Serrano* v. *Priest* (1971), *Horton* v. *Meskill* (1977), and similar cases, state courts have mandated the goal of equality in educational resources. Often only fiscal reforms have been considered as means to achieve the ideal. However, structural reforms may also be effective means to maximize equality with a minimum of costs.

Overall, the findings in the present research support key arguments in the fiscal-zoning theory. Nevertheless, it should be stressed that these findings are intended to inspire, not preclude, further analysis. They are not intended to provide final answers to the numerous issues involved in the fiscal-zoning debate, let alone the many other issues raised by advocates and critics of the wide-ranging public-choice literature (Golembiewski 1977; Ostrom 1977).

Fiscal-zoning theory requires much further analysis and refinement. Further research should explore many other policy antecedents for exclusionary zoning and residential segregation in urban areas, and should measure their contributions to interjurisdictional differences in private and public resources. Additional controls should be introduced for other social, economic, and psychological variables that may also affect exclusionary zoning, residential segregation, and fiscal imbalance in metropolitan areas. Alternative indexes for complex phenomena such as residential segregation and expenditure inequality should be computed and correlated with each other and with their varied causes and consequences.

Obviously the results of this future research cannot be predicted with any great precision. Nevertheless, based on present research it would seem reasonable to predict one general set of findings. How local governments are organized and financed can help shape patterns of exclusionary zoning and residential segregation in urban areas and, subsequently, can contribute to inequality in the distribution of urban-service capacities.

Court Cases

Beal v. *Lindsay*, 468 F. 2d 287, 2d Cir. (1972).

Berger et al. v. *New Jersey and the Borough of Mantoloking*, 364 A 2d 993 (1976).

Borough of Morris Plains v. *Department of the Public Advocate*, 169 NJ Super 403 (1979).

Burner v. *Washington*, C.A. No. 242–71 D.D.C. (1972).

Hawkins v. *Town of Shaw*, 461 F 2d 1171 (1972).

Home Builders League of South Jersey, Inc. v. *Township of Berlin*, 81 NJ 127 (1979).

Horton v. *Meskill,* 172 Conn 615 (1977).
In Re Appeal of Kit-Mar Builders, Inc., 439 Pa 466, 268 A. 2d 765 (1970).
National Land and Investment Company v. *Kohn,* 419 Pa 504, 215 A 2d 597 (1965).
Oakwood at Madison, Inc. v. *Township of Madison,* 371 A 2d 1992 (1973).
Oakwood at Madison, Inc. v. *Township of Madison,* 72 NJ 481 (1977).
Robinson v. *Cahill,* 303 A 2d 273 (1973).
Serrano v. *Priest,* 483 P 2d 1241 (1971).
Southern Burlington County NAACP v. *Mt. Laurel,* 236 A 2d 713 (1975).
Urban League of Greater New Brunswick v. *Cartaret,* 359 A 2d 879 (1976).

References

Alol, F., and Goldberg, A.A. 1971. "Racial and Economic Exclusionary Zoning: The Beginning of the End?" *Urban Law Annual.*

Alol, F.; Goldberg, A.A.; and White, J. 1969. "Racial and Economic Segregation by Zoning: Death Knell for Home Rule?" *University of Toledo Law Review* 1.

Altshuler, A.A. 1970. *Community Control.* New York: Pegasus.

Babcock, R., and Bosselman, F.P. 1963. "Suburban Zoning and the Apartment Boom." *University of Pennsylvania Law Review* 3.

——. 1973. *Exclusionary Zoning: Land Use Regulations and Housing in the 1970s.* New York: Praeger.

Benson, C.S., and Lund, P.B. 1969. *Neighborhood Distributions of Local Public Services.* Berkeley: Institute of Governmental Services, University of California.

Bish, R.L. 1971. *The Public Economy of Metropolitan Areas.* Chicago: Markham.

Block, P.B. 1974. *Equality of Distribution of Police Services: A Case Study of Washington, D.C.* Washington, D.C.: Urban Institute.

Branfman, E.J.; Cohen, B.I.; and Trubeck, D.M. 1973. "Measuring the Invisible Wall: Land Use Controls and the Residential Patterns of the Poor." *Yale Law Journal* 82:483–508.

Fisk, D., and Lancer, C.A. 1974. *Equality of Distribution of Recreation Services: A Case Study of Washingtin, D.C.* Washington, D.C.: Urban Institute.

Frederickson, G. 1973. *Neighborhood Control in the 1970s.* New York: Chandler.

Golembiewski, R.T. 1977. "A Critique of 'Democratic Administration' and Its Supporting Ideation. *American Political Science Review* 71:1488–1507.

Hamilton, B.W. 1973. "Property Taxation's Incentive to Fiscal Zoning." In G.E. Peterson, ed., *Property Tax Reform,* pp. 125–139. Washington, D.C.: Urban Institute.

Hamilton, B.W.; Mills, E.; and Puryear, D. 1975. "The Tiebout Hypothesis and Residential Income Segregation." In E.S. Mills and W.W. Oates, eds., *Fiscal*

Zoning and Land-Use Controls, pp. 101-118. Lexington, Mass: Lexington Books, D.C. Heath and Company.

Harrison, R.S. 1976. *Equality in Public School Finance.* Lexington, Mass.: Lexington Books, D.C. Heath and Company.

Hill, R.C. 1974. "Separate and Unequal: Governmental Inequality in the Metropolis." *American Political Science Review* 68:1557-1568.

———. 1976. "The Social Stratification and Governmental Inequality Hypothesis: A Rejoinder." *American Political Science Review* 70:154-159.

Kirby, R.F.; deLeeuw, F.; and Silverman, W. 1972. *Residential Zoning and Equal Housing Opportunities.* Washington, D.C.: Urban Institute.

Levy, F.S., and Meltsner, A.J. 1974. *Urban Outcomes.* Berkeley: University of California Press.

Lineberry, R.L. 1974. "Mandating Urban Equality: The Distribution of Municipal Services." *Texas Law Review* (December):25-58.

———. 1977. *Equality and Urban Policy.* Beverly Hills, Calif.: Sage Publications.

Merget, A.E. 1979. "Equity in the Distribution of Municipal Services." In H. Bryce, ed., *Revitalizing Cities,* pp. 161-191. Lexington, Mass.: Lexington Books, D.C. Heath and Company.

National Comitttee against Discrimination in Housing and Urban Land Institute. 1974. *Fair Housing and Exclusionary Land Use.* Washington, D.C.

Neiman, M. 1976. "Communications: Social Stratification and Governmental Inequality." *American Political Science Review* 70:149-154.

Netzer, D. 1974. *Economics and Urban Problems.* New York: Basic Books.

N.J. Department of Community Affairs. 1970. *Zoning in New Jersey.* Trenton, N.J.

Orr, L.L. 1975. *Income, Employment, and Urban Residential Location.* New York: Academic Press.

Ostrom, V. 1972. "Polycentricity." Paper prepared for delivery at the 1972 Annual Meeting of the American Political Science Association. Washington, D.C., 5-9 September.

———. 1977. "Some Problems in Doing Political Theory." *American Political Science Review* 71:1508-1525.

Rich, R.C. 1977. "Equity and Institutional Design in Urban Service Delivery." *Urban Affairs Quarterly* 12(March):383-410.

———. 1979. "Neglected Issues in the Study of Urban Service Distributions: A Research Agenda." *Urban Studies* 16(June):143-156.

Rose, J.G. 1979. "Myths and Misconceptions of Exclusionary Zoning Litigation." *Real Estate Law Journal* 8(Fall):99-124.

Sagalyn, L.B., and Sternlieb, G. 1972. *Zoning and Housing Costs.* New Brunswick, N.J.: Center for Urban Policy Research.

Sager, L.G. 1970. "Tight Little Islands: Exclusionary Zoning, Equal Protection and the Indigent." *Stanford Law Review* 21, no. 4: 767-800.

Schaefer, R. 1975. "Exclusionary Land Use Controls: Conceptual and Empirical Problems in Measuring the Invisible Wall." Discussion paper, Harvard University Department of City and Regional Planning.

Seidel, S.R. 1978. *Housing Costs and Government Regulations.* New Brunswick, N.J.: Center for Urban Policy Research.

Sternlieb, G., and Listokin, D. 1976. "Exclusionary Zoning: State of the Art, Strategies for the Future." In U.S. Department of Housing and Urban Development, *Housing in the Seventies,* vol. 1, 325-350. Washington, D.C.: U.S. Government Printing Office.

——. 1970a. *Census of Housing.* Washington, D.C.: U.S. Government Printing Office.

——. 1970b. *Census of Population.* Washington, D.C.: U.S. Government Printing Office.

U.S. Bureau of Census. 1976. *Census of Government.* Washington, D.C.: U.S. Government Printing Office.

U.S. National Commission on Urban Problems. 1968. *Building the American City.* Washington, D.C.: U.S. Government Printing Office.

Williams, N. 1955. "Planning Law and Democratic Living." *Law and Contemporary Problems* 20.

——. 1970. "The Three Systems of Land Use Control." *Rutgers Law Review* 25, no. 1.

Williams, N., and Norman, T. 1970. "Exclusionary Land Use Control: The Case of North Eastern New Jersey." *Syracuse Law Review* 22, no. 2.

Williams, N., and Wacks, E. 1969. "Segregation of Residential Areas along Economic Lines: Lionshead Lake Revisited." *Wisconsin Law Review.*

Windsor, O.D. 1979. *Fiscal Zoning in Suburban Communities.* Lexington, Mass.: Lexington Books, D.C. Heath and Company.

Windsor, O.D., and James, F.J. 1975. "Breaking the Invisible Wall: Fiscal Reform and Municipal Land Use Regulation." In R. Lineberry and L.H. Masotti, eds., *Urban Problems and Public Policy,* pp. 87-106. Lexington, Mass.: Lexington Books, D.C. Heath and Company.

Part II
City Finances and
Service Distributions

7 The Distribution of Urban Services in a Declining City

E. Terrence Jones

Many of the major U.S. cities have experienced hard times since World War II. A brief burst of expansion in the first few years after 1945 was followed by a decline that has yet to end. Cities' population declined, their economies shrank, their housing deteriorated, and their crime rates increased. The people who stayed in central cities were increasingly poor, economically and socially dependent, and—usually—nonwhite. The changes in the demographic and economic character of these cities has created a new agenda for their governments. Smaller populations and fewer jobs mean a reduced tax base; yet the people who remain have a greater per capita need for public services. Paradoxically, as the implicit (and often explicit) demand for government assistance has risen, governments' financial ability to provide goods and services has declined.

In such a setting, urban governments confront many problems. Examples include squeezing more blood out of the same revenue turnips, digging up previously undiscovered nonanemic turnips, avoiding excessive debt, and re-examining the intracity allocation of existing services.

This chapter deals with this last issue. As fiscal push comes to service shove, which areas of the city pay the price? Is the burden spread evenly, or do certain areas suffer a disproportionate decline in their share of services? If specific areas are required to pay most of the piper's bill, which ones are they? These two questions are applied to the city of St. Louis's distribution of uniformed police personnel and street-maintenance services between 1950 and 1974.

Previous Research

One can find appropriate pieces of previous research to support any desired answer to these questions. Will whatever inequity existed in 1950 persist until 1974? The notion of incrementalism, propounded by Lindblom (1965) and tested successfully by many others, seems to suggest that inequity would not be likely to change substantially over time. For a great many reasons (such as the inertia in any system), radical changes are unlikely.

In fact, however, incrementalism can be used to argue either side of the question. If the incrementalism applies to a given set of policy outputs (for example, the number of police personnel by district) and consequently there is little alteration in personnel distribution even when conditions (for example, the number of persons living in the district) change, then incremental policies can lead to nonincremental outcomes—a sharp increase in net inequity. If, on the other hand, incrementalism applies to a more general "mutual partisan adjustment" among the city's areas, then the consequent bargaining would tend to incorporate the changing conditions and to reproduce essentially the same inequity outcome year after year.

If inequity increases, will certain types of areas—especially those with growing nonwhite populations and those with persons whose incomes are not keeping pace with the society's norms—bear most of the burden? Existing research on urban-service-delivery patterns suggest not. What Lineberry (1977) has labeled the *underclass hypothesis* has received scant support. This proposition holds that neighborhoods having lower socioeconomic status, minority racial chararacteristics, and less political power are less likely to receive their share of urban services than are neighborhoods having higher socioeconomic status, majority racial characteristics, and more political power. As Lineberry summarizes:

> While one could easily find exceptions in all areas, the cumulative weight of the evidence seems clear. Distribution studies are more likely than not to find either roughly equal or even compensatory patterns than to find discriminatory patterns . . . the weight of the evidence compels the conclusion that overt, measurable discrimination in the distribution of conventional city services has been overstated by anecdotal commentary and conventional wisdom. [1977, p. 186]

These findings, however, are based on studies using a cross-sectional design. The data typically have represented the allocation pattern for one time period rather than distributions over many time periods. Although an area that is substantially nonwhite or extremely poor might get its share of the service pie, it does not necessarily follow that an area that is changing from white to black or one that is in economic decline will also fare well at the service table. These areas, which are being abandoned by the middle class, may very well also be neglected by urban government. Indeed, Anthony Downs has recommended such an approach. Adopting the triage strategy of medical emergencies, Downs (Lachman 1975) has argued that city officials should ignore areas that are beyond saving (as well as those that will survive unattended) and concentrate their efforts on the salvageable. In terms of the modern central city, the salvageable area is one in which social and economic decline is in its incipient stage.

The Setting

St. Louis has been among the hardest hit of the more mature central cities of the United States in the post World War II period. One frequently used index incorporating unemployment, dependency, education, income, housing crowdedness, and poverty places St. Louis sixth worst out of fifty-five in comparison with its surrounding metropolitan area and second worst (to Newark) compared with other central cities (Nathan, 1976).

Table 7-1 quantitatively describes the twenty years of decline between 1950 and 1970. Overall, St. Louis became smaller, blacker, and—compared with the rest of the country—poorer. The city's population dropped by more than 27 percent, from 856,296 in 1950 to 622,200 in 1970; the nonwhite share of the population more than doubled, going from 18.0 percent in 1950 to 41.3 percent in 1970; and the median income, in constant 1967 dollars, increased only modestly, from $4,078 in 1949 to $5,618 in 1969.

These demographic changes, however, were not spread uniformly throughout St. Louis. Table 7-1 also gives the population, racial, and income data for each police district, one of the two areal units used in this analysis. There is considerable variation around the citywide averages. At one extreme, Districts I and VI had relatively stable population levels; at the other, Districts III and IV dropped by more than 35 percent. Racial transition covered the gamut: District I remained virtually all white; District II remained at a constant 3-to-1 integration level; Districts V and VI went from almost completely white to 40- to 50-percent nonwhite; District VII changed from almost all white to virtually all nonwhite; and District VII increased its nonwhite majority from two-thirds to nearly 100 percent. Finally, the rate of increase in median incomes ranged from 17 percent in District V to 47 percent in District I.

The city of St. Louis's accounting system is sufficiently archaic that no one can accurately chart revenue and expenditure trends. Nevertheless, it has become

Table 7-1
Police-District Demographics, 1950, 1960, 1970

District	Population			Percentage Nonwhite			Median Income[a]		
	1950	1960	1970	1950	1960	1970	1950	1960	1970
I	69,431	71,114	66,940	1.3	1.0	0.9	$4,987	$6,580	$7,320
II	197,798	171,796	143,545	23.7	22.6	25.1	4,399	5,480	5,964
III	220,261	182,034	135,688	6.2	6.2	12.2	3,989	5,048	5,226
IV	80,130	60,497	37,355	48.6	55.4	68.6	2,268	2,633	3,500
V	51,035	41,392	35,664	0.5	8.5	38.9	4,087	5,216	4,776
VI	62,028	58,168	59,764	0.4	6.5	49.7	5,109	6,415	6,991
VII	96,227	92,398	83,701	2.1	62.1	91.0	4,464	4,871	5,525
VIII	79,386	72,488	59,543	64.4	92.5	98.6	3,282	4,109	4,358
Total/ average	856,296	749,887	622,200	18.0	28.8	41.3	$4,078	$5,060	$5,618

[a]Median income is for families and unrelated individuals and is expressed in 1967 dollars.

increasingly evident that service demands are outstripping local revenue sources. Indeed, as one recent review noted, only substantial federal aid in the 1970s has prevented the situation from reaching crisis proportions:

> To say that the city has become a ward of the national government is too strong a statement; to say that it has become heavily dependent on federal funds to maintain its basic services and cope with its critical revitalization needs is no exaggeration. The city would be placed in an impossible position were federal assistance to cease or be drastically reduced. [Schmandt, Wendel, and Tomey 1979, p. 58]

This analysis focuses on two traditional urban services: police and street maintenance. The distribution of each service was calculated for the five five-year periods between 1950 and 1974. The specific measure for police services was the number of uniformed personnel in each police district. The street-maintenance measure was the number of square yards resurfaced. This factor was aggregated for twenty-six sets of census tracts, and each set's share for each five-year period was determined. The twenty-six sets of census districts have had the same boundaries over the period 1950–1970 and correspond relatively well to the neighborhood distinctions established by the city of St. Louis Community Development Agency.

Findings

The first question is whether the distribution of uniformed police and street maintenance has become more inequitable between 1950 and 1974. Before this question can be answered, one or more standards for determining equity must be established. This analysis uses one standard (population) for street maintenance, and three criteria (population, reported personal crime, reported property crime) for police. Traffic counts or total street surface would have been better standards for street maintenance, but measures for these criteria are all unavailable. Population, however, is a workable proxy for both factors. For population, perfect equity would be the identical amount of services (square yards resurfaced or uniformed police) per capita. For personal and property crime, maximum equity would be an equal number of police per reported personal crime and per reported property crime.

All these standards were applied to the five service distributions. Population estimates for each time period were obtained by interpolating the 1950, 1960, and 1970 figures, except for the 1970–1974 period, for which the 1970 estimate was used. The crime data were aggregated for each five-year segment. Coulter's (1980) Index of Inequity was used to measure the overall degree of equity. This procedure—a variant of chi square—captures the difference between each area's allocation and its expected value (if perfect equity obtained). The Index of

Inequity can range from 0 to 100, and Coulter suggests the following numerical-to-verbal translation: 0 = perfect equity; 1-10 = virtual equity; 11-20 = minor inequity; 21-30 = serious inequity; 31-50 = severe inequity; and greater than 50 = extreme inequity.

Table 7-2 gives the results of these equity calculations. Overall, there have not been sustained and substantial inequities in the distribution of street-maintenance and police service in St. Louis during the postwar period, nor has there been a noticeable trend toward more or less inequity. Street resurfacing has touched the serious-inequity border during the early 1950s and the late 1960s, but has stayed in the mid-teens for the remaining years. Police-personnel distributions have been even less inequitable, especially when property crime is used as the criterion. Whatever the standard, there does not appear to have been any major trend toward more or less inequity in police distributions between 1950 and 1974. Although the index scores have varied very modestly during the twenty-five years, the variation has not moved steadily in one direction or another.

The second question is whether each area's service allocation changes over time and, if so, whether the shifts are connected with changes in the area's racial composition and economic situation. To discover this for police services, ratios of the proportion of service allocated (uniformed police personnel) to the proportion of the equity standard (population, personal crime, property crime) were calculated for each police district for each five-year period. These ratios are given in table 7-3. A ratio greater than 1.0 means that a district has more uniformed police than the equity standard would warrant, and a ratio less than 1.0 indicates that the area has fewer police officers than the equity criterion would justify.

Although the results are not clear cut, they suggest that areas undergoing white-to-black transition and lower-than-average increases in per capita income are a bit more likely to have negative trends in receiving their share of police services. From a racial perspective, the two districts (I and III) that are largely white have been consistently underserved by the population standard but regularly overserved by the two crime criteria. The one district that began and ended the period with a nonwhite majority (District VIII) moved from under-served to proportionally allocated by the population and property-crime stand-ards but stayed consistently underserved in terms of personal crimes.

The three districts experiencing rapid racial transition from white to non-white (Districts V, VI, and VII) fared less well over time. By the personal-crime standard, they declined either from overserved to underserved (V and VII) or from overserved to proportionally served (VI). Using the property-crime crite-rion, they stayed proportional (V) or underserved (VII), or declined from over-served to underserved (VI). The district that maintained a relatively constant white/nonwhite ratio went from underserved to proportionally served on one standard (personal crime), moved in the opposite direction on another criterion

Table 7-2
Overall Inequity for Street-Maintenance and Police Services, 1950-1974

Service	Standard	Years				
		1950-1954	1955-1959	1960-1964	1965-1969	1970-1974
Street maintenance	Population	19.48	15.28	11.86	20.88	13.42
Police personnel	Population	12.63	13.01	13.02	13.53	11.56
Police personnel	Personal crime	12.32	9.06	9.63	8.64	10.45
Police personnel	Property crime	6.58	8.06	6.29	6.67	7.21

Table 7–3
Trends in Police-Distribution Equity, 1950–1974

	Service/Standard Ratio[a]				
District/Standard	1950–1954	1955–1959	1960–1964	1965–1969	1970–1974
I: Population	0.77	0.63	0.66	0.65	0.68
Personal crime	2.83	3.17	3.20	3.05	3.17
Property crime	1.86	1.63	1.36	1.34	1.33
II: Population	1.05	1.04	0.97	0.92	0.87
Personal crime	0.75	0.79	0.85	0.94	1.10
Property crime	0.98	1.03	0.95	0.99	0.91
III: Population	0.69	0.70	0.69	0.67	0.73
Personal crime	1.39	0.91	1.25	1.03	1.01
Property crime	0.93	0.75	0.94	0.98	0.98
IV: Population	2.01	2.21	2.34	2.63	2.48
Personal crime	0.82	1.06	1.13	1.29	1.60
Property crime	1.14	1.37	1.33	1.42	1.66
V: Population	1.63	1.51	1.50	1.39	1.54
Personal crime	1.52	1.43	1.11	0.81	0.74
Property crime	1.09	0.95	0.94	0.84	0.86
VI: Population	0.99	0.79	.75	0.80	0.95
Personal crime	2.32	3.33	2.54	1.76	1.10
Property crime	1.06	1.43	1.24	1.06	0.81
VII: Population	0.76	0.88	0.94	1.09	1.04
Personal crime	1.40	1.15	0.68	0.74	0.66
Property crime	0.64	0.77	0.74	0.79	0.85
VIII: Population	0.86	0.95	1.11	1.02	1.03
Personal crime	0.53	0.65	0.69	0.71	0.76
Property crime	0.79	0.97	0.95	0.86	1.09

[a]A ratio less than 1.0 indicates that the district is being underserved, and a ratio greater than 1.0 indicates that the district is being overserved.

(population), and stayed proportional on the third standard (property crime). The final district (IV) ended the period being overserved, but these results are affected by the fact that this area includes the central business district.

From the standpoint of each district's economic situation, the two areas having the lowest rate of increase in per capita income (Districts V and VII) went from overserved to underserved on the personal-crime standard, stayed either proportionally served (V) or underserved (VII) on the property-crime criterion, and remained overserved (V) or went from underserved to evenly served (VII) on the population standard. The two areas having the highest rate of increase (Districts I and IV) for the most part either stayed high or moved upward in their share of police-personnel allocations. The one exception is that, by the population standard, District I remained underserved throughout the period. The other four districts all had about the same rise in per capita income, and their allocation trends cover all the possibilities.

In order to assess the relation between racial changes and the distribution of street-maintenance services, service/standard ratios were calculated for four types of racial change (remained white, remained nonwhite, full transition from white to nonwhite, partial transition from white to nonwhite) experienced by the various census districts. Similarly, the twenty-six census districts were divided into three economic-change groups (low, medium, and high) and the resurfacing/population ratio was computed for each set.

The results are displayed in tables 7-4 and 7-5. Areas experiencing substantial racial transformation have received less than their per capita share of street resurfacing. The deficit, however, does not seem to increase as the district moves from white to black but, rather, persists throughout the entire postwar period. Areas undergoing partial racial transition usually have fared rather well, with the exception of the 1970-1974 segment. The consistently white areas usually get the most and are never grossly underserved. Nonwhite areas have a sporadic record, but when the central business district is excluded from this set, the remaining black areas almost always receive less than their share.

Economic change bears a comparable relationship to the service/standard ratios. Districts with minor increases in real income have—with one exception (1955-1959)—been underserved. Medium-change areas have done relatively well, and their ratios have never gone below 0.90. Districts with larger increases in median income have tended to have the most street resurfacing. Their ratio has been as high as 1.76 and has always exceeded 1.0. As with racial change, the more impoverished areas are disadvantaged throughout the postwar era rather than having their ratios go from better to worse as their relative situation declines.

Table 7-4
Racial Change and Street-Maintenance Equity, 1950-1974

Districts' Racial Change	Service/Standard Ratio[a]				
	1950-1954	1955-1959	1960-1964	1965-1969	1970-1974
Remained white	1.81	0.95	1.30	1.38	1.68
Remained nonwhite[b]	0.27	2.18	1.20	0.73	0.43
Full transition, white to nonwhite	0.58	0.44	0.54	0.40	0.71
Partial transition, white to nonwhite	1.20	1.20	1.03	1.74	0.68

[a]A ratio less than 1.0 indicates that the area is being underserved, and a ratio greater than 1.0 indicates that the area is being overserved.

[b]This category includes the central business district. If it is excluded, the ratios for the five five-year periods become, respectively, 0.32, 1.05, 0.77, 0.66, and 0.49.

Table 7-5
Economic Change and Street-Maintenance Equity, 1950–1974

Districts' Economic Change[b]	Service/Standard Ratio[a]				
	1950–1954	*1955–1959*	*1960–1964*	*1965–1969*	*1970–1974*
Low (0–25%)	0.67	1.20	0.95	0.69	0.75
Medium (26–40%)	1.32	0.90	1.15	0.90	1.34
High (> 40%)	1.49	1.35	1.04	1.76	1.33

[a]A ratio less than 1.0 indicates that the area is being underserved, and a ratio greater than 1.0 indicates that the area is being overserved.

[b]Economic change is the percentage gain in constant (1967) median income for families and unrelated individuals between 1949 and 1969.

The fact that areas with full racial transition and low economic growth have tended to be underserved during the entire 1950–1974 period should not obscure the point that discrimination is therefore increasing. Since, for example, areas going from white to black were underserved for all five time segments, this means that the relationship between racial composition and service/standard ratio is rising. As white underserved areas become black, this raises the Pearson product-moment correlation between percentage nonwhite and service/standard ratio from -.44 in 1950–1954 to -.65 in 1970–1974.

Moreover—and I am indebted to Richard Rich for this insight—the street-maintenance results probably understate the inequity in street quality. Since for the most part black and low-income persons live in the city's older portions, their street-repair needs tend to be greater. Therefore, even an equal allocation of street maintenance would yield an unequal distribution of street conditions.

Conclusion

This examination of the distribution of police and street-maintenance services in St. Louis between 1950 and 1974 does not reveal any massive reallocation of resources as areas experienced different rates of racial and economic change. The overall amount of inequity remained relatively constant and rather modest during the twenty-five years. Nevertheless, areas moving from white to black and areas faring less well on increases in income tended to have slightly less favorable trend patterns in receiving uniformed police and street resurfacing. The pattern is not strong or steady enough to support a firm conclusion that members of the underclass were being systematically deprived. The findings do suggest, however, that a longitudinal perspective might provide more positive evidence than does a cross-sectional analysis for the notion that racial minorities and the economically impoverished do less well in getting their share of public services.

References

Coulter, P.B. 1980. "Measuring the Inequity of Urban Public Services: A Methodological Discussion with Applications." *Policy Studies Journal* 8:683-698.

Lachman, L.M. 1975. "Planning for Community Development: A Proposed Approach." *Journal of Housing* 32:56-60.

Lindblom, C.E. 1965. *The Intelligence of Democracy*. New York: Free Press.

Lineberry, R.L. 1977. *Equality and Public Policy*. Beverly Hills, Calif.: Sage Publications.

Nathan, R.P., and Adams, C. 1976. "Understanding Central City Hardship. *Political Science Quarterly* 91:47-62.

Schmandt, H.J.; Wendel, G.D.; and Tomey, E.A. 1979. *The Impact of Federal Aid on the City of St. Louis*. St. Louis, Mo.: St. Louis University Center for Urban Programs.

8 Urban Public Benefits and Fiscal Retrenchment: The Distributional Impacts of Municipal-Expenditure Reductions

Harold Wolman

The distribution of benefits and imposition of burdens among different segments of the population has long been recognized as a fundamental concern for any society. In fact, many define political science as the study of who gets what, how, and why, and economics as the study of how society chooses what goods to produce, how, and for whom. Despite this definitional obeisance that political science and economics pay to distribution, the question of how the benefits and burdens of public-sector activity are distributed has been studied by political scientists much less than questions of political process and behavior and by economists much less than questions of the efficient allocation of resources.[1]

In addition, nearly all the empirical research on distribution has assumed or been conducted under conditions of public-resources growth. Yet the present fiscal environment is one of public-resources constraint. Urban fiscal problems have come to dominate public debate in the 1970s as urban racial, poverty, and social issues (which were viewed more explicitly as distributional or equity questions) did in the 1960s. Distributional considerations should be of even greater importance in a constrained environment, as cities struggle to make difficult fiscal readjustments that often result in real-expenditure cutbacks.[2]

However, existing studies on the distribution of benefits from public expenditures yield little information, even by implication, on the probable distributional consequences of municipal-expenditure cutbacks. Such studies are usually cross-sectional rather than longitudinal. They provide a snapshot of the distributional pattern at a point in time but give no information about the change in distributional patterns over time, let alone on possible variables in changes of distributional patterns over time resulting from different causes. Additionally, these cross-sectional distribution studies do not provide unambiguous findings.[3]

The distributional consequences of municipal-expenditure reduction thus pose an increasingly important challenge for future research. This is particularly so in view of legal decisions such as *Hawkins* v. *Town of Shaw*, which held that inequality in the provision of local public services to black and white neighborhoods is constitutionally prohibited by the Fourteenth Amendment (see Merget and Wolff (1976) for a discussion of these decisions and their policy

113

implementations). There is good reason to believe that the distributional patterns of public services under conditions of growth—where everyone wins to some extent and side payments are possible to participants perceived as losers in the process—are likely to change significantly under conditions of scarcity.

The equity of distributional consequences of spending cuts are not at all obvious. First, since the rhetoric of U.S. local politics emphasizes policymaking in the "public interest," these distributional questions are seldom explicitly addressed in local policymaking. In addition, recent research suggests that the actual distribution of local services is often determined by the decision rules and professional norms of bureaucrats charged with administering the service rather than by the expressed desires of high elected and appointed policymakers (Jones 1977; Jones and Kaufman 1974; Levy, Meltsner, and Wildarsky 1974; Antunes and Mladenka 1976; Lineberry 1977; Mladenka 1977).

The resistance of local bureaucracies and their adherence to bureaucratic decision rules can frustrate the will of elected officials even when, as happens during times of crisis or changes in leadership, overt efforts are made at the policymaking levels to change resource-distribution patterns (Antunes and Mladenka 1976). Thus it may be that the actual distributional consequences of the strategy adopted do not match those that were expected. The foregoing clearly suggests that the distributional consequences of fiscal readjustment strategies are likely to be strongly affected by the way in which these strategies are implemented by local bureaucracies and, in particular, by the effect these strategies have on bureaucratic decision rules.

Thus, for several reasons (the lack of research on *changes* in service-distribution patterns over time, the paucity of work on local fiscal behavior under conditions of contraction rather than growth, and the nonobvious nature of service-distribution patterns), the existing literature on distribution does not yield a set of convincing and consistent hypotheses about the distributional consequences of municipal-expenditure cutbacks.

Instead, I will turn first to the much less rigorous literature on responses to fiscal stress and will search it for statements—both speculative and empirical—on the likely distributional consequences of fiscal retrenchment. I will then examine some of the empirical work that has been carried out at the Urban Institute on municipal-expenditure reductions in order to probe any implications it might hold for distributional consequences. Finally, I will suggest a design for pursuing further research focused directly on the distributional consequences of municipal-expenditure reductions.

Distributional Consequences of Expenditure Cutbacks: Some Hypotheses

Most a priori speculation from researchers and analysts seem to reflect popular wisdom that the poor and minorities and their neighborhoods will suffer disproportionately from service cuts. Ladd (1978), in discussing they likely impact

of Proposition 13, observes: "While further research would be useful in identifying the services most likely to be cut back in the event of controls and the distributional consequences of such cutbacks, the presumption must be that the
impact of service level reductions will fall more heavily on poor households than
on rich within any one jurisdiction" (p. 10). Danziger (1979) notes: "The commonly held assumption has been that, ultimately, the services most likely to be
substantially curtailed are those that redistribute resources toward the 'underclass'—the poor, the underemployed, and unemployed (p. 63)." Lineberry and
Massoti (1976), Gans (1975), and Drewett (1979) agree, the latter two noting
that social services are the most likely candidates for expenditure reductions.

Shefter (1977) argues, somewhat differently, that the political logic of expenditure cutback dictates that the most recently enfranchised groups will be
the most adversely affected—hence, the New York City expenditure reductions
fell most heavily on blacks, Hispanics, and civil servants. Pascal and Menchik
(1979, p. 89) suggest a similar process. They argue that just as the expansion of
local services in the last two decades disproportionately benefited minorities and
the poor, elderly, and handicapped, so these groups' lack of political power will
make them the first to lose in an era of service cutbacks.

Initial commentary on the reaction to Proposition 13 in California indicates
that the poor may be bearing a disproportionate share of the burden, at least in
terms of first-year readjustments. Reischauer (1979) notes:

> California has tended to hold harmless basic services directed at the
> middle class or the majority of the population. For example, elemen-
> tary and secondary education will be largely unscathed, because the
> state is distributing a large amount of new aid next year, which will
> provide school districts with almost 90 percent of their expected fiscal
> 1978-1979 budget. Although summer schools and some special pro-
> grams will have to be trimmed, basic education will continue much
> as planned before the passage of Proposition 13. However, state cate-
> gorical aids were cut back by 10 percent when the state instituted its
> economy moves. That cut will affect a number of state-financed redis-
> tributive programs such as the program for disadvantaged youth educa-
> tion, compensatory education, special reading programs, bilingual
> education programs, child nutrition programs, and urban impact aid.
>
> Provisions in the state bail-out laws also ensure that basic police and fire
> services will not be reduced. The mandate that jurisdictions receiving
> state aid maintain their existing levels of protective services implies
> budget cuts in other services. . . . Whether this pattern of cutbacks
> disproportionately affects the poor and underprotected is not clear.
> However, the action that California recently took in the area of welfare
> is clearly unequitable. To save state monies, California cancelled the
> 7.55 percent cost-of-living increase in welfare benefits that was sched-
> uled to occur this past July. [p. 16]

Stumpf and Terrell (1979) also argue that the poor have been most severely
affected, although their conclusions are not based on an analysis comparing the
impact on the poor with that on other groups. Rather, they argue that it is those

population groups that are most dependent on publicly provided services that suffer most—groups such as working women and their children, the elderly, and ethnic and racial minorities. Stumpf and Terrell (1979, pp. 106-107) cite a series of service cutbacks that "increase the day in and day out burden of poverty, [and] undermine opportunities for economic advancement" for relatively service-dependent groups.

It is difficult to generalize from these preliminary and tentative studies of California to the distributional consequences of municipal fiscal readjustment elsewhere. The first-year readjustments in California have involved *both* local-expenditure changes and massive increases in state aid (as the state surplus is drawn down) of a sort that have not occurred and are not likely to occur for localities in other states facing fiscal pressure.

Not all the literature suggests that the poor will be the most severely affected. White (1978) argues that high- rather than low-income groups will bear the brunt of public-expenditure cutbacks. She notes that most locally produced public goods have at least partial private-market substitutes (for example, privately purchased security systems are a partial substitute for publicly provided police service). White terms these services *quasi public goods* and notes that since higher-income groups have a higher marginal propensity to consume such goods, they are more likely to be able and willing to substitute increased private for reduced public inputs. She thus reasons that local governments will try to differentiate spatially, cutting back services most severely in high-income areas.

Glassberg (1978) hypothesizes that expenditure reduction ought to reinforce the existing distribution of services since, he argues, the only politically viable approach to expenditure reduction is across-the-board percentage cuts. He thus predicts that after a budget crisis local government budgets would remain essentially unchanged in their allocation of resources among various services, but would be reduced in size.

Distributional Consequences of Expenditure Reductions: Empirical Findings

The empirical determination of the distributional effects of reductions in local spending is not an easy task. There is not necessarily any reason to believe that the value of the public-service benefit being conferred coincides with the cost of producing it. Thus, for example, a reduction in real local expenditure for garbage collection brought about by a wage freeze for public employees may result in no reduction in the level or distribution of services provided and thus of benefit received, whereas a reduction of similar size brought about by work-force cuts may require a reduction in service levels and thus in benefits. In order to determine the distributional effects by income class of these benefit reductions, however, we would have to examine actual changes in activity by areas—for example, was collection reduced more in low-income than in middle-income area?

The empirical data for this chapter are drawn from work performed by the author and colleagues at the Urban Institute. The work includes a survey of responses to fiscal pressure in twenty-five municipalities (funded by the Charles F. Kettering Foundation) and case studies of four state governments (New Jersey, New York, Michigan, and California) and a fiscally stressed municipality and county in each state (funded by the U.S. Department of Health and Human Services). These studies were not designed directly to yield information on changes in the distribution of public benefits; they did, however, yield information on changes in the allocation of expenditures by function, which will in some cases permit inferences to be drawn about changes in the distribution of benefits.

Distributional Effects of Expenditure
Reductions by Program

It is frequently asserted that the poor and minority groups will bear a disproportionate share of the burden of expenditure reductions since these groups are relatively disorganized politically and since the human-service programs designed to serve them are thought to have low levels of public support. If this assertion is correct, then the human-service programs would be expected to receive disproportionate reductions.

In fact, human-service programs did not appear to suffer disproportionate reductions. It appears that any propensity to reduce expenditures for these programs is strongly mitigated by two factors. First, the human-service programs are also the most heavily federally funded programs and thus are least likely to suffer reductions. Second, most human-service programs are the responsibility of county or state rather than of municipal government; most cities simply do not have the opportunity to reduce local spending for human-service programs very substantially. Thus even a finding that cities reduced spending in human-service areas by a greater *percentage* than in other areas would not necessarily indicate major reductions in the amount of such services received by city residents. In any case, such a finding did not occur; for the thirteen cities in our survey that reduced real operating expenditure in fiscal-year 1978 or fiscal-year 1979, public works received the largest average expenditure reduction (7.7 percent), followed by general government (4.5 percent), then social services (4.2 percent), and finally public safety (2.9 percent). Our intensive examination of Trenton, Buffalo, and Detroit suggested that parks, recreation, libraries, and cultural facilities are likely to receive the largest percentage cuts.

County governments, the local governmental units that are most likely to provide human-service programs, are generally in better fiscal condition than their central cities and thus are less driven to make massive expenditure reductions. In addition, counties also finance a substantial portion of their human-service expenditures from intergovernmental sources. Where local governments —whether cities or counties—do spend their own funds for human-service purposes (other than as matching funds for intergovernmental assistance), these expenditures *do* appear to experience substantial reductions.

If the state in which the locality is located is experiencing fiscal difficulties, local recipients of some human services in fiscally constrained cities may find benefits reduced even though their local government is not facing fiscal pressure. The state determines benefit levels for AFDC and other income-support programs. Our studies indicate that one of the most common means by which states respond to fiscal pressure is to reduce state expenditures for income support by simply not increasing benefit levels to keep pace with inflation. In New York State these benefit levels have not changed since 1974; in New Jersey these levels have increased by only 7.6 percent for AFDC since 1976 and not at all for general assistance, an indication of the lack of political strength of these groups.

Overall, however, it appears that budget reductions do not occur systematically in programs targeted to poor and minority groups. This does not necessarily imply that the poor do not bear a disproportionate portion of the burden. If they do, however, it is likely to be through a mechanism other than cutting programs aimed at the poor. It is possible, for example, that the reductions in the more traditional locally funded programs—public safety, public works, parks, and so on—are disproportionately focused on poor and minority neighborhoods. As noted earlier, we do not have evidence to test this possibility. We will return to this question later.

In addition, a proportionate decrease in all services or even one spread equally across all income groups or neighborhoods may provide a greater burden for the poor, particularly if reductions are in essential services. In many instances the nonpoor have the option of substituting private goods for declines in the quantity of public services, whereas such an option is by definition much more limited for the poor. Thus wealthier individuals may substitute private schools for reductions in public-school programs, home security systems for reductions in police service, and book purchases for reduced library services.

Distributional Effects of Municipal-Employment Reduction

We now turn to an examination of the distributional impacts of various means of expenditure reduction. The two most prevalent strategies are (1) to reduce the size of the municipal work force and (2) to reduce real wages of municipal employees. Municipal employees are likely to be disproportionately minority. Peterson (1980, p. 28) presents data for seven large cities in five of which the percentage of black employees exceeds the percentage of blacks in the population.

In addition, minorities are likely to be an even higher percentage of recently hired workers. Reischauer (1979, p. 18) presents data indicating that in 1976, 15.3 percent of all state and local noneducational employees hired before the previous year were black, compared with 18.7 percent of workers hired during the previous year. Since layoffs usually occur on a seniority basis ("last hired—first fired"), a disproportionate burden of layoffs is likely to fall on the minority population. Hiring freezes have the same effect since they close off employment opportunities open disproportionately to minorities.

At least until recently, however, reductions in numbers of municipal employees in many cities have been offset substantially by CETA-funded personnel. Federal CETA regulations requiring the employee to have been previously unemployed and low income result in a high proportion of minority members in the CETA program. (National Commission on Manpower Policy 1979). Consequently, the net effect of reduction in number of municipal employees and partial replacement by CETA employees may in the short run have led to an increase in minority employment in the total city work force (municipally funded plus CETA). However, reductions in federal funding for CETA and in the number of CETA jobs suggests that the long-term burden of municipal-employee reduction will indeed rest disproportionately on minority groups.

Distributional Effects of Municipal Wage Reduction

Real-wage reductions for municipal employees are also likely to fall more heavily on minorities, again because minorities represent a disproportionate share of municipal employees. However, it is questionable whether such real-wage reductions disproportionately affect lower-income people. Average local public-employee earnings exceed average earnings for all nonpublic employees. In October 1978 average annual earnings for local public employees were $13,536, compared with an average wage for all domestic employees in 1978 of $13,272 (U.S. Department of Commerce 1978, pp. 320, 925). Reischauer (1979, p. 17) presents data showing that state- and local-government employees are better off in terms of both earnings and family income than are workers in general.

Distributional Effects of Shifts of Service Responsibility

One strategy for reducing local expenditures is to attempt to shift the responsibility for providing and financing a service to another (usually higher) level of

Table 8-1
Racial Composition of Public-Sector Employees

City	Percentage Black Population (1970)	Percentage Black Population (1974)
Baltimore	46.4	59.6[a]
Boston	16.3	5.9[a]
Chicago	32.7	23.0
Detroit	43.7	45.7
Newark	54.2	68.1
New York	21.1	31.4
Philadelphia	33.6	42.0

Source: R. Reischauer, "Intergovernmental Responsibility for Meeting the Equity Considerations of Proposition 13: The Federal Role," in Selma J. Mushkin, ed., *Proposition 13 and Its Consequences for Public Management* (Cambridge, Mass.: Abt Books, 1979), p. 18. Reprinted with permission of Evaluation Research Society, Washington, D.C.

[a]School system only.

Table 8-2
Distribution of All Workers and of State- and Local-Government Workers by Earnings and by Total Family Income
(percentage)

Income and Earning Range	By Earnings		By Total Family Income	
	All Workers	State and Local Workers	All Workers	State and Local Workers
$1,000–4,999	40.4	35.0	20.9	7.1
$5,000–7,499	14.4	13.7	12.1	7.6
$7,500–9,999	12.1	14.7	11.1	9.9
$10,000–12,499	11.3	14.0	10.9	11.0
$12,500–14,999	6.5	8.1	9.1	10.6
$15,000+	15.3	14.6	36.0	53.9
Total	100.0	100.0	100.0	100.0

Source: Estimates from the U.S. Bureau of the Census, *Survey of Income and Education*, 1976. Taken from R. Reischauer, "Intergovernmental Responsibility for Meeting the Equity Considerations of Proposition 13: The Federal Role," in Selma J. Mushkin, ed., *Proposition 13 and Its Consequences for Public Management* (Cambridge, Mass.: Abt Books, 1979), p. 17.

government, or to the private sector. Concern is frequently expressed that when central-city services are shifted to the county or metropolitan level or to the private sector, the focus of these services on the lower-income, minority population of the central city will be diluted. Thus, it is argued, although the financing of these services is likely to be more progressive, the distribution of services is likely to be more regressive with a net redistribution effect that may vary in each specific case. We have no data that would permit us to evaluate this argument.

Distributional Effects of Reduction in Capital
Outlays and Maintenance Spending

It is possible that reduction in capital outlays and maintenance spending for streets, parks, and so on occurs disproportionately in poor areas. These kinds of reductions are, at least initially, likely to be relatively invisible to citizens and unlikely to be announced in the way that program reductions (such as reduced library hours) would be. Higher-income citizens may be more sensitive to deterioration of quality because they have higher expectations with respect to infrastructure quality. Consequently, they may complain more about lack of maintenance and thus receive additional service. If poor and wealthy neighborhoods do complain equally, the city may nonetheless respond by reducing maintenance to a lesser extent in wealthier neighborhoods, either because these neighborhoods have better political access and influence or because the city does not wish to encourage its wealthier residents to migrate to the suburbs.

For whatever reasons, it would seem plausible to expect capital outlay and maintenance reductions to occur disproportionately in low-income and minority neighborhoods. However, this tendency is mitigated by another factor: the existence of the Community Development Block Grant (CDBG) program, which requires 75 percent of the funds to be spent in low- and moderate-income neighborhoods. CDBG funds are usually used quite heavily for capital facilities and maintenance purposes.

Studying the Retrenchment-Induced Change in the Distribution of Benefits

The research described so far stops short of examining actual changes in service-distribution patterns brought about by expenditure cutbacks. In this concluding section I set forth a brief design for such research. In order to examine changes in the distribution of output characteristics brought about by various municipal-expenditure-reduction strategies, some adaptations in the traditional manner of studying service distribution will be necessary.

As has been noted, previous distributional studies have been cross-sectional; we are interested in the change in distribution brought about as a result of expenditure reduction. It would appear, therefore, that we are interested in determining the difference in the distribution of benefits between two points in time: at time A, a point just prior to the municipal-expenditure reductions, and at time B, a time after the cutbacks have had their distributional impact. Conceptually, however, our real concern is with the difference between the distribution of benefits at time B and the distribution of benefits that would have occurred at time B in the absence of expenditure reduction. This conceptualization assumes that the distribution is changing over time in response to a variety of forces other than retrenchment. Figure 8–1 illustrates the sequence. Where the onset of fiscal distress occurs between t_2 and t_3, the reduction in municipal

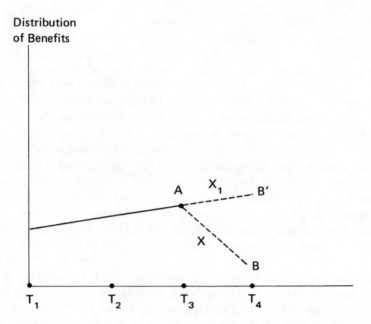

Figure 8-1. Longitudinal Design for Service-Distribution Studies

expenditures occurs at t_3, and A measures the distribution of benefits at the time expenditure reductions occur. (The measure may be the percentage of benefits received by a specific group, or it may be a more comprehensive distribution measure such as 1-gini coefficient. The gini coefficient is a measure of deviation from absolute equality. Gini-coefficient values vary from 0, which is absolute equality, to 1, which is absolute inequality. The example should not be taken to imply that the distributional impact is *necessarily* away from equality.)

X is the set of service responses resulting from the expenditure reduction.

X_1 is the behavior the government would have undertaken had fiscal stress not occurred and the government not responded by reducing expenditures.

B is the distribution of benefits at t_4, a time after which the service responses have had their distributional impact.

B' is the distribution of benefits that would have resulted at t_4 had fiscal stress and expenditure cutbacks not occurred. (B' therefore assumes an extension of the distributional curve that is fitted to the distributional measures from t_1 to t_3.)

The methodology for determining service distribution would be similar to that of the service-distribution studies. These studies gather data on output attributes by area (usually clusters of census tracts) through intensive examination of local records and interviews with local administrators, and attempt to determine through correlation analysis whether differences in service outputs among areas are related to demographic characteristics of areas such as race or income.

However, the concern with *change* in the distribution of service outputs adds a further complication, for we must distinguish between B', the expected distribution of benefits at t_4 had there been no response or set of responses to fiscal distress, and B, the actual distribution of benefits at t_4. For some services we might safely assume that B' would coincide with A—that there would be no reason to expect changes because service distribution patterns had been constant for a long period of time. In these cases we must simply ascertain A in order to compare with B. However, for services in which distributional changes might be expected, we would have to attempt to estimate B'. Thus some part of modeling exercise would be necessary, combined with interviews with officials concerning their planned distribution of outputs prior to imposition of a fiscal restraint.

Such research would be both tedious and difficult, but ultimately rewarding.

Notes

1. Until quite recently distributional questions were largely ignored by social scientists studying urban politics or urban public services. Writing in 1964 in reference to the literature of economics, and in particular public finance, Carl Shoup (1964) noted: "little is known about distribution of government services by location, race, religion, income class, or other category" (p. 383). Hirsch (1968) closely echoes these remarks, as does Gold (1974). Jones and Kaufman (1974) come to the same conclusion with respect to political-science literature, observing: "we have few studies of the distributional aspects of urban public services, and we know even less about the causes of existing patterns of distribution" (p. 227). And E.S. Savas (1978), after stating that equity is an important measure of service performance, concludes nonetheless that "management scientists have tended to focus their efforts on the issues of efficiency and effectiveness and have paid relatively little attention to the issues of equity" (p. 802).

Recent work (particularly Levy, Meltsner, and Wildavsky 1974 and Lineberry 1977) tend to soften these judgments. However, in a recent review of the municipal-service-distribution literature, Antunes and Mladenka (1976) still are able to comment that it is hazardous to generalize from the existing studies, partly because "too few studies of the allocation of municipal services have been conducted" (p. 160).

2. Not all of these readjustments occur on the expenditure side. Many municipalities respond by increasing revenues. Such responses include, despite the current tax-revolt environment, increases in tax rates and user fees. For a discussion of the variety of readjustment strategies cities employ, see Wolman,

"Local Government Strategies to Cope with Fiscal Pressure," *Sage Yearbook in Politics and Public Policy* (in press).

3. The findings derived from the literature on service distribution vary widely according to (1) service studied, (2) measures of service used, and (3) the city or cities in which the study occurred. Lineberry, for example, concludes (1977): "While one could find exceptions in all areas, the cumulative weight of the evidence seems clear. Distribution studies are more likely than not to find either roughly equal or even compensatory patterns than to find discriminatory patterns" (p. 186). Levy, Meltsner, and Wildavsky conclude, from their study of Oakland (1974): "We found a distribution pattern that favored both extremes. Some mechanisms were biased toward the rich. Other mechanisms favored the poor. We discovered no examples of mechanisms that favor the middle" (p. 219). See Rich (1979), Lineberry (1977), and Antunes and Mladenka (1976) for reviews of this literature.

References

Antunes, G., and Miladenka, K. 1976. "The Politics of Local Services and Service Distribution." In L. Massot and R. Lineberry, eds., *The New Urban Politics,* pp. 147-169. Cambridge, Mass.: Ballinger.

Danziger, J. 1979. "Rebellion on Fiscal Policy: Assessing the Effects of Proposition 13," *Urban Interest* 1:59-67.

Drewett, R. 1979. "Urbanization Trends in Selected OECD Countries." Paper prepared for and edited by OECD Secretariat, Paris.

Gans, H.J. 1975. "Planning for Declining and Poor in Cities." *Journal of the American Institute of Planners* 41:305-307.

Gillespie, W.I. 1965. "Effect of Public Expenditures on the Distribution of Income." In Richard Musgrave, ed., *Essays in Fiscal Federalism,* pp. 122-185. Washington, D.C.: Brookings Institution.

Glassberg, A. 1978. "Response to Budgetary Stringency: New York and London." Paper prepared for presentation to North World Congress of Sociology, Uppsala, Sweden.

Gold, S. 1974. "The Distribution of Government Services in Theory and Practice." *Public Finance Quarterly* 2:107-130.

Hirsch, W. 1968. "The Supply of Urban Public Services." In H. Perloff and L. Wingo, eds., *Issues in Urban Economics,* pp. 477-526. Baltimore, Md.: John Hopkins University Press.

Jones, B. 1977. "Distributional Considerations in Models of Government Service Provision." *Urban Affairs Quarterly* 12:291-312.

Jones, B.D. and Kaufman, C. 1974. "The Distribution of Urban Public Services." *Administration and Society* 6:337-360.

Ladd, H.F. 1978. "An Economic Evaluation of State Limitations on Local Taxing and Spending Powers." *National Tax Journal* 31:1-18.

Levy, F.; Meltsner, A.; and Wildavsky, A. 1974. *Urban Outcomes.* Berkeley: University of California Press.

Lineberry, R. 1977. *Equality and Urban Policy.* Beverly Hills, Calif.: Sage Publications.

Lineberry, R. and Massoti, L. 1976. "Introduction." In L. Massoti and R. Lineberry, eds., *The New Urban Politics,* pp. 1-15. Cambridge, Mass.: Ballinger.

Merget, A.E. and Wolff, W.M., Jr. 1976. "The Law and Municipal Services: Implementing Equity." *Public Management.* 58:2-8.

Mladenka, K. 1977. "Citizen Demand and Bureaucratic Response: Direct Dialing Democracy in a Major American City." *Urban Affairs Quarterly* 12:273-290.

National Commission on Manpower Policy. 1979. "Monitoring the Public Service Employment Program: The Second Round." Special report no. 32 (March).

Pascal, A.H., and Menchik, M.D. 1979. "Fiscal Containment: Who Gains? Who Loses?" Santa Monica, Calif.: Rand Corporation.

Peterson, G. 1980. "The Fiscal Outlook for Cities." Unpublished paper, Urban Institute, Washington, D.C.

Reischauer, R. 1979. "Intergovernmental Responsibility for Meeting the Equity Considerations of Proposition 13: The Federal Role." In J. Mushkin, ed., *Proposition 13 and Its Consequences for Public Management,* pp. 13-22. Cambridge, Mass.: Abt Books.

Rich, R. 1979. "The Distribution of Services: Studying the Products of Urban Policymaking." In D.R. Marshall, ed., *Urban Policymaking,* pp. 237-260. Beverly Hills, Calif.: Sage Publications.

Savas, E.S. 1978. "On Equity in Providing Public Services." *Management Science* 24:800-808.

Shefter, M. 1977. "New York's Fiscal Crisis: The Politics of Inflation and Retrenchment." *Public Interest* 48:98-127.

Shoup, C. 1964. "Standards for Distributing a Free Government Service: Crime Prevention." *Public Finance* 19:383-392.

Stumpf, J., and Terrell, P. 1979. "Proposition 13 and California Human Services: First Year Impacts on Budget, Personnel and Clients." Millbrae, Calif.: National Association of Social Workers, California chapter.

U.S. Department of Commerce, Bureau of the Consul. 1978. *Statistical Abstract of the United States.* Washington, D.C.: U.S. Government Printing Office.

White, M. 1978. "Government Response to Spending Limitations." Paper prepared for Conference on Tax and Expenditure Limitation, Santa Barbara, Calif.

Wolman, H.L. 1980. "Local Government Strategies to Cope with Fiscal Pressure." In C.H. Levine and I. Rubin, eds., *Fiscal Stress and Public Policy*, pp. 231–248. Beverly Hills, Calif.: Sage Publications.

Wolman, H.L., and Peterson, G. 1980. "Policy Consequences of Local Expenditures Constraints." *Urban Interest* 2:75–82.

9

Inequality of Urban Services: The Impact of the Community Development Act

Dennis R. Judd and
Alvin H. Mushkatel

Over the last two decades the policy priorities of city politics have been thoroughly altered. In the 1960s a social crisis was evidenced by repeated urban rebellions.[1] In 1968 the report of the National Advisory Commission on Civil Disorders referred to "an explosive mixture which has been accumulating in our cities since the end of World War II" (*Report of National Advisory Commission* 1968, p. 9) and cited a long list of grievances that, if left uncorrected, would "make permanent the division of our country into two societies; one, largely Negro and poor, located in central cities; the other, predominantly white and affluent, located in the suburbs and in outlying areas" (*Report* 1968, p. 22). Much rhetoric and money were expended on the war on poverty, the Model Cities program, and other initiatives to solve the urban crisis and "save the cities."

According to Douglas Yates, this agenda has been replaced by one that emphasizes " 'service delivery' as the central issue and problem of urban policy making" (Yates 1974, p. 213). But even if, as Yates maintains, attention has been redirected toward the normal, relatively mundane services supplied by local governments, the political issues involved are far from mundane. As Robert Lineberry (1977, p. 13) has pointed out, "virtually all the rawest nerves of urban political life are touched by the distribution of urban service burdens and benefits." Urban services were cited by the Kerner commission as one of the principal aspects of the urban revolts of the 1960s (*Report* 1968, pp. 80-83).

Issues not only of quality and cost, but also of equity and efficiency, are important in public services. Race, poverty, and inequality were the chief components of the urban crisis of the 1960s, and they are also central to debates about the distribution of urban services. To a large extent, the newfound interest in urban services is related to the rising expectations encouraged by the social programs of the 1960s. Traditionally, cities provided a standard list of services such as garbage collection, education, sewage treatment, water distribution, and police and fire services. As a result of the vastly expanded federal role of the 1960s, cities took on—usually through participation in grant-in-aid programs—a host of new programs such as summer youth employment, expanded recreational opportunities, transportation for the elderly, special-education programs, expanded welfare services, housing rehabilitation, and others.

The replacement of large numbers of grant-in-aid programs by revenue sharing and block grants has not reduced the federal presence. In the city budgets of 1978, one dollar in four originated at the state or federal levels. (Judd 1979, p. 322). Equally important, in the 1970s, it became difficult and often impossible to separate urban services supplied strictly at the local level from those originating in state and federal programs. It is doubtful that any significant service supplied by a large city in 1980 is supported solely by funds or by program guidelines controlled completely by local government. Consequently, any study of municipal services should attempt to assess the influence exerted by bureaucracies or political constituencies outside the municipality. This study traces the influence of the Community Development Act and the Department of Housing and Urban Development (HUD) on housing-rehabilitation programs implemented by local governments. Using Denver's rehabilitation program as an example, we will demonstrate that federal influence has engendered a program that results in the least well off urban areas receiving a lower level of services than those that are better off.

Even without outside intervention and influence, the new services undertaken by cities entailed a new politics. Local participation in social services led to local participation in the complex political problems that ensued. "The services demanded in the 1960's . . . were intrinsically difficult to allocate and also difficult to deliver effectively. In contrast to earlier demands for either essentially private or essentially public goods, service demands in the 1960's centered on what might be called neighborhood goods." As a consequence, "urban policy makers were forced to decide what constituted a neighborhood, what the relative needs of different neighborhoods were, and what constituted equity in service delivery" (Yates 1977, pp. 80-81). To some extent, the divisive issues that characterized national politics in the 1960s became bound up in service delivery at the local level in the 1970s.

It would seem that a larger federal influence, a new emphasis on the issue of equity in local service delivery, and a revitalized local politics would make urban bureaucracies more sensitive to the political impact of their service activities. One could expect that services would not be delivered in an obviously inequitable fashion to the wealthier, more privileged segments of the city. In fact, one of the primary goals of several of the Great Society programs was to make city halls and their assorted bureaucracies more sensitive to minorities and the poor (Judd 1979, pp. 298-305). Although the federal government may have failed to accomplish its manifest purposes—an end to poverty, the creation of model cities and so on—its programs did shake up local political processes (Piven and Cloward 1971; Fischer 1973; Bachrach and Baratz 1970).

Research on municipal services in most cities, therefore, ought to find few instances of manifest discrimination against minorities, the poor, or their neighborhoods. In his research on San Antonio, Robert Lineberry concluded that urban services were distributed in an "unpatterned inequality"; that is, local services did not discriminate on the basis of race, class, political and economic position, or even ecological characteristics of neighborhoods. Lineberry summarized: "If . . . bureaucracies in San Antonio somehow deliberately set about to design service allocations to favor particular groups of the powerful or the wealthy, they do a poor job of it" (Lineberry 1977, pp. 193-194). From his review of research conducted in other cities, Lineberry concluded that except in the case of library services, there was little evidence that San Antonio was exceptional in this respect (Lineberry 1977, p. 185), and that the "weight of evidence compels the conclusion that overt, measurable discrimination in the distribution of conventional city services has been overstated by anecdotal commentary and conventional wisdom" (Lineberry 1977, p. 186). He explains the delivery of services in San Antonio and elsewhere as the end result of the decisional rules employed by local bureaucracies that have become substantially insulated from local political processes but show no tendency to turn this insulation into discrimination.

Even if we were to accept Lineberry's conclusions about the predilections of local bureaucracies, we would not be so sanguine in interpreting the actions of the federal government over the last several years. Our research shows that the federal government, specifically in administering the Community Development Act and its associated programs, has strongly encouraged and sometimes coerced cities to allocate services, especially those financed by the federal government, in a manner that would *disadvantage* the least well-off urban dwellers. To restate the case: if, for the sake of argument, we accept Lineberry's thesis, we can point to a process under way in which the federal government, through the Community Development Act, actively encourages cities to abandon the equitable delivery of services on the basis of race, class, and ecological characteristics of neighborhood.

The Federal Impact

When the Community Development Act was formulated, there was considerable confusion about its purposes. Since a major objective of the CDA was to encourage local discretion, local governments were granted a large degree of autonomy in the expenditure of funds. In the early program guidelines, the federal government specified that target areas be established so that the expenditure of funds could be tracked. As the Community Development Block Grant (CDBG) program evolved, HUD became concerned that local governments were using their discretion in favor of neighborhoods and families with higher than low or moderate incomes. To counteract this trend, HUD proposed that CDBG funds be used to principally benefit "low and moderate income families" (Housing and Community Development Act of 1977, P.L. 95-120, section 104 (B).(1)). This wording marked a change from the original 1974 legislation, which designated the beneficiaries to be low *or* moderate income (Keating and LeGates 1978, p. 709).

The social objectives pursued by HUD stood in direct contradiction to other objectives that the federal government also promoted. These were (1) an increased emphasis on leveraging private investment in the inner city, (2) a continued focus on core economic development, and (3) a focus on stabilization and conservation of middle- and upper-income residential areas. The focus on leveraging appeared very early in HUD's strategies and, in fact, was a central component leading to the Community Development Act. During the debates over the act, and before its passage, Anthony Downs, as a consultant for HUD, recommended that urban programs be targeted to maximize their potential for securing private investment that would turn deteriorated neighborhoods around (Nathan et al. 1977, p. 332; Van Horn 1979, p. 127; Judd 1979, p. 346). His "triage" model was based on a comparison with the treatment of wounded French soldiers during World War I. Medical personnel classified the wounded into three groups: those who were so badly wounded that they could not be saved (prescribe pain killers)—translate to fully deteriorated neighborhoods; those who would die without treatment, but who would probably live with it (maximum effort)—translate to partially deteriorated neighborhoods; and those wounded who would survive even without medical care, or with minimal care—translate to basically healthy neighborhoods. Downs recommended that the middle category receive the largest dose of public funds and that public funds be used primarily to leverage the investment of private funds. Through this process a permanent investment strategy would be set in motion that would restore marginal neighborhoods to full health.

With HUD's encouragement, a large number of communities concentrated their CDA efforts in transitional neighborhoods (U.S. Department of Housing and Urban Development 1978, p. 44; Nathan et al. 1977, p. 331; Dommel et al. 1978, p. 243; Dommel et al. 1980, chap. 2). Although in its 1977 amendments Congress expressed concern about the social effects of the CDA funds, and the legislation was followed up by HUD action to ensure that more money went to low- and moderate-income families, the contradictions in the CDA strategies were left intact. In 1977 one program goal was to implement "neighborhood development in order to induce higher income persons to remain in or return to the community" (Keating and LeGates 1978, p. 709). A second goal required cities to establish *neighborhood strategy areas* (NSAs), which would be comprehensive neighborhood-revitalization areas (Dommel et al. 1980). Although originally the NSAs may have been designed to ensure—if possible—a simultaneous accomplishment of leveraging *and* emphasis on service delivery to low- and moderate-income families, in 1978 Congress effectively made it impossible for HUD to enforce the priority on low- and moderate-income families.

In 1977 HUD had announced an intention to adopt a "75–25" rule in evaluating local programs. According to this guideline, at least 75 percent of the locale's CDBG funds would be earmarked for "low and moderate income families" (Van Horn 1979, pp. 129–130; Dommel et al. 1980, chap. 2). Amendments passed by Congress in 1978 forced HUD to retreat from applying this rule and also thwarted HUD's efforts to make the CDBG program a redistributive policy by prioritizing social targeting (Van Horn 1979, p. 109). Thus, NSAs became firmly ensconced within a triage approach rather than a social-targeting approach. In the city of Denver, for example, this guaranteed an increasing emphasis on transitional areas and, in some cases, a loss of funds to the most deteriorated areas of the city.

The Distribution of Community-Development Funds: Housing Rehabilitation and Neighborhood Revitalization

The effects of targeting funds into neighborhood strategy areas, combined with a triage approach, can be examined by looking at how CDBG funds are distributed to provide public services in Denver. Housing rehabilitation and neighborhood revitalization are the two largest community-development programs in the city. The allocation of funds for these two programs demonstrates that, first, CDA funds are being targeted primarily to transitional areas, and second, that in some instances targeting of funds has resulted in a net loss in the proportion of funds flowing to the most deteriorated areas of the city, with a concomitant rise in the proportion of funds allocated to moderate and well-off areas. Finally, it is clear that targeting services by designating NSAs, both in principle and in fact, increases inequity in service delivery at the local level.

Community-Development Housing-Rehabilitation Program

The largest single program utilizing CDBG funds is housing rehabilitation (Dommel et al. 1980, pp. 118–125; Dommel et al. 1978, pp. 243–253). The Denver CDA spends 40 percent of its budget on this housing program. Many of these rehabilitation programs combine income requirements with targeting of certain areas within the city. Denver's Community Development Rehabilitation Program (CDRP) makes use of both income eligibility requirements (social targeting) and the designation of certain priority areas within the city to receive funds (geographic targeting). Employing both types of targeting has a dramatic effect on the distribution of funds and on the selection of areas in the city to receive rehabilitation services.

Prior to the adoption of HUD regulations requiring cities to designate neighborhood strategy areas, Denver's Community Development Agency (CDA) already had begun to target its CDRP funds geographically. In late 1977 a task force to establish criteria for awarding rehabilitation loans was established. Its deliberations eventually led to the designation of five priority areas within the city. The CDA offered assurances that funds would be distributed in such a manner that "every community within the city receives its fair share according to its own needs in relation to the rest of the city" (CDA, City and County of Denver 1978, p. 1). Perhaps realizing that HUD would soon be implementing something like an NSA requirement, the planners on the task force developed formal criteria for selection of target areas.

The selection process involved ranking census tracts according to five need indicators that fell into three basic areas: income, age, and condition of housing stock, and the housing market in an area as measured by the percentage of conventional loans for mortgages there (CDA, City and County of Denver 1978, pp. 7–9). Census tracts were then assigned to one of six ranked categories, with group 1 containing areas of greatest need, and group 6 those of least need. All the neighborhoods in groups 1–3, which presumably demonstrated greater than average need, were designated a revitalization area. From within this designated revitalization area, the CDA selected five target areas. The allocation of funds based on this "need" model began in January 1979, just when HUD's NSA requirements took effect.

All five of the CDRP target areas have median incomes below 80 percent of the SMSA's median income, thereby satisfying HUD requirements to qualify as low- and moderate-income areas. According to the CDA's classification, two of these target areas come from group 1, two from group 2, and one from group 3 (CDA, City and County of Denver 1978, app. B). Only two of the target areas, then, come from the group defined by the CDA as demonstrating the *greatest* need. The other three target areas, though still in the revitalization area, are less needy than many other tracts, falling into what has been described as transitional areas (groups 2 and 3)—in need of some revitalization (unlike groups 4–6) but not the worst off. (For an additional discussion of the characteristics of these areas see Mushkatel and Lasus 1980, pp. 8–10.)

What has been the effect of targeting on the provision of rehabilitation services in Denver? Have services been shifted away from the neediest areas of the city to moderate-income areas? The data used to investigate these questions consist of records of every loan or grant made for the entire duration of the CDRP, from FY 1975–1976 through March 1980. The records include the dollar value of each loan, the location of the housing unit receiving the loan, and other information.

The sites of these loans and grants have been coded by census tract, and each tract has been identified by whether or not it falls below 80 percent of the median family income for the SMSA. This definition of low or moderate income is consistent with HUD's use of the term. It should be noted, however, that HUD's definition is very generous to the Denver CDA, because using the SMSA's median-income figure tends to inflate the number of areas within the city that fall into the low- or moderate-income categories (Rosenfeld 1978, p. 32). For

Denver, the city's median income is lower than that for the SMSA (SMSA median income = $10,777; city median income = $9,654). During the first four-and-a-half years of the Denver CDRP, the CDA has spent $11,236,150.

Our data allow us to examine the effects of targeting rehabilitation funds by examining dollar allocations before targeting is adopted as a formal strategy by the CDA and comparing these allocations with spending patterns observed after the policy was adopted. For this analysis, the period prior to targeting runs from 1975 through 1977, and the period subsequent to the implementation of targeting extends from January 1978 through March 1980. Table 9-1 presents the allocation of funds during each time period for low- and moderate-income areas, for tracts above moderate income, and for the five target areas.

The findings reported in table 9-1, which allow us to observe the target areas as a distinct group, show a clear pattern. Tracts falling above 80 percent of the SMSA median income increase their proportion of funds by 15 percent. Where did these funds come from?

The poorer areas of the city lost a substantial proportion of the funds received prior to targeting as a result of the formal adoption of geographic targeting. Almost 25 percent of the proportion of funds allocated to these neediest areas in the period prior to targeting is lost after targeting is implemented.

The effect of targeting of the poorest areas of the city is even more clearly visible after examining table 9-2. Table 9-2 provides data on the per capita expenditures for the CDRP before and after the program changes. Although one must be cautious in interpreting these figures since they are not weighted by need of the area, the pattern that emerged from table 9-1 is reinforced. Tracts above 80 percent of the SMSA median income lose only 8.79 percent of their per capita expenditures after the program change. The target areas show an

Table 9-1
Distribution of CDRP Funds before and after 1978 Program Changes by Income of Census Tracts, with Target Areas Reported Separately

	Period before 1978 Program Changes		Period after 1978 Program Changes	
Tracts above 80% of SMSA median income $N = 43$, pop. = 215,103	$1,543,867	(22.5%)	$1,406,869	(32.0%)
Tracts below 80% of SMSA median income $N = 33$, pop. = 156,300	$4,476,384	(65.3%)	$1,788,472	(40.7%)
Tracts composing five target areas $N = 6$, pop. = 29,278	$ 825,233	(12.1%)	$1,195,325	(27.2%)
Total	$6,845,484		$4,390,666	

Table 9-2
Per Capita Distribution of CDRP Funds before and after 1978 Program Changes
by Income of Census Tracts, with Target Areas Reported Separately

	Per Capita Expenditures, Period before 1978 Program Changes	Per Capita Expenditures, Period after 1978 Program Changes	Percentage Loss or Gain in per Capita Expenditures
Tracts above 80% of SMSA median income N = 43, pop. = 215,103	$ 7.17	$ 6.54	−8.79
Tracts below 80% of SMSA median income N = 33, pop. = 156,300	28.63	11.44	−60.04
Tracts composing five target areas N = 6, pop. = 29,278	28.18	40.82	+44.85

increase in per capita expenditures of 44.85 percent. This increase is gained largely from the poorest areas of the city, which show a loss in per capita expenditures of 60.04 percent. In short, poorer areas of the city lost a high proportion of their total and per capita allocations to pay for the proportional increases among the transitional target areas of Denver. We will now see that a similar trend emerged in the CDA's Neighborhood Revitalization Program.

Neighborhood Revitalization Program

Approximately 20 percent of Denver's CDA funds are allocated to its Neighborhood Revitalization Program (NRP). This program provides funds for construction and rehabilitation of neighborhood facilities including senior-citizen centers, parks, neighborhood centers, child-care centers, health centers, crisis centers, alley paving, and sidewalk repair (CDA, City and County of Denver 1980, NF-1-74). In addition, city funds are expended in services closely connected to these projects.

During the five years' operation of the neighborhood program, seventy-four projects either have been funded or will be funded after the city receives its year 6 grant. Denver has designated three NSAs plus three additional target areas for this program. The NSAs receive priority for three years and the target areas for one year. In its December 1979 application for CDBG funds, the Denver CDA formally stated that one of its goals was the "targeting of public services and public works maintenance to older deteriorating neighborhoods" (CDA, City and County of Denver 1979, p. 1).

In determining which census tracts would be selected as NSAs and targets in its NRP, the CDA relied heavily on the six categories of need established for implementing the CDRP. In fact, three of the five target areas in the CDRP are either NSAs or target areas in the NRP. Of the six areas chosen to receive priority funding for services in this program, three are from group 1, two are from group 2, and one from group 3. Again, at least half the areas chosen for special attention are transitional areas rather than areas of most need.

The data for the NRP lend themselves to the same type of analysis as was applied to the CDRP data. Once again, the data for budgeted spending (as opposed to drawn expenditures) have been divided into time periods, one before and one after the implementation of targeting (NSAs and target areas). Table 9-3 presents the planned budget expenditures during each time period for low- and moderate-income areas, for tracts above moderate income, and for the six targeted areas.

A pattern very similar to that observed for the CDRP allocations emerges for the NRP. Once again, the targeted areas increase their proportion of funds in the second time period. Only a 10-percent increase is observed, but the targeted areas appear to be receiving a large share of funds even before officially being designated NSAs. The budgeted allocations for the moderate-income areas are not affected and hold steady at about 25 percent of the funds. The biggest losers are the neediest areas of the city, which lose about 10 percent of their proportion of the funding received in the first time period. This proportion is picked up by the targeted areas.

The neediest areas' loss can be confirmed through examining the per capita expenditure patterns in table 9-4. This table needs to be interpreted with caution because per capita expenditures are not weighted by need and because of

Table 9-3
Distribution of Budgeted Neighborhood-Revitalization Funds before and after 1979 Program Changes by Income of Census Tracts with NSA and Target Areas Reported Separately

	Period before 1979 Program Changes	Period after Changes (Budgeted)
Tracts above 80% SMSA median income $N = 13$, pop. = 63,882	$ 3,694,133 (25.4%)	$1,372,000 (25.3%)
Tracts below 80% of SMSA median income $N = 10$, pop. = 51,531	3,424,141 (23.5%)	$ 721,000 (13.3%)
Tracts composing six target areas $N = 10$, pop. = 52,436	7,419,618 (51.0%)	$3,317,784 (61.3%)
Total	$14,540,932	$5,410,784

Table 9–4

Per Capita Distribution of Budgeted Neighborhood-Revitalization Funds before
and after 1979 Program Change by Income of Census Tracts, with NSA and
Target Areas Reported Separately

	Per Capita Expenditure before 1979 Program Change	Per Capita Expenditure after Change (Budgeted)	Percentage Loss in Per Capita Expenditure
Tracts above 80 percent SMSA median income N = 13, pop. = 63,882	$ 57.82	$21.47	−62.87
Tracts below 80 percent of SMSA median income N = 10, pop. = 51,531	66.44	13.99	−78.94
Tracts composing six target areas N = 10, pop. = 52,436	141.49	63.27	−55.28

the large difference in dollar allocations between the two time periods, which results in per capita losses to all three types of areas. The biggest losers are the
poorest areas in the city. The cost of targeting the NRP, just as with the CDRP,
is borne disproportionately by the neediest areas.

The analysis of fund allocations for the two largest Denver CDA programs,
accounting for about half of the agency's total expenditures, reveals some interesting results. First, although adopting a targeting approach to fund allocation
may be, according to a bureaucracy that adopts a triage approach, the most efficient way to provide services, the effect of the strategy is to place a disproportionate burden on those areas of the city least able to afford a decline in funds
and services. At least in Denver, the targeting of funds seems to be paid for by
the most needy areas of the city while the areas of moderate income either increase their proportion of funds or at least maintain levels established prior to
targeting.

Changing Priorities in Local Service Delivery

From his research, Lineberry concluded that most urban services in San Antonio
were distributed through bureaucratic "decisional premises" about the "rational" distribution of public services in the city. Further, he indicated that
these decisional premises did not result in services being delivered in a discriminatory fashion on the basis of race, social-class background, economic or political influence, or ecological characteristics of neighborhood. In Denver, however,

the CDA experience has been very different than Lineberry's findings would have led us to anticipate.

HUD's guidelines for distribution of CDA funds resulted in monies being carefully and systematically targeted to neighborhoods specifically defined on the basis of their ecological and social-class (income) characteristics. Our analysis of the Denver's CDA's programs indicate that this targeting resulted in a substantial proportional loss of funds by the most needy areas of the city.

The Community Development Act has been developed by HUD as a national program that provides considerable autonomy to local governments but is administered with strong emphasis on a triage model of urban policy. Usually more than CDA funds are involved; the federal government not only attempts to use federal funds to leverage private investment, but also strongly encourages city governments to coordinate the provision of local city services with services and programs financed through federal funds. In fact, it would make no sense if this were not the case since leveraging with federal money is all the more effective if the full range of neighborhood services is coordinated with housing rehabilitation and other services. The city of Denver explicitly promised to coordinate its public services with the expenditure of CDA funds.

The chief characteristic of federal policy—the triage strategy, with the resulting targeting of city services in neighborhood strategy areas—provides significant insight into service delivery in the 1980s. Either by design or by accident, a trade-off has been accepted not only by the federal government but also by local governments. This trade-off favors efficiency over equity. Triage and coordination of city services into targeted areas may facilitate the maximum impact of programs in designated areas of the city. But the criteria used in the triage strategy also result in the most needy areas of the city being overlooked. If Denver's experience is representative, the 1980s may witness more "efficient" but less equitable delivery of services. The definition of efficiency here is a narrow economic one that assumes that the most efficient use of governmental (public) resources is the leveraging of private investment. Other definitions of efficiency are certainly plausible, however, and these would include calculations of social costs and benefits.

Note

1. There is abundant evidence that race, ethnicity, and poverty still have the potential to ignite social unrest in the cities. The riots in Miami during June 1980 were remarkably similar to those of the 1960s. According to Meranto and Mosqueda (1979), the conditions that brought about the urban riots continue to characterize the cities. The relative quiet of the last several years may be only a temporary hiatus.

References

Bachrach, Peter, and Baratz, Morton S. 1970. *Power and Poverty: Theory and Practice*. New York: Oxford University Press.

Community Development Agency, City and County of Denver. 1978. "Community Development Rehabilitation Program 1978." Unpublished report.

——. 1979. "Community Development Block Grant Program Application" Unpublished application.

——. 1980. "Community Development Project States: April 30, 1980." Unpublished report.

Dommel, P.; Bach, V.; Liebschultz, S.; and Leonard Rubinowitz and Associates. 1980. *Targeting Community Development*. Washington, D.C.: U.S. Government Printing Office.

Dommel P.; Nation, R.; Liebschultz, S.; and Margaret Wrightson and Associates (1978) *Decentralizing Community Development*. Washington D.C.: U.S. Government Printing Office.

Fischer, Paul B. 1973. "The War on Poverty and the 'Blackening' of Urban Bureaucracies—Observations from a Case Study." Paper delivered at the American Political Science Association Meetings, Chicago, 4–8 September.

Judd, Dennis R. 1979. *The Politics of American Cities: Private Power and Public Policy*. Boston: Little, Brown.

Keating, D., and LeGates, R. 1978. "Who Should Benefit from the Community Development Block Grant Program?" *Urban Lawyer* 10, no. 4:701–736.

Lineberry, Robert L. 1977. *Equality and Urban Policy: The Distribution of Municipal Public Services*, Sage Library of Social Research, vol. 39. Beverly Hills, Calif.: Sage Publications.

Meranto, Philip, and Mosqueda, Lawrence. 1979. "Toward Revolution in Urban America: Problems and Prospects." Paper delivered at Annual Convention of American Political Science Association, Washington, D.C., 3 September.

Mushkatel, Alvin, and Lasus, Howard. 1980. "Geographic Targeting of Community Development Funds in Denver: Who Benefits?" Paper presented at Annual Meeting of the Social Science Association, Albuquerque, N.M., 23–26 April.

Nathan, R.; Dommel, P.; Liebschutz, S.; and Milton D. Morris and Associates. 1977. "Block Grants for Community Development." Washington, D.C.: U.S. Government Printing Office.

Piven, Frances Fox, and Cloward, Richard A. 1971. *Regulating the Poor: The Functions of Public Welfare*. New York: Pantheon Books.

Pressman, Jeffrey L., and Wildavsky, Aaron B. 1973. *Implementation*. Berkeley: University of California Press.

Report of the National Advisory Commission on Civil Disorders. 1968. New York: Bantam Books.

1 copy
pp 69 – 82
103 – 140

Thks

[signature]

To _Susan_

WHILE YOU WERE OUT

From _Eli_
Affirmative Action

Phone _3417_

| Area Code | Number | Extension |

Urgent		Phoned		Came in	X
Returned your call		Will call again			
Wants to see you		Please call			X

Message

_Needs a deadline
date of Visiting
Hanfield Prof._

Taken by	Time	Date

Rosenfeld, R. 1977. "National and Local Performance in Community Development Block Grants: Who Benefits?" Paper presented at the Annual Meeting of the American Political Science Association, Washington, D.C., September.

U.S. Department of Housing and Urban Development. 1978. *Community Development Block Grants: Third Annual Report.* Washington, D.C.: U.S. Government Printing Office.

Van Horn, Carl. 1979. *Policy Implementation in the Federal System.* Lexington, Mass.: Lexington Books, D.C. Heath and Company.

Yates, Douglas. 1974. "Service Delivery and the Urban Political Order." In Willis D. Hawley and David Rogers, eds., *Improving the Quality of Urban Management.* Beverly Hills, Calif.: Sage Publications.

_____. 1977. *The Ungovernable City: The Politics of Urban Problems and Policy Making.* Cambridge, Mass.: MIT Press.

10 Community Distribution of Federal Funds: The Community Development Block Grant Program

John F. Sacco

With the emergence of the block-grant programs as a new approach for allocating federal funds to local governments, and with the corresponding latitude these programs afford local jurisdictions, one of the central distributional issues is the extent to which city governments are directing block-grant dollars to the most needy neighborhoods and persons. A fundamental concern in some quarters is that localities will use this extension of policy latitude to spread the dollars throughout the community rather than to direct or target these funds to the greatest need. Similar concerns were not as relevant under earlier categorical programs such as urban renewal or model cities since the federal government had tighter control over project selection and location.

In line with these new distributional questions, the purpose of this chapter is to examine within-city distributional patterns in the Community Development Block Grant (CDBG) program legislated under the Housing and Community Development Act of 1974 (Public Law 93–383). Three facets of the block-grant distributional issue are examined. The first pertains to whether there was more or less local targeting to need under previous categorical grants than under CDBG. The second covers community targeting practices over the first five years of CDBG, 1975 to 1979. The third looks at changes over time in the block-grant program, focusing particularly on those changes associated with the effort by the federal government to encourage greater targeting by local jurisdictions. Running through each of these questions is the effect of federal legislation and regulations on local practices.

For the most part this analysis of targeting is based on a large sample of cities in order to provide a national picture of targeting. Case material and city-by-city patterns are introduced to shed light on the processes and factors affecting local distribution, although the focus is not on the politics of distribution in any one jurisdiction.[1]

Although the intent of the block-grant concept was to provide expanded latitude to local governments vis-à-vis federal control, the CDBG system, both as legislated and as it has evolved, exhibits competing strains. These competing strains permeate practically all aspects of the program, including the issue of targeting versus spreading.

The national CDBG legislation (as a result of sharp differences between the Republican administration and the Senate) offers differing guidelines on the question of targeting to need. In one provision (Sec. 101 c), the legislation supports a relatively rigid targeting goal by stating that the primary objective of the program is to direct assistance so that low- and moderate-income persons are the principal beneficiaries. At the same time, the legislation also provides a much broader set of criteria for approval of local programs. Under this provision (Sec. 104 b 2), localities can use income, physical conditions, or urgency to justify a project. It is these wider criteria that permit local distribution of federal block-grant dollars to a wide spectrum of areas and households.

In addition, the federal implementing regulations, devised by the U.S. Department of Housing and Urban Development (HUD), carry the same dualism exhibited in the national legislation. During the first two years under the Republican administration, 1975 to 1976, the broader and more flexible criteria mentioned earlier were followed by HUD. With the change in administration in 1977, the emphasis of the HUD regulations shifted. For this period, 1977 to 1979, considerably more pressure was put on the cities to target to needy areas and needy populations. The regulations made it clear that the primary emphasis was on low- and moderate-income households (24 Code of Federal Register 570.302 b 3).

Added to the competing demands at the national level, there are rival demands at the jurisdictional level. At the local level, however, the bias would appear to favor spreading. The design of the legislation, which gives distributional authority to the city council and mayor and also opens the distributional process to all interests in the city, makes spreading a strong possibility (Kettl 1979). The history of the legislative struggle—namely, the effort to gain more flexibility for the cities—also gives the local government a further rationale for spreading CDBG funds.

In short, there are pressures favoring both targeting and spreading in this intergovernmental system. The question is whether one or the other dominates, or whether there are mutual adjustments and accommodations.

Measuring Targeting and Community-Development Needs

Census tracts provide the basic unit of analysis for assessing the degree to which localities target CDBG funds. The census tract is chosen because it is a unit small enough to differentiate subareas of need within cities. Additionally, comparable data are available to permit the ranking of census tracts by degree of distress.

The primary indicators used to gauge need at the census-tract level are income, age of housing, and home ownership. Income is measured by the percentage of persons in poverty in 1969 and median family income in 1969; age of housing is indicated by the percentage of the houses built prior to 1939; and home ownership is measured by the percentage of the dwellings that are owner occupied in 1970. Using all four indicators, the level of distress in each census tract is indexed by calculating how much better or worse the tract conditions are than the average conditions in the city as a whole. The worse off a tract is relative to the city average, the lower the score given; the better off; the higher the score.[2]

Assessment of the degree to which CDBG funds are targeted to census tracts of different distress levels is gauged in three ways. The first simply reflects whether the census tract was covered in the CDBG plans, regardless of the amount of dollars budgeted. The second is the total dollars budgeted to a census tract. This measure shows level of effort. The third extends the analysis to include the nature of the activity undertaken. Six types of activities are distinguished: acquisition, demolition, and clearance of property; public works, including street and sewer installation and repair; rehabilitation of substandard housing; open spaces and recreation, which entails beautification and park improvements; public services, including projects such as job training, child care, and legal services; and public facilities, including improvements to municipal property.

It is these three elements—tract coverage, dollars invested, and activities selected—that communities can use to develop different distributional strategies and at the same time address different pressures. Cities can, for example, cover most of the tracts in the jurisdiction, yet budget the bulk of the dollars to a few selected tracts. Similarly, certain activities can be located in one set of tracts and others in a different set of tracts.

Sample and Data Base

To study these targeting questions, data from over 4,000 census tracts in 151 cities are examined.[3] The cities represent a stratified random sample from all metropolitan cities (numbering about 600) in the CDBG program.

The data on distribution of CDBG funds come from plans submitted by each city.[4] Five years' data (1975-1979) are used. This analysis includes both five-year funding totals and annual outlays for 1976 and 1979. The two annual outlays are used to examine change over time, particularly change resulting from the 1977-1978 federal regulatory modifications.

Some difference in targeting is expected between the earlier categorical programs and the CDBG efforts because the categorical grants had stricter requirements for project selection and location. To some degree the results show greater targeting to the most distressed tracts under the previous categorical programs. With respect to these former programs, tract coverage (although generally low) is heavily concentrated in the most distressed tracts and drops off substantially between the most distressed and the moderately distressed tracts. Specifically, percentage of the tract covered, as shown in table 10-1, falls by a factor of almost four, going from 47 percent in the most distressed tracts to 12 percent in moderately distressed tracts (distress level 5). For CDBG the decline, though evident, is considerably less, going from 96 percent in the most distressed tracts to 78 percent in moderately distressed tracts (distress level 5). The slopes for this distress range, 1 to 5, also show the greater targeting under previous categorical grants. For the previous categorical grants the slope is -8.5, compared with -4.5 for CDBG (table 10-2).

Over the entire range of distress (1 to 10), CDBG distribution, not categorical distribution, exhibits more noticeable targeting. However, most of the targeting under CDBG occurs in moderately to lightly distressed tracts (as indicated by slope for this 6-10 distress range, which is -8.0), not in the seriously to moderately distressed tracts (slope, -4.5) (table 10-2).

Table 10-1
Percentage of Census Tracts Covered within Each Distress Level, by Type of Program: Prior Categorical and CDBG

		Most			Moderate				Least	
	1	2	3	4	5	6	7	8	9	10
Prior categorical	47	40	24	24	12	8	5	4	4	2
CDBG	96	96	92	86	78	74	62	57	49	40

Note: The categorical programs covered are urban renewal, Model Cities, and neighborhood development.

Table 10-2
Slopes for Percentage of Census Tracts Covered

	1-5	6-10	1-10
Prior categorical[a]	-8.5	-1.5	-5.5
CDBG	-4.5	-8.0	-6.6

Note: Slopes are unstandardized regression coefficients. The slopes in this case can be expressed in percentages. For example, the slope of -8.5 means a predicted decline of 8.5 percent for each of the first five levels of distress.

[a]Categorical programs include the same listed in table 10-1.

In light of this evidence, the difference between the two programs is not one of targeting versus no targeting. Rather, the evidence shows a change in targeting strategy occurring between the former urban programs and CDBG. Under the previous categorical programs, efforts were heavily concentrated in the worst-off areas; under CDBG targeting has been extended to the moderately distressed areas in the cities. In all likelihood the differences and the complexity of the differences between the programs reflect the fact that the CDBG legislation is neither totally devoted to nor completely neglectful of the block-grant concept. On the one hand, communities are not required to place projects into the most distressed area; but on the other hand the goal of targeting is not abandoned.

More light is shed on targeting patterns under CDBG by examining and comparing the percentage of tracts covered and per capita dollars budgeted to these tracts. If these two indicators are used, the results show that both strains in the program—spreading and targeting—are being addressed. This is being accomplished by the fact that at least some amount of dollars, no matter how small, are budgeted to almost all areas regardless of distress (table 10-1), while at the same time most of the dollars are placed in the worst-off tracts, distress level 1 to 3 (table 10-3). Illustrative of this is the fact that 78 percent of the tracts in distress level 5 are covered; yet these same moderately distressed tracts receive only 8.7 percent of the CDBG funds.

A look at several individual communities provides specific examples of this duality of spreading and targeting. In St. Louis, Missouri, almost all tracts are covered regardless of the level of distress, which indicates spreading. By contrast, the distribution of dollars is more highly targeted. Over $300 per capita is placed in the most distressed tracts and slightly more than $100 in the better-off tracts. Similar patterns hold for York, Pennsylvania, and Gary, Indiana, although there are deviations within the cities (table 10-4).

Table 10-3
Distribution of CDBG Dollars by Distress Levels of Census Tracts

| | Distress Level | | | | | | | | | |
| | Most | | | Moderate | | | | Least | | |
	1	2	3	4	5	6	7	8	9	10
Per capita dollars[a]	310	193	150	111	81	63	47	29	17	18
Percentage of all dollars	23.8	18.8	16.1	11.9	8.7	7.1	5.5	3.4	2.3	2.4

[a]Per capita dollars are five-year totals. All tracts, whether funded or not, are included in the per capita calculation.

Table 10–4
Distribution of CDBG Funds for Selected Cities, Dual Pattern

	Distress									
	Most			Moderate				Least		
City	1	2	3	4	5	6	7	8	9	10
St. Louis										
Dollars per capita	337	206	193	98	97	74	103	47	181	118
Percentage coverage	100	100	100	100	100	100	100	100	94	100
York										
Dollars per capita	247	132	66	42	–	75	0	19	140	56
Percentage coverage	100	100	100	100	–	75	0	100	100	100
Gary										
Dollars per capita	339	825	389	130	110	590	70	34	6	41
Percentage coverage	100	100	100	100	100	80	100	100	100	100

Note: – indicates that the city has no tracts at this particular level of distress.

The cities taking this dual approach—that is, budgeting for most tracts but concentrating dollars in the worst-off tracts—are dealing with the competing strains in the block-grant system. In St. Louis the city council during the initial four years of the program viewed the CDBG dollars as an outside source of funds to be divided among the electoral districts. Neighborhood groups, too, put considerable pressure on the council and the local community-development office to budget funds in the various areas of the city. Additionally, even the less distressed areas in this city are in need, providing a further rationalization for the spreading. As a result of these pressures, all tracts receive some attention.

In York the dispersion of coverage was more a result of the decision of the city council. The elected officials wanted to show the local citizens that these new federal funds, in contrast to the categorical programs, could be distributed to moderately and less distressed areas.

Notwithstanding this spreading to many tracts, the distribution of dollars in these and other cities is still targeted to the worst-off areas. Part of the reason is the pressure from the federal government to target. Not only must all projects be reviewed by federal officials, but local groups also can take their complaints to the federal area offices. Other factors also enter. These include carryover projects from previous categorical projects (which were usually located in the most distressed areas), current pressures from vocal neighborhood groups residing in these distressed areas, and the sheer force of the areal distribution of community-development need.

The dual approach to distribution, though dominant, does not exclude other patterns. Some communities target on both tract coverage and dollars invested, whereas others target on neither (table 10-5).

The practice of targeting on tract coverage and tract funding appears to occur where need is not pervasive throughout a community. In Colorado Springs, for example, there is a clear demarcation between the most needy and less needy areas. As a result, the local planners have been able to avoid the spreading.

Failure to carry out targeting in terms of either coverage or investment can occur when many areas are in economic and physical decline but when advocacy groups are unable to secure funding for the worst of these areas. Birmingham fits this pattern. During the first three to four years of the program, the city used CDBG funds to carry out capital-improvement efforts throughout the community, regardless of the overall distress of the areas.

Changing Patterns, 1976-1979

The various strains in the CDBG program have not remained constant for the first five years of implementation. To begin with, many of the projects carried over from the categorical program were completed in the initial years of CDBG. Although this gave cities greater options in planning, the federal government negated some of these options by setting more rigorous targeting standards in 1977 and 1978.

Table 10-5
Distribution of CDBG Funds for Selected Cities, Other Patterns

| | Distress | | | | | | | | | |
| | Most | | | Moderate | | | | Least | | |
	1	2	3	4	5	6	7	8	9	10
Birmingham										
Dollars per										
capita	80	82	85	79	87	66	166	67	17	52
Percentage										
coverage	100	100	100	100	100	89	100	100	100	78
Colorado Springs										
Dollars per										
capita	278	142	10	55	19	8	0	2	3	0
Percentage										
coverage	100	100	100	100	75	60	0	14	25	0

The pattern of distribution changed to some extent between 1976 and 1979. The amount of spreading declined, as is particularly evident when the coverage of tracts is examined. Comparing the slopes for 1976 and 1979 shows greater targeting in 1979. According to table 10-6, the overall slope for 1979 is steeper than for 1976, -7.3 versus -6.0.

Decrease in spreading is also the case for per capital dollars, but the decrease is not large. The dollars going into the most distressed tracts (distress levels 1, 2, and 3) in 1979 are somewhat greater than those budgeted in 1976, 61 percent compared with 57 percent. Over the entire range of the distress levels, however, the lack of difference is evidenced by the similarity of slopes for 1976 and 1979, -2.5 versus -2.6 (table 10-7).

Shifts to slightly greater targeting of CDBG funds are also apparent when the income element of tract distress is singled out (the HUD regulatory changes were directed mainly at this facet of distress). Table 10-8 shows that four percent more of the dollars are budgeted to the low- and moderate-income tracts (that is, less than or equal to 80 percent of the SMSA family median income) in 1979 than in 1976.[5] This is about the same level of gain experienced in the most distressed tracts.

Although more dollars are being budgeted for poorer areas, it is important to note that the change along the income dimension has taken place mainly in the moderate-income tracts (66-80 percent of the SMSA median income), not in

Table 10-6
Percentage of Census Tracts Covered by Level of Distress, 1976 and 1979

| | Level of Distress | | | | | | | | | | |
| | Most | | | Moderate | | | | Least | | | |
Year	1	2	3	4	5	6	7	8	9	10	Slope
1976	74	74	77	71	67	56	48	40	35	23	-6.0
1979	76	74	70	59	52	44	32	29	19	17	-7.3

Table 10-7
Percentage of CDBG Funds Distributed by Level of Distress, 1976 and 1979

| | Level of Distress | | | | | | | | | | |
| | Most | | | Moderate | | | | Least | | | |
Year	1	2	3	4	5	6	7	8	9	10	Slope
1976	22	19	16	12	9	6	6	4	2	3	-2.5
1979	26	19	16	12	8	7	5	3	2	2	-2.6

Table 10-8
Distribution of CDBG Funds by Income Level, 1976 and 1979
(percent)

Income Level	1976	Cumulative	1979	Cumulative
LE 50%	10.9	10.9	10.5	10.5
51–65%	22.8	33.7	22.8	33.3
66–80%	27.7	61.4	31.5	64.8
81–100%	26.5	87.9	25.6	90.4
101–125%	8.5	95.4	7.5	97.9
GT 125%	3.5	99.9	2.0	99.9

the low-income tracts (less than or equal to 50 percent of the SMSA median income). Specifically, the percentage of dollars in the moderate-income tract increased from 27.7 percent in 1976 to 31.5 percent in 1979, whereas the percentage of dollars in the poorest tracts remained almost the same, near 10.9 percent (table 10-8). This again reflects the multiple targeting strategies of local governments, wherein there is greater targeting yet not without a tendency to resist large federally requested changes.

When the CDBG data for tract coverage and per capita investment are examined without respect to project type, the results show a dual strategy of targeting and spreading. A similar dualism emerges when the CDBG data are decomposed by type of activity. In this case the dual approach is achieved by greater targeting for some of the activities than for others. In particular, demolition, clearance, and acquisition of property are most likely to go into distressed areas, and beautification and parks are most likely to go into better-off areas. Housing rehabilitation falls in between the two, with substantial amounts going into both heavily and moderately distressed areas (table 10-9).

This differential placement of activities suggests, at least in the view of some, that communities are following a practice of tearing down in the worst-off areas and one of preservation in the better-off neighborhoods. This is and has been an issue of considerable controversy in the practice of urban development (Anderson 1964).

Although there is indeed some differential placement, and it is controversial, many communities defend these practices. First, part—perhaps a large part—of this type of distribution is explained by commitments cities had from prior categorical programs, urban renewal in particular. These urban-renewal efforts frequently involved acquisition and assemblage of large parcels of land in the worst-off areas of the city for the purpose of commercial or housing development. Cities that undertook these projects prior to CDBG were often obligated to complete at least part of the project. As a result, much of the early CDBG effort was oriented to acquisition, demolition, and clearance in distressed areas of the city.

Table 10–9
Slopes of CDBG Activities against Distress Level

	Per Capita Distribution	Percentage Distribution[a]
Acquisition/demolition	−9.9	−3.2
Public works	−6.9	−2.0
Rehabilitation	−5.5	−2.1
parks	−0.8	−1.4
Public services	−2.9	−2.4
Public facilities	−2.2	−2.0

[a]The steeper the slope, the more the activity is located in highly distressed tracts.

With the passage of time, however, less is seen of large clearance efforts localized in the most distressed areas. Examination of the size of these acquisition projects over the first five years of the program, as shown in table 10-10, suggests that execution of these projects is diminishing.

Localities also rationalize heavy acquisition and demolition projects in distressed areas on the grounds that much (39 percent) of the publicly funded housing built or committed since the initiation of CDBG has gone into these very same distressed areas. Although this housing may not cover the same structures removed or may not replace all the units lost, it nonetheless shows that replacement is occurring.

To further show that efforts under CDBG have not been solely directed to tearing down in distressed areas, cities point to the fact that infrastructure improvements—streets, sewers, and sidewalks—are highly targeted to distressed tracts. Table 10-9 supports this contention. In short, cities argue that although acquisition and demolition are concentrated in distressed areas, this does not imply a sole reliance on these activities. Building and preservation are also taking place.

The other and more critical view is that localities are indeed taking a narrow approach to treatment of the most distressed areas.[6] This case rests on the relatively heavy placement of housing rehabilitation and public works in moderately distressed areas. As seen in table 10-11, housing repair and public works are the major activities in moderately distressed tracts, whereas acquisition and clearance (supplemented by other undertakings) are the major activities in the worst-off areas. This, in the view of the critics, is a form of triage—namely, saving the moderately ill while not giving treatment of the same quality to the most ill.

The controversial approach of targeting heavily for certain activities and less for other activities has diminished somewhat. The overall difference in targeting among all activities has decreased between 1976 and 1979. In 1976 the difference between the highest (-2.2) and lowest slope (-0.15) was 2.1, whereas in

Table 10–10
Percentage of Acquisition/Demolition Funds by Project Size

	Project Size	
Year	LT $100,000	GE $500,000
1975	3.8	60.0
1976	4.7	56.8
1977	6.2	63.0
1978	5.3	53.4
1979	7.6	45.4

Note: Project size is based on dollars budgeted at the census-tract level.

Table 10–11
Per Capita Distribution of CDBG Funds for Selected Activities, by Tract Distress
(dollars)

	Distress									
	Most			Moderate				Least		
	1	2	3	4	5	6	7	8	9	10
Acquisition/ demolition	122	52	36	23	13	9	7	4	2	4
Public works	77	51	40	32	22	21	15	10	7	7
Housing rehabilitation	51	42	35	28	21	16	11	7	3	2

1979 the difference, as shown in table 10–12, was down to 1.3. Equally important, there is less concentration of acquisition and demolition and slightly more placement of rehabilitation in the most distressed areas, reducing the use of the dual strategy. Table 10–12 shows that between 1976 and 1979 the regression coefficient for acquisition and demolition declined from -2.2 to -1.5, whereas the regression coefficient for rehabilitation went up slightly from -1.4 to -1.5. Again, however, there is a tenacity of movement in the important area of housing rehabilitation.

A number of factors account for what reduction in the dual approach there is. The tightening of the federal regulations is among these. Not only do the regulations encourage cities to coordinate and balance activities, but the regulations also stress placement of these coordinated undertakings in the poorer neighborhoods (CFR 507.301 c and 570.302 3).

Table 10–12
Activity Per Capita Dollars by Distress, 1976 and 1979

| | Regression Coefficients | |
Activities	1976	1979
Acquisition/demolition	−2.2	−1.4
Public works	−1.2	−1.5
Rehabilitation	−1.4	−1.5
parks	−.15	−.23
Public services	−.56	−.56
Public facilities	−.42	−.50
Difference	2.1	1.3

The slowness associated with movement of housing repair into the most distressed areas appears to be a result of local reluctance as well as of the inertia that accompanies any change. With respect to reluctance, the localities contend that it is difficult to pursue aggressive rehabilitation programs in poorer areas. Home ownership is low and incomes are not sufficient to pay off even low-interest loans. Added to this, cities have been slow in finding innovative ways to deal with these problems. In many communities only in the fifth year has the CDBG program started to use CDBG dollars for repair of multifamily rental units.

City governments, on their own, have been moving toward neighborhood preservation (which consists mainly of housing rehabilitation and public works) as a central approach for areas of all types, and away from the former renewal, acquisition-dominated, strategies. Interviews with city officials plus the CDBG data support this.[7] Table 10–13 compares and contrasts growth in neighborhood preservation with area renewal. In 1976 neighborhood preservation was used mostly in moderately distressed tracts. In that year 47 percent of all CDBG funds budgeted in moderately distressed tracts were allocated to preservation, compared with a third of the funds in the worst-off tracts. In contrast, area redevelopment, which derives from the former urban-renewal projects and consists primarily of acquisition and demolition, was heavily employed in the most distressed tracts in 1976. As of 1979, however, it was the preservation approach that consumed most of the dollars in the seriously distressed areas, as well as in the other distress levels.

Summary and Conclusions

The central question addressed in this chapter is whether communities are targeting federal CDBG dollars to areas of greatest need under this new

Table 10–13

Distribution of Funds for Neighborhood Preservation versus Neighborhood Redevelopment, by Tract Distress

(percentage)

Revitalization Strategy	Distress		
	Most	*Moderate*	*Least*
Neighborhood preservation			
1976	33	47	45
1979	45	48	46
Renewal			
1976	36	18	14
1979	19	17	13

Note: Distribution is a column percentage. Columns do not add to 100 percent since not all strategies are presented.

block-grant arrangement or whether the funds are being spread. Integral to this analysis is the effect of federal legislation and regulations and the impact of changes in federal guidelines. The distributional patterns at the subcity level present a complex pattern reflecting the various federal and local pressures operating in the block-grant intergovernmental system. The complex practices show that there is a dual pattern of targeting to needy areas; yet evidence of spreading is still present. Additionally, movement away from spreading has been slow.

Two sets of local strategies appear to be used to accomplish this dualism. In the first set, spreading and targeting are achieved by affecting how much money goes where. In essence, many parts of the city receive at least some dollars, but most funds are reserved for the highly distressed areas. The spreading permits the city government to serve citizens in all areas of the city. The targeting of dollars meets federal pressure for focusing on the most needy areas as well as local pressure for this goal.

The basis of the second set of local strategies is careful selection of the types of activities that go into each level of distress. For the worst-off tracts, although these are receiving most of the dollars, the character of the effort is somewhat narrow, consisting mainly of property acquisition and demolition. This is among the most controversial of the targeting issues.

This propensity to pursue a multiple strategy with respect to the distress of the tract has declined somewhat since 1976. The worst-off areas now receive more attention and a wider complement of activities, although the movement has been slow.

Case and comparative material from various sources suggests the interplay that is taking place behind these distributional results. First, the general finding of multiple strategy (spreading and targeting) is the result of the clash between local control and federal regulations. Both parties, however, have made accommodations in a pattern of classical mutual adjustment, with neither side totally dominating. Second, the movement toward greater targeting is the result of increased federal pressure, although once again the speed of that movement is mutually adjusted.

Two particular studies cast further light on the dynamics and results of these interactions. In an analysis of sixty-four communities, the Brookings Institution shows that HUD is perceived to be gaining slightly more influence in local decisions in the fourth year (1978) of the program than in the second year, but the gain does not indicate a dominance.[8] During this more recent period, HUD area-office visits to the cities became more frequent, city plans were reviewed more carefully by HUD, and formal notices and actions against the cities became more common. Similar patterns were found in a twenty-four-city study conducted for HUD in 1978 by Westat Inc. Cities took cognizance of federal initiatives in terms of moving toward more targeting, but not without holding on their own agendas.

In all, although targeting is evident in a number of respects, there are noticeable elements of spreading. Further, the gains in targeting are taking place slowly. This suggests an adjustment in the direction of the federal targeting initiatives rather than a predominance of the federal position.[9] In this sense localities are still holding their options, although the options are now more limited.

Notes

1. Three case studies were conducted by the author: St. Louis, Missouri; York, Pennsylvania; and Bethlehem, Pennsylvania. These were supplemented by a larger fund of over seventy-five case studies.

2. To calculate the index, the standard score for each of the variables—income, poverty, age of housing, and home ownership—was subtracted from the city average for that variable and the differences were added to yield an aggregate distress score for each census tract. In adding the scores, greater weight was assigned to the income variables, since income predominates in the federal criteria. The tracts were then grouped in ten equal intervals, with the first interval representing the most distressed tracts and the last interval the least distressed tracts.

3. The sample varies slightly from year to year. The data base was developed and organized by the staff of the Office of Evaluation, Community Planning and Development, U.S. Department of Housing and Urban Development.

4. Called the CDBG application, the plans represent a relatively detailed description of projects the city expects to implement. Similar detail is not readily available on the actual execution of the plans.

5. Tracts that have 50 percent or more of the families with median incomes less than or equal to 80 percent of the SMSA median family income are defined as low- and moderate-income census tracts by HUD.

6. In a recent report, *Monitoring Community Development: The Citizen's Evaluation of CDBG, National Citizen Monitoring Project, t*he CDBG program received criticism on a number of fronts, including place of projects in non-low- and moderate-income areas.

7. HUD has provided a report on CDBG each year. Case material based on perceptions of local officials was included in the *Fourth Annual Report, 1979*, chap. 5.

8. A longitudinal monitoring of CDBG since the initial year of the program has been done by the Brookings Institution. Their third report, which provides an assessment of the changes in the HUD regulations, is *Targeting Community Development* (Washington, D.C.: U.S. Department of Housing and Urban Development, 1980). See chap. 3 for a discussion of changes in federal influence.

9. These national patterns fit with the political theory of partisan mutual adjustment, as well as with the notion of the power of local government in a federal system. See Lindblom (1965); see also Straub (1980) for a broad assessment of local response during the first two years of the CDGB program.

References

Anderson, Martin. 1964. *The Federal Bulldozer.* Cambridge, Mass.: MIT Press.

Brookings Institution. 1980. *Targeting Community Development.* Washington, D.C.: U.S. Department of Housing and Urban Development.

Bunce, Harold. 1979. "CDBG Formula: An Evaluation." *Urban Affairs Quarterly* 14:443–464.

Bunce, Harold, and Goldberg, Robert. 1979. *City Need and Community Development Funding.* Washington, D.C.: U.S. Department of Housing and Urban Development.

Housing and Community Development Act of 1974. Public Law 93-383.

Kettl, Donald. 1979. "Can Cities be Trusted?" Memorandum, Columbia University.

Lindblom, Charles. 1965. *The Intelligence of Democracy.* New York: Free Press.

Straub, John. 1980. "Implementation of the CDBG Program In Local Politics." Ph.D. diss., University of Pennsylvania.

U.S. Department of Housing and Urban Development. 1978. *Third Annual Report to Congress on the Community Development Block Grant Program.* Washington, D.C.: U.S. Government Printing Office.

——. 1979. *Fourth Annual Report to Congress on the Community Development Block Grant Program.* Washington, D.C.: U.S. Government Printing Office.
24 Code of Federal Register. Section 570.

11

The Costs of Service Equalization: Standards of Service Equity and Their Impacts on Municipal Budgets

David L. Cingranelli

The federal courts in the United States have viewed distributions of services that grossly discriminate against predominantly black neighborhoods as violations of the equal-protection clause of the Fourteenth Amendment to the U.S. Constitution. Some rough standard of input equality or equality of service efforts across neighborhoods has been the judicial standard applied. So far the federal courts have refused to use an equal-results standard that would place much greater burdens on government. Furthermore, they have not ruled on how much inequality of inputs across neighborhoods is tolerable.

Service equalization issues—those involving the redistribution of service resources or benefits, supposedly in the interests of fairness or equity—are likely to be a concern of the governments of large U.S. cities for many years to come. The Warren Court, in *McDonald* v. *Board of Commissioners* (1969), not only upheld racial classifications as "constitutionally suspect," but also hinted that classifications based on wealth were suspect as well. The Burger Court's treatment of service-equalization cases has shown far more restraint; and, largely for this reason, concern about service equalization in noneducational service areas has decreased. As Lineberry (1974, p. 26) notes, despite the present lull, "the legal questions surrounding service distribution are no more a dead issue than those concerning public school financing. If anything, in future years challenges to service allocations are likely to grow with the increasing political sophistication of minority groups and the deepening fiscal problems of major cities."

This chapter deals with some practical issues surrounding the service-equalization process. First, some factors other than race and wealth that may have a systematic effect on the distribution of services are considered in terms of constitutional strictures. Alternative approaches to service equalization are then discussed. Finally, using the distributions of police- and fire-protection resources in Boston, Massachusetts, as an example, price tags are placed on different equalization approaches. Assigning price tags to service-equalization options graphically illustrates the nature and magnitude of the urban-service maldistribution problem. Price tags allow us to estimate, for example, the extent to which an existing allocation of service resources among recipient units would have to be disrupted in order to redress inequities in the distribution due to classifications of neighborhoods on the basis of racial, political, or economic considerations.

Suspect Classifications and Service-Delivery Rules

As defined by Bish (1976), a *suspect classification* is a classification that serves
no useful purpose and that often implies a stigma or majoritarian abuse toward
a group so classified. Race is clearly a suspect classification of neighborhoods
when used by service administrators for the purpose of allocating larger shares
of neighborhood-oriented service resources to predominantly white neighborhoods. Some feel that wealth should also be a suspect classification when used in
service-delivery rules—regularized procedures for allocating service resources—to
favor wealthy neighborhoods. In general, however, the courts have held that as
long as a government policy does not infringe on some fundamental interest or
differentially treat a suspect class, it need only serve some rational purpose—that
is, be related in some reasonable way to the achievement of a public goal—to be
considered constitutional.

In the delivery of municipal services some classifications of neighborhoods
are necessary. For example, neighborhoods are commonly classified according to
their needs for particular types of services. Areas of high crime rates need more
law-enforcement resources than areas of low crime rates, and research has shown
that police departments take this factor into account when allocating police
manpower. Similarly, service administrators commonly consider neighborhood
"service conditions"—the variety of physical, human, financial, and legal factors
that can make it harder or easier to provide services of a specified quantity or
quality to neighborhoods (Hirsch 1968). For example, because of high levels of
traffic congestion, which slow response time, it is likely that it will cost a municipal fire department more money to deliver a given level of fire protection to
the central business district than it will cost to provide the same level of protection to a less congested residential area of the city.

Usually, there is little objection to the employment of the need or service-
condition criteria when service inputs are distributed, but some types of indicators of "relative need for services" can produce perverse distributive outcomes.
Utilization rates, for example, when used as indicators of need for services, are
especially likely to produce distributive outcomes that reinforce and, over time,
exaggerate existing distributive patterns (Levy, Meltsner, and Wildavsky 1974).
Even though classifications of neighborhoods according to their relative needs
for services or their peculiar service conditions may in some contexts produce
unfortunate results, few would argue that service administrators should abandon
such classifications or that the courts should treat them as legally suspect. However, two types of biases evident in the service-delivery rules of some cities are at
least morally suspect and may be the subject of future litigation. These are (1)
differential service treatment of neighborhoods designed to promote business
interests, and (2) differential service provision designed to maintain or enhance
urban electoral coalitions. The former type of bias is well known and widely
accepted in the U.S. political system. The latter type is considered less legitimate

but, though difficult to document, is widely suspected. Both represent interesting philosophical and practical problems for future service-equalization debate.

Promoting Industry and Commerce

The degree of bias in favor of industrial and commercial interests is difficult to measure in any city because it is manifested in so many ways, but the existence of biases in favor of business interests is clear in most cities that are concerned about economic development and are at all threatened with financial insolvency. Examples of local policies showing favoritism to areas of the city with relatively high levels of industrial and commercial activity include:

1. property-tax forgiveness programs for new and/or expanding business enterprises—usually manufacturing
2. special capital improvements to accommodate business interests (traffic improvements, the purchase of new fire-fighting equipment, and so on)
3. the use of urban-renewal and community-development money by many cities almost exclusively for central-business-district development
4. lower tax assessments for businesses or lower tax rates for business properties
5. zoning policies that favor business development
6. special low-interest credit arrangements (local bonds) to finance the construction of facilities for lease or sale to private firms
7. provision of relatively high levels of neighborhood-oriented service expenditures to commercial and industrial areas of the city.

The logic in favor of a distributive policy providing preferential treatment to areas of existing or potential commercial or industrial development is quite compelling. Relatively high levels of neighborhood-oriented services and public improvements to downtown areas of the city create a good business climate, encouraging business interests to increase private investment. Since increased investment has a multiplier effect on the local economy, many new jobs are created and increased tax revenues generated. The new tax revenues allow the cycle to continue as a positive-feedback loop—each cycle producing better economic consequences for the local economy (Peterson 1979; Judd 1979).

This rationale not only is important to many, if not most, local elected officials, but also is central to much current federal policy toward cities. For example, according to Patricia R. Harris, former secretary of the Department of Housing and Urban Development, the specific intent of HUD action programs was to stimulate new and increased private investment in cities while establishing private-sector confidence that would protect existing business investment (Joller 1977). Urban elected officials and service administrators are attentive to such sentiments because HUD administers much of the competitive categorical and block-grant programs for community development available to local governments.

Why are urban policies that favor business interests acceptable, whereas policies explicitly biased in favor of predominantly white or upper-income neighborhoods would almost certainly be subject to challenge in the courts? This is a question of considerable relevance to future urban policy. Although it may be true that what is good for commercial and industrial areas within cities is good for the city as a whole, the net effect of such policies is regressively redistributive. Areas of existing accumulated wealth receive the greatest benefits.

Promoting Electoral Interests

Just as there is a compelling logic behind distributive policies that promote business interests within the city, there are equally compelling reasons for elected municipal officials and service administrators of major city departments to promote their electoral interests. Although there is little systematic evidence to link electoral politics with the distribution of municipal services, in the city of Boston the level of support each neighborhood provided to the winning candidate for mayor in 1967 was found to be positively related to the subsequent levels of fire- and police-protection resources each received.

Space limitations do not permit a full explanation of this finding, but a link between electoral politics and the distribution of resources within a political jurisdiction is not surprising. Voters make electoral choices and through these choices give officeholders the power to make distributive decisions and to delegate such decisions to appointed administrators. The particular officeholders who have been elected make personnel appointments and distributive decisions that may differ from those that would have been made had an alternative set of representatives been chosen. Voters, observing the distributive decisions of elected representatives and their designees, act in the next election at least partly on the basis of their satisfaction or dissatisfaction with the decisions made.

But could this competitive process result in a denial of equal protection of the laws? If so, which is more important—the democratic process or the equal-protection standard? This question is not purely academic. Cities across the United States have experienced a precipitous decline in voter turnout over the past decade. There is good reason to believe that a disproportionate share of the nonvoting group consists of black and low-income voters. If elected officials make key decisions by calculating the best way of ensuring success in the next election, black and low-income nonvoters are likely to receive short shrift from those decisions.

Options for Service Equalization

Because of political realities and bureaucratic inertia, a particular service distribution, once established, is not easily changed. Planned redistributions are possible, however, either as short-term solutions (in order to comply with a court ruling, for example) or over the long run. Regardless of the service-delivery area or the amount of time available, redistributive policies can basically take only three directions—*leveling down, leveling up,* or the *elimination of extremes.*

The equal-protection standards used by the courts require equality of treatment but do not imply that a minimum level of services must be supplied to each neighborhood or subgroup within the city. Therefore, one possibility for equalizing services would be to reduce the level of service provision to all recipients to the level provided the least advantaged recipients (leveling down). For example, a city ordered to make its public-transportation system equally accessible to handicapped and nonhandicapped passengers could conceivably respond by going out of the public-transportation business. A city could respond in the same way to an order requiring new public-transportation routes in areas with large socially and economically disadvantaged populations. The leveling-down option would be most attractive to financially distressed urban areas that are forced to respond quickly to service-equalization court decisions.

The leveling-up option—increasing the level of service provision for all recipients to the level enjoyed by the most advantaged recipient—is much more palatable to citizens but is also much too costly in all but the most unusual circumstances. Where the amount of variance across recipient units is slight, however —as may be the case in regard to sewers, street lighting, or trash collection—this option may be more attractive than it would appear at first glance.

However, the most likely course of action leading to service equalization in this period of increasing scarcity of resources is the elimination of extremes— bringing the level of service provision supplied to each neighborhood closer to the mean level of service provision across all recipient units. This appears to be the option that most state governments are pursuing in attempting to equalize state aid to local school districts in the wake of the *Serrano* and *Rodreguez* federal court cases in the early 1970s challenging state educational-finance systems that were tied to local property taxes. Intradistrict differences within cities in school quality (which are subject to manipulation by local policymakers) are most likely to be equalized through the elimination of extremes as well. The elimination of extremes is a no-cost, incremental approach that is most reasonable in a legal environment where the courts have not stated the level of inequality of treatment that is tolerable within the equal-protection guidelines.

It is useful to consider these three options in the context of the distribution of services in a U.S. city—Boston, Massachusetts. A simple statistical exercise will illustrate the degree of disruption in the 1970-1971 allocation of police- and fire-protection expenditures to Boston neighborhoods that would have occurred if any of the three options outlined previously had actually been implemented. Table 11-1 presents some basic information concerning variation in per capita police and fire expenditures across Boston's 120 residential census tracts.

Boston had 147 census tracts in 1970, but this analysis excludes the central business district—tracts in which 45 percent or more of the land area was used for industrial or commercial purposes—because per capita expenditure comparisons between downtown and residential neighborhoods can be misleading. The denominator of the expenditure ratio consists of nighttime population only; but in business areas of a city, services are being provided to a large, transient, daytime population as well. Although it is sensible to make per capita expenditure comparisons across residential areas or, perhaps, even across business areas within a city, lumping the two types of areas together creates an "apples and oranges" situation.

Expenditures for police protection in Boston's residential census tracts totaled $21,493,110 in 1971, whereas expenditures for fire protection in the same neighborhoods totaled $15,742,840 in 1970. All the cost figures for police and fire protection are expressed in 1971 and 1970 dollars, respectively. These figures exclude administrative and other overhead costs that could not be directly allocated to census tracts. Police and fire expenditures were allocated to census tracts through the following procedure.

For each of eleven police districts, the salaries of all police officers were totaled. Central administrative expenditures were allocated in proportion to the allocation of manpower expenditures. The expenditures allocated to each of the police districts were divided by the number of patrol-car sectors within the district to derive an estimate of the crime-prevention and control expenditures for each car sector. Then, using census-tract maps, with the boundaries of police-car sectors superimposed, the amount of patrol activity that each census tract received from the various car sectors serving the tract was estimated. With the cost of each car sector estimated as described earlier, the police expenditures within the tract were computed. Finally, the expenditures were divided by the population of the tract to derive per capita expenditure estimates.

Table 11-1
Per Capita Costs of Supplying Police and Fire Protection to Boston's Residential Census Tracts

	Mean	Highest	Lowest	Standard Deviation
Fire expenditures (1970)	$29.83	$163.65	$6.04	$22.84
Police expenditures (1971)	43.42	239.70	2.70	32.87
N = 120				

The allocation of fire expenditures to census tracts was similar to the allocation of police expenditures but was not based on as much detailed information about the salaries of fire fighters. Instead of data on districts and patrol-car sectors, information on seventy-two land-based engine and ladder companies was utilized. Since each company has roughly the same number of men, the figure for total fire-fighting expenditures was divided by the number of companies to estimate the cost per fire-fighting company. Using census-tract maps and superimposing the boundaries of fire-fighting companies, the amount of fire-fighting coverage that each census tract received from the various fire companies serving the tract was estimated. Based on the estimated cost of a fire company, indicated earlier, fire-fighting expenditures for each tract were then computed. The assumption is that if a census tract is within the boundaries of several fire companies, it will be physically close to several fire stations and therefore receive a relatively high level of fire-protection services.[1]

Per capita service expenditures are often used when actual service distributions are described, but these figures are usually computed for units such as census tracts, which vary widely in population. In Boston the residential census tracts varied in population from 696 to 14,963. The mean was 4,859, and the standard deviation was 2,744. These differences in population make a big difference when the costs or savings associated with each option are calculated. As can be seen in table 11-2, the leveling-up option in Boston would have had a huge impact on the municipal budget there because relatively high amounts of police and fire expenditures per capita were being provided to residential neighborhoods with relatively small populations.

If the individual service recipient rather than the census neighborhood has served as the unit of analysis, there would have been no costs or savings associated with the elimination-of-extremes option. But police and fire services are neighborhood oriented—that is, they are designed to provide protection in differential amounts to spatially defined areas. Within those areas differential treatment of individuals is uncommon; in other words, variation in treatment is

Table 11-2
Costs and Savings Associated with Leveling Up, Leveling Down, and Elimination of Extremes in Boston

Expenditure Category	Leveling Up (Costs)	Leveling Down (Savings)	Elimination of Extremes (Costs)
Fire protection (1970)	$ 79,681,966	$12,221,298	$1,651,122
Police protection (1971)	118,276,679	19,918,732	3,825,222
$N = 120$			

probably greater across neighborhoods than within them. For this reason, the neighborhood is the more realistic unit of analysis here, and because of population differences among neighborhoods in Boston, even the elimination-of-extremes option would have had moderate costs attached to it.

Equality or Equity?

Input equality is not necessarily a good standard to use in judging the equity of a service distribution. Inherent in the concept of equity are the notions of fairness and justice, which are not necessarily implied by the concept of equality. To give each recipient group an *equitable* share of services may be different from supplying an *equal* share to each (Rich 1979). As noted earlier, there are some acceptable and noncontroversial reasons (such as differences in needs and technical service conditions) for allocating higher levels of service inputs per capita to some neighborhoods rather than to others. It may be far less costly and far more equitable to reallocate resources so that discrimination against one type of neighborhood attribute is eliminated than it would be to mandate input equality.

The distribution of police services to Boston neighborhoods can be used to provide a rough illustration. The following is an estimating equation for per capita police expenditures to Boston's residential census tracts.

$$\text{POL EXP} = -3.449 + .28 \text{ CRIME} - .17 \text{ DENS} + .52 \text{ IND/COM}$$
$$\phantom{\text{POL EXP} = -3.449 +} (.03) \phantom{\text{ CRIME}} (.06) \phantom{\text{ DENS}} (.17)$$

$$+55.5 \text{ POL} - .19 \text{ BLACK}$$
$$(22.4) \phantom{\text{ POL}} (.10)$$

$$\bar{R}^2 = .54 \text{ (standard errors in parentheses)}$$

where	POL EXP	= police expenditures per capita
CRIME	= part I and part II crime rates
DENS	= population density
IND/COM	= percentage of land area used for industrial or commercial activity
POL	= percentage of registered voters who voted in the previous mayoral election (turnout) multiplied by the percentage of votes delivered to the winning mayoral candidate (loyalty)
BLACK	= percentage black

These results indicate that not only were neighborhood needs (CRIME) and service conditions (DENS) important determinants of the distribution of police expenditures to Boston's neighborhoods, but that neighborhood economic (IND/COM), political (POL), and racial (BLACK) attributes were important as well.[2] As noted earlier, economic and political classifications are in some ways suspect when used as resource-distribution criteria. Race has already been found to be an illegitimate classification when used for this purpose.

Using the unstandardized regression coefficients from the foregoing equation, the costs of removing the effects of these inappropriate criteria from the 1971 police-service allocations can be estimated. Removing the effects of a particular neighborhood characteristic from the distribution of per capita police expenditures can be accomplished by calculating the dollar amount of each neighborhood's allocation that is due to its deviation from the mean on that particular characteristic. This procedure is a variation of the elimination-of-extremes approach, where, for example, if one wishes to estimate the dollar costs of eliminating the racial bias that exists in the distribution of services across neighborhoods, each neighborhood's service-expenditure allocation is estimated as though it contained a percentage of black residents equal to the mean percentage of black residents across all neighborhoods. Then the difference between each neighborhood's actual and estimated resource allocation is calculated. The resulting figure represents the level of extra expenditures provided or the amount of expenditures denied because of the racial composition of the neighborhood. The sum of this calculation for all residential neighborhoods in the city is the amount of dollars that would have had to be reallocated if the effects of that characteristic had been removed from the observed allocation of service expenditures to neighborhoods.[3] Table 11-3 illustrates how much the 1971 allocation of police expenditures to Boston would have been disturbed if the illegitimate effects of racial composition, economic composition, or political characteristics were removed in this manner.

Removing the effects of probusiness bias on neighborhood police expenditures would have required a reallocation of slightly more than 7 percent of the $21,493,110 spent in 1971 to provide police protection to Boston's 120 predominantly residential neighborhoods. Removing the effects of either of the other neighborhood classifications would have cost even less. Only in the redress of racial imbalances would the number of neighborhoods losing expenditures have been higher than the number of gainers. Since the emphasis of the elimination-of-extremes approach is on reallocation—taking from some neighborhoods and giving to others—the actual impact on the municipal budget to remove the effects of any (or all) of these attributes on the distribution of police expenditures would have been very small.

Conclusions and Policy Recommendations

These simple calculations regarding the narrowly defined dollar costs associated with service equalization in one U.S. city help to illustrate three points. First, input equality is a ridiculous standard for the evaluation of service distributions.

Table 11-3
Dollar Reallocation Required to Remove Racial, Economic, and Political Effects from Neighborhood Police Allocations in Boston, 1971

Neighborhood (NBH) Characteristic	Number of NBHs Losing Expenditures	Average Loss/ NBH	Number of NBHs Gaining Expenditures	Average Gain/NBH	Total Amount Reallocated[a]	Additional Expenditures Required[b]
Racial composition	86	$18,614	34	$34,095	$1,159,230	None[c]
Percentage industrial-commercial activity	45	28,114	74	22,681	1,533,735	$144,659
Political-power index (1967)	44	34,083	76	20,971	1,499,652	94,144

[a]The amount that would have to be taken from some neighborhoods and given to others.

[b]The amount of additional expenditures or costs that would be entailed in removing the effects of a variable from the distribution of expenditures to neighborhoods.

[c]Removing the effects of neighborhood racial composition from the 1971 allocation of police expenditures actually could have saved the city $441,574.

Although there was considerable variation in police- and fire-protection expenditures per capita across Boston's neighborhoods in the early 1970s, comparatively little of this variation in treatment could be attributed to classifications of neighborhoods on the basis of political tendencies, the level of business activities they contained, or their racial compositions. Some input inequality is necessary to produce service equity or fairness of treatment so that no city will need to pursue any of the disruptive options (leveling up, leveling down, or elimination of extremes) available to achieve input equality.

Second, equity or fairness in the distribution of services to recipients requires only that legally or perhaps morally suspect classifications of recipients not be used as criteria when service resources of all types are distributed. If the evidence from Boston in the early 1970s is at all illustrative of the distribution of service expenditures across neighborhoods in other large U.S. cities, this requirement would not appear to be too costly for even the most financially hard-pressed cities.

Thus the courts and urban policymakers would be well advised to turn their attention away from the input-equality standard and to replace it with an *input-equity* standard. One approach policymakers might take would be to mandate the use of explicit formulas in determining allocations of municipal-service resources to each neighborhood within an urban area. The courts would not have to develop formulas for each category of service provision but would simply require that cities make service-distribution rules explicit and public, allowing citizens to challenge them first within each service agency and, ultimately, in the courts. If the courts decided that the service-distribution rule employed in a particular case included a classification not appropriate as a criterion for distribution, the court would order that the effects of only the unjustified variable be removed from the distribution standard. The assumption would be that all other factors affecting the distribution of resources were legally acceptable.

My guess is that few service-equalization cases would ever reach the courts, because public, explicit distribution rules would allow service-equalization issues to be debated intelligently within the normal political process. The present system of service distribution in most cities impedes such debate because (1) information about the distribution of service resources to neighborhoods is rarely released; (2) when it is released, each service agency has its own set of administrative districts, which makes it difficult for residents to compare treatment; and (3) the criteria for disbursement of service resources are rarely made public.

Notes

1. The procedure for allocating police and fire expenditures to census tracts is explained in some detail in Podoff, Primont, and Esposito (1973, pp. 110–114).

2. Explained variance is adjusted for degrees of freedom and reported as $\bar{R}^2$.

3. The actual formula used to calculate the size of the reallocations needed to remove the effects of any variable from the police-expenditure equation was as follows:

$$\sum_{i=1}^{N} B_{EQ} (\bar{Q}_i - Q_i) \times \text{Pop}_i$$

where E = per capita police or fire expenditures

        Q = the illegitimate variable to the removed

        B = the unstandardized regression coefficient of E on Q

        i = 1

      Pop = population of the census tract

All positive totals were summed and all negative totals were summed. The grand sum equaled the total reallocation that would have been required. The calculations in table 11-3 do not indicate the number of dollars that would have to be reallocated or the total additional expenditures that would be required if the effects of all three illegitimate neighborhood characteristics were removed from the 1971 allocation of police expenditures to residential neighborhoods in Boston. Because there is some correlation between these neighborhood characteristics, removing the effects of one neighborhood characteristic would also remove some of the effects of another. See Duncan (1969).

References

Bish, R.L. 1976. "Fiscal Equalization through Court Decisions: Policy-Making without Evidence." In E. Ostrom, ed., *The Delivery of Urban Services*, pp. 75-102. Beverly Hills, Calif.: Sage Publications.

Duncan, O.D. 1969. "Inheritance of Poverty or Inheritance of Race." In D.P. Moynihan, ed., *On Understanding Poverty*, pp. 85-110. New York: Basic Books.

Hirsch, W.Z. 1968. "The Supply of Urban Public Services." In H.S. Perloff and L. Wingo, Jr., eds., *Issues in Urban Economics*, pp. 138-149. Baltimore, Md.: Johns Hopkins University Press.

Joller, R.L. 1977. "Hud Secretary Quiets Critics." *St. Louis Post-Dispatch*, 18 April, p. 38.

Judd, D.R. 1979. *The Politics of American Cities: Private Power and Public Policy*. Boston: Little, Brown.

Levy, F.S.; Meltsner, A.J.; and Wildavsky, A. 1974. *Urban Outcomes*. Berkeley: University of California Press.

Lineberry, R.L. 1974. "Mandating Urban Equality: The Distribution of Municipal Public Services." *Texas Law Review* 53:26–59.

Peterson, P.E. 1979. "A Unitary Model of Local Taxation and Expenditure Policies," In D.R. Marshall, ed. *Urban Policy Making,* pp. 113–130. Beverly Hills, Calif.: Sage Publications.

Podoff, D.; Primont, D.; and Esposito, L. 1973. *Substandard Housing and the Cost of Providing Housing-Related Services.* Boston: Boston Urban Observatory.

Rich, R.C. 1979. "Neglected Issues in The Study of Urban Service Distribution: A Research Agenda," *Urban Studies* 16:143–166.

Part III
Can We Learn from
Comparisons?

12

Transforming Needs into Services: The Japanese Case

Ronald Aqua

Students of urban-service delivery in Japan usually approach their subject with a set of assumptions about the context of local decision making that is quite different from the framework employed by students of the Western democracies. Whereas observers of those other systems have increasingly begun to analyze the delivery of public services in terms of distributive issues involving particular jurisdictions (or between the center and periphery of metropolitan areas), observers of the Japanese case are more accustomed to studying the redistributional impact of national policies across major regions. Moreover, whereas in the West local distributive decisions have usually been thought to emanate from a pluralistic configuration of civic-action groups, neighborhood associations, organized business and professional interests, local notables, and individual voters, in Japan such pluralistic forces are not thought to be as significant in explaining policy outcomes as are local authorities' dependence on and integration into a fairly rigidly structured set of linkages to higher administrative levels.

The study of regional imbalances and the impact of central grants on local development lie outside the scope of this chapter, which is concerned primarily with the level of service delivery within communities.[1] I will examine how local administrators process the demands made by their constituencies for various services and weigh those demands against standards of performance set by higher levels of government. This basic question has received little systematic attention in Japan, or elsewhere. I hope this chapter will stimulate closer examination of the relationship between bureaucratic decision making and the distributional outcomes discussed in some of the other chapters of this book.

There are a number of ways to approach the question of how standards of performance are determined, each derived from a different model of allocative decision making. According to a model commonly used in studying the United States, local residents' perceptions of the need for certain types of services are transformed into the actual delivery of services through such democratic processes as public hearings, debates, and elections. In this model, centrally imposed standards may serve as a yardstick in measuring performance but are not the ultimate determinants of local outcomes. Rather, local planners and administrators set standards of performance that reflect local political realities. According to a second model, one that is less commonly seen in the United States but is the prevailing paradigm in Japan, the determination of need is made on the basis of quantitative measures that reflect standards of performance established by the central government. Such measures are usually derived from various statistical indexes of socioeconomic phenomena and may or may not be related to the needs articulated by local residents. A third model posits that the attitudes and values held by local bureaucrats—not necessarily their perceptions of the needs defined by local residents or by central officials— determine local allocative decisions. According to this model, the decisions made by local administrators may not be influenced by public debate and are not necessarily matched against standardized evaluative criteria.

In all three models, the determination of need is a crucial step in the chain of decision making that ultimately produces a distributive outcome. When top local officials try to map out new services or cut back on existing ones, many factors may color their decisions. The second model suggests that perceptions of need may be based on such widely used indicators as the average response time for emergency fire and police calls or the area of classroom space for each school-age child in the city. But even when quantifiable needs may be apparent, the first model suggests that they do not necessarily form the sole basis for allocative decisions. For example, police officials in a city with a low crime rate might deliberately overreact to a relatively minor wave of petty crimes in order to assist the mayor in preserving a law-and-order image. And according to the third model, it is conceivable that a program such as sewer construction may not be given high priority in a rural community, not because modern sewage facilities are not needed, but because administrators decide to rely on traditional means of sewage disposal.

Here I examine the relative usefulness of these three models with data from a sample of thirty-seven medium-sized Japanese municipalities.[2] The purpose of the analysis is to test the hypothesis that in the local decision-making environment thought to characterize the Japanese system, the performance criteria established by the central government determine local administrators' perceptions of need. These perceptions should then be translated into the delivery of public services. In this analysis, *need* will be defined as the difference between the quantity of service units already being provided in a particular locality and the number of such units that citizens and public officials deem desirable for that locality.

Three Models of Local Decision Making

The *democratic* decision-making model, assumes that the relationship between the articulation of needs by residents (as mediated through elected officials) and the actual delivery of services is immediate and direct. Thus demands from residents should result in higher levels of service or in the creation of new services. To determine whether such a relationship exists, I have selected the example of public playgrounds.

In this case, the dependent output variable was operationally defined as the extent of municipal-playground construction relative to a standardized measure of performance. The independent variable was defined as residents' articulation of the need for children's playgrounds, as derived from public-opinion surveys commissioned by Japanese cities that had tapped the dimension of "citizen satisfaction with existing levels of services." Typically, respondents were asked to list the public services with which they were most dissatisfied, or which, if unavailable, were desired. The responses to these questions convey some notion of imbalance between actual and desired levels of performance (need).

Of eleven cities in the sample that had commissioned surveys probing this particular dimension of need, respondents in seven cities identified children's playgrounds as among the three most desired services. To test for the relationship between this perceived need and actual performance, I first rank ordered the eleven cities according to the degree of citizen dissatisfaction with playground facilities, and then with respect to the extent to which playground facilities were available in comparison with other cities in the same general population range. Finally, I made paired comparisons of these two rank orderings. In so doing, I hypothesized (according to the democratic model) that cities in which local residents articulated the least dissatisfaction with children's playgrounds should also display the highest levels of performance; conversely, cities in which residents were least sanguine about the quality of children's playground facilities should have the poorest overall performance for this type of service.

The findings of this paired-comparison analysis indicated that in all but a few cases citizen dissatisfaction was not closely related to the level of performance. This is, admittedly, a crude and limited test of a very complicated model; but I have demonstrated that the relationship between citizen demands and service delivery is not necessarily direct or automatic.

The second model posits that *socioeconomic* factors are the most important determinants of local performance. This presupposes that bureaucrats' (and citizens') perceptions of need are mediated through standards of performance set by the central government and calibrated according to the particular socioeconomic characteristics of local populations.

Again I devised a simple test to measure the strength of these relationships. This time I considered the delivery of educational services, as this program area is often thought to display highly standardized levels of performance relative to need in Japan. *Need* was defined here as the student-teacher ratio in elementary schools in 1971 for the thirty-seven cities in the sample. This indicator reveals a community's ability and willingness to provide financial support for high-quality public education and is, in that sense, a socioeconomic measure.

On the output side, two measures of performance were used. The first was the percentage of total local spending for elementary education contributed by the central and prefectural governments, and the second, the percentage of total local spending for elementary education devoted to capital improvements. Central and prefectural subsidies represent a substantial portion of local-government school budgets, and school-aid formulas are closely tied to such standardized measures as student-teacher ratios. Furthermore, it is reasonable to expect levels of capital spending to be closely related to the perceived need for more classroom space. Thus, if student-teacher ratios can be regarded as indicators of socioeconomic need, then the two performance indicators should be strongly associated with this need.

The cities were clustered according to whether they were "higher than average" or "lower than average" for each of the three indicators. The groupings were arranged in such a way that all the cities that had higher than average student-teacher ratios were paired with "higher than average" rankings for either of the two performance indicators. The same was done for those cities that had lower than average student-teacher ratios. This method of pairing identified cities that scored consistently higher than average or consistently lower than average across all three measures. Proceeding in this manner revealed the following patterns of association:

First, seventeen cities ranked "higher than average" in student-teacher ratios, and twenty ranked "lower than average."

Second, there were two instances in which cities ranked "higher than average" across all three indicators.

Third, there was only one instance in which a city ranked "lower than average" across all three indicators.

There are several ways to interpret these findings. If it is assumed that only a similarly high or low ranking across all three indicators suggests a strong degree of association between a certain socioeconomic level and certain types of spending decisions, then the relationship revealed here is very weak indeed. If, on the other hand, similar rankings between student-teacher ratios and only one of the performance indicators could be regarded as indicative of a strong association, then it would be possible to conclude that socioeconomic factors do have a strong influence on at least one aspect of performance; there were, in fact, only three cases in which neither performance variable was closely associated with the socioeconomic indicator.

The two performance indicators in this analysis were selected advisedly. One, the percentage of central-prefectural financing, is heavily dependent on centrally determined formulas for apportioning funds. The other is different, however. Local spending decisions for capital improvements in Japan involve considerable local discretion in deciding on the optimal mix of revenues from various sources, including central or prefectural grants-in-aid, local borrowing, and revenues derived from local public enterprises such as gambling. It is in this qualitative distinction between the two performance indicators that the most potentially useful finding emerges from this analysis—namely, that in the group of cities with lower than average student-teacher ratios, nearly twice as many were lower than average in the percentage of capital spending as were lower-than-average in the percentage of central-prefectural financing. This suggests that the strongest association between socioeconomic factors and outputs, at least on the negative side, derives from local choices about investment alternatives rather than from criteria based on central standards.

The third model stands in sharp contrast to the prevailing mode of analysis that tends to look more at organizational or structural variables than at individual perceptions of needs and of the availability of local resources to meet those needs. According to this administrative perceptions model, there should be a demonstrable relationship between administrators' personal perceptions and actual performance outcomes. Because local planners are assumed to rely heavily on objective indicators in evaluating their city's needs, I first decided to test the hypothesis that socioeconomic (environmental) factors have the strongest influence on such evaluations. Although I have already demonstrated that the direct relationship between socioeconomic indicators and performance is not necessarily strong, it is nonetheless possible that knowledge of these indicators is reflected in the thinking of local bureaucrats. If this proves to be the case, then it is reasonable to expect that bureaucratic perceptions would be only weakly related to actual outcomes.

I began this inquiry by determining how local administrators perceived the needs of their city. I next examined the relationship between these perceived needs and four clusters of independent variables, including a number of socio-economic indicators.[3] For the analysis I drew on data from a survey of about 350 local bureaucrats that I conducted in the thirty-seven sample cities during 1975 and 1976.

I asked respondents to identify which policy items (in a list of thirty-three) received less attention in their city than such items "should have been receiving." This question addressed the issue of need in reflecting a feeling of disjuncture between desired and actual levels of performance. The rate at which respondents chose even one item was far below the response rate for an earlier question in the survey on priorities, suggesting that bureaucrats are generally satisfied with the policy priorities of their local administrations or, at least, are not inclined to express their dissatisfaction with the status quo. Despite this low response rate, however, the items of greatest perceived need were also those selected as receiving the highest priority—namely, those in the education sector. The second-ranking group of issues, in the public-works sector, had also been regarded as receiving high priority in many cities. From this it might be inferred that priorities reinforce perceptions of need and occasionally generate dissatisfaction with existing levels of service.

I next measured the strength of association between these perceptions of need and the four clusters of independent variables by constructing contingency tables to derive the Cramer's V for each paired relationship.[4] The results of the Cramer's V analysis revealed patterns of association that were completely at odds with the predicted findings. The independent factors most strongly associated with perceptions of need were not environmental but were, rather, respondents' personal background (their years of administrative experience and their self-anchoring on an ideological "thermometer" across the conservative-progressive spectrum). The weakest associations were with the cluster of socio-economic (environmental) factors. The single most important factor associated with perceptions of local program needs was the ideological disposition of individual respondents. The influence of pressure activities from the local Communist camp was also considerable, whereas city-assembly activities seemed to be among the least important. Several political-linkage factors, notably the partisan channels of the mayor, local assemblymen, and members of the Diet, were significant in their impact but far outdistanced by respondents' ideological proclivities.

The primacy of personal political views in coloring bureaucratic perceptions of need warrants closer scrutiny, not only because of the presumed apolitical nature of the Japanese bureaucracy, but also because the possible relationship between personal ideology and service delivery suggests an extremely complex model of bureaucratic decision making. It will be recalled that when the democratic model was subjected to an empirical test, it was found that citizens' perceptions of need do not always reflect actual performance levels. To what extent, then, do bureaucratic perceptions mirror citizen views? If there is some divergence between the two, then it is at least possible for bureaucrats' perceptions to be more closely tied to actual performance, for reasons not related to the partisan loyalties or ideological inclinations of local residents.

The results of attitudinal surveys commissioned by a number of cities in the sample were helpful in considering this issue. One question common to nineteen such surveys probed for the types of programs that residents regarded as deserving more attention in city hall. This particular dimension is roughly comparable to the question in my own survey dealing with policy areas thought to have been neglected in the past.

The results of the nineteen surveys of citizens contrast greatly with the bureaucratic responses elicited in my survey. Whereas local administrators placed the greatest emphasis on education, local residents wished to see sewage and sanitation projects emphasized, followed by social welfare and environmental protection. Thus it would seem that, in the aggregate, local administrators formulate judgments of need quite independently of the views expressed by local residents.

In the context of the earlier finding that bureaucrats' personal background characteristics and, in particular, their ideological self-anchoring, are major influences on perceptions of local need, I will now attempt to describe the way in which the local policymaking environment affects personal ideology as bureaucrats set goals for the delivery of municipal services. To accomplish this, I will turn to another question in my survey, in which respondents were asked to specify the perceived degree of responsiveness of their city's administration to certain types of problems common to most municipalities. This question is related to the earlier question probing attitudes toward perceived neglect in certain program areas. Thus it is not surprising in examining the responses to find that those areas that were thought to be the most neglected were viewed in this instance as being the most "weakly" pursued. These include such programs as support for small and medium-sized industries and for the promotion of commerce in general. Programs that had been perceived as being least neglected, on the other hand (including child welfare, old-age assistance, and environmental protection), were here regarded as being "strongly" pursued.

What kinds of factors might influence such perceptions? Presumably, in addition to ideological self-anchoring, they might include the respondent's age ("wisdom"), his educational background ("knowledge"), and his years of experience as a local administrator. The relative influence of each of these in determining satisfaction with local accomplishments was measured by cross-tabulating them with the responses to this question. The results of this tabulation, again using Cramer's V, indicate that the single factor most strongly associated with the program areas overall is ideological self-anchoring. This strengthens the impression that personal political views override or at least subsume accumulated administrative experience in shaping bureaucratic perceptions of local performance.

Determining the process by which bureaucrats formulate a personal political ideology might help explain some of the differences across various policy areas that were uncovered in this analysis. I thus explored the ideological component further by cross-tabulating the ideological-thermometer question in the survey with a number of other responses reflecting personal attitudes toward central-government authority, local pressure groups, and mayoral leadership style, as well as with the partisan affiliation of the mayor. As a control in this test, I also cross-tabulated ideology with educational and experiential background factors.

These calculations showed that ideology was most strongly linked with "mayoral conservative linkage," followed by "priority relation to higher levels" and "reaction to salary warning."[5] The first of these factors encompasses both the partisan affiliation and the electoral experience of the incumbent mayor. The second and third factors measure attitudes toward central-government authority over important local issues. The latter two factors are closely related to the first, in that they reveal an administrative posture toward central incursions into the local policymaking arena that are invariably tied to the mayor's own political relationships with higher-level actors. This in turn suggests that the mayor's stance with respect to the problem of defending local interests against central-government interests is closely related to the ideological posturing of local bureaucrats, which ultimately colors their perceptions of need.

The importance of this finding lies in its relationship to a finding that the mayor's partisan linkages to political and bureaucratic actors at other levels are not associated with various types of performance outcomes (Aqua 1979, chap. 2). It would seem that a mayor's progressive or conservative posture, as well as his formal partisan identification, relate to the degree of separation he seeks to communicate to his constituents in defining his relationship with higher-level bureaucrats and politicians. It is often the case in Japan, as elsewhere, that a posture of distance from the central government can be a valuable asset under certain electoral circumstances. Thus "progressive" mayoral candidates may wish to be viewed as reformist and independent in relation to the ruling Liberal Democratic Party (LDP), whereas conservatives may hope to ingratiate themselves with voters by appearing to be closely linked to the LDP. Neither posture is necessarily an accurate reflection of the ties that may actually bind the mayors to central authorities. But in both cases mayoral candidates have adapted to and adopted localistic norms of political conduct, and this obviously has an impact on local bureaucrats and on their subsequent decisions regarding service delivery.

What is most striking about this model is the degree to which local political forces predominate over national politics. To say that a mayor is progressive or conservative or that he has been affiliated with a particular political party for a certain number of years is simply not enough. It is also important to know how he and his policy staff hope to trade off the interests of higher-level actors against political pressures generated from below. In this sense ideology relates less to deeply held convictions about the proper role of the state in society than to an instrumental view that regards symbols of central authority and power in terms of more immediate and personal political gain.

One last question remains—the extent to which local administrative perceptions of performance, colored as they may be by an ideology that might be termed localism, reflect the actual level of service delivery in particular cities and for particular programs. To answer this, I first selected three types of services that are readily amenable to physical measurement (roads, libraries, and parks), and defined standardized performance indicators for these services as follows: (1) roads = the proportion of paved road area to total road area; (2) libraries = the number of books per local resident in the public library system; and (3) parks = the area of public park space per local resident. Next, a question from the survey of local administrators asking how the quality of certain services compared with the standard set in other cities for the same services was introduced into the analysis.

These performance and survey data were then brought together in the following manner: first, with respect to the physical performance data, each city's level of performance was classified as "low," "medium," or "high" relative to the average across all thirty-seven cities in each of the three service areas; second, with respect to the survey data, each city's "response tendency" was classified as "low," "medium," or "high" according to the plurality opinion among the bureaucrats surveyed in each city hall regarding the level of performance for each type of service; and third, each city's physical performance was compared with the evaluation given by its administrators.

The results of this pairing revealed that local administrators generally have very accurate perceptions of performance levels. This stands in marked contrast to residents' perceptions, which, it should be recalled, were at variance with actual outcomes. Such a finding supports the proposition that administrative perceptions of need are an essential link in the process whereby political pressures are transformed into policy outputs. A causal chain between local politics and service delivery has thus been demonstrated.

Summary and Conclusion

Unlike most of the other contributions to this book, this chapter does not specifically address the large range of methodological and theoretical issues concerned with the equitable distribution of public services within and across local jurisdictions. In part this reflects the lower salience of these issues to researchers working in the Japanese setting, where outward migration to suburban areas has not resulted in inner-city deterioration and where neighborhoods cannot be readily classified according to racial or socioeconomic characteristics. But it also reflects a more basic need to understand the process whereby the articulation of demands for services is transformed into tangible service-delivery outcomes. There is little awareness of this process in Japan, and there is certainly much to learn in the broader comparative landscape.

As some of the other chapters so ably demonstrate, many factors influence patterns of service distribution, including the imposition of new rules by higher tiers of government (structural), the availability of local resources (environmental), and the definition and measurement of performance criteria (political). All too often, however, the interrelationships among these factors have not been clearly defined or explicated. This does not necessarily indicate a poor research design; rather, it underlines the sheer complexity of the processes we have attempted to delineate.

In much of the research to date, there has been a noticeable tendency to dwell on the structural or environmental determinants of distributive outcomes, and to assign to an unspecified residual category those political factors that elude measurement on linear scales or defy unambiguous definition. This chapter obviously represents a departure from that research tradition in attempting to probe the innermost circuitry of the political "black box." No strong claim is made for the applicability of these findings to other cases, and there is not yet enough evidence to assert that similar processes operate in jurisdictions in Japan that are significantly larger or smaller than the medium-sized cities in the sample. Still, it is clear that local political factors do make a significant difference in the distribution of public services in Japan, and that such factors are more important in accounting for differences than either structural or environmental factors.

Do local politics matter in the determination of distributional outcomes? Our findings suggest not only that they *do* matter, but also that the question is worth asking. If there is inequality in performance (as much of the evidence in this book suggests), and if such inequality is persistent over time, then it may be as important to search for the roots of that inequality in the complex sets of relationships between elected officials, bureaucrats, and local residents as it is to document the level of disparity between neighborhoods or localities. The Japanese case attests to the importance of local political forces in what is thought to be a highly structured administrative system with strong centralistic tendencies. At this juncture one can only speculate about the extent of political localism and its impact on distributive outcomes in the less centralized U.S. system.

Notes

1. The major work in English on this subject is Glickman (1979).

2. These cities were selected on the basis of their variation with respect to geographical location, socioeconomic structure, and political history (notably the party affiliation of mayors since the end of World War II). They were drawn from a larger sample of eighty-eight medium-sized cities that make up the universe of Japanese cities with a "densely inhabited district (DID)" population of between 100,000 and 500,000 according to the 1970 national census.

3. The factors that make up each grouping are described in appendix 12A. The responses to several questions from the survey of local bureaucrats appear among these factors as "response to question."

4. Cramer's V is a modified version of ϕ and can be used for contingency tables larger than those in a two-by-two format. This particular measure of association does not impute the direction of causal flow and does not attribute more than nominal-level significance to the variables. The effect of each independent variable on the dependent variable, controlling for the effects of the other independent variables, cannot be measured using this technique. Still, it is possible to test for the existence of associative relationships that are stronger than might be expected were purely random factors influencing the dependent variable.

5. See appendix 12A for the operational definition of these terms.

References

Aqua, R. 1979. "Politics and Performance in Japanese Municipalities." Ph.D. diss., Cornell University.

Glickman, N.J. 1979. *The Growth and Management of the Japanese Urban System.* New York: Academic Press.

Appendix 12A: Derivation of Separate Factors in Each of the Four Independent-Variable Clusters

I. Central-Local Linkages

Name (Code name in parentheses)	Method of Calculation	Sub-Categories	Frequency (Percentage)
Mayor conservative linkage	Determine political camp (conservative or progressive) of present mayor (1975) and total number of years of electoral political experience.	1. Conservative with 10 or more years experience 2. Conservative with less than 10 years experience 3. Progressive with 10 or more years experience 4. Progressive with less than 10 years experience	105 (29.2) 85 (23.7) 91 (25.3) 78 (21.7)
Quality of Lower House Diet representation	Summation of +cabinet minister from district = 5 points +total number of years all LDP Dietmen held office (current roster, 1975), greater than 15 = 4 points +average per member years in office for entire delegation (1975), greater than 5 = 3 points +1 point each for members born in city +1 point each for members with local (city only) political experience	Point total of 11 or more 5 to 10 1 to 4 0	42 (11.7) 69 (19.2) 149 (41.5) 99 (27.5)
Degree of dependency on general grant (Local Allocation Tax) in total revenues, 1973	Low = 5.9% or less of total revenues derived from LAT Medium = 6.0–11.9% of total revenues derived from LAT High = 12.0% or more of total revenues derived from LAT	Low Medium High	103 (28.7) 155 (43.2) 101 (28.1)
Priority relationship to higher levels	Response to question: What was the relationship between the selection of these programs as priority items and central- or prefectural-governmental policies?	Reflect only local initiatives Reflect central and prefectural policy Reflect only central policy Other Reflect only prefectural policy	296 (82.7) 44 (12.3) 8 (2.2) 8 (2.2) 2 (0.6)
Central government as valued information source	Response to question: When you plan programs, which source of information do you value most highly? (multiple answer, no more than 3 from list of 11)	Respondents who selected "central government" Respondents who did not select "central government"	92 (25.6) 267 (74.4)
Dietmen as preferred negotiating channels	Response to question: When your city conducts negotiations with various central government	Respondents who selected "Diet members"	233 (64.9)

Variable	Response / Category	N (%)
agencies regarding such financial matters as revenue sharing, bonding authorization, and categorical grants-in-aid, to which of the following are you most likely to turn for assistance if you encounter difficulties? (multiple answer, no more than 3 from list of 12)	Respondents who did not select "Diet members"	126 (35.1)
National City Mayors Association as preferred negotiating channel	Response to same question as "Dietchan"	
	Respondents who selected "National City Mayors Assn."	183 (51.0)
	Respondents who did not select "National City Mayors Assn."	176 (49.0)
"Direct contacts" as preferred negotiating channels	Response to identical question	
	Respondents who selected "direct city connection to agency"	169 (47.1)
	Respondents who did not select "direct city connection to agency"	190 (52.9)
Reaction to salary warning	Response to question: In 1975 the Ministry of Home Affairs issued an administrative directive warning that the salary levels of local civil servants were higher than those of national civil servants and therefore too high. How is your city reacting to this?	
	"Salaries" not direct cause of fiscal crisis	194 (54.5)
	We agree with MOHA analysis	107 (30.1)
	City has no fiscal problems	39 (11.0)
	Other	16 (4.5)
Mayor's administrative ability	Educational and career background	
	College graduate, civil-service career	48 (13.4)
	High-school graduate, civil-service career	85 (23.7)
	College graduate, non-civil-service career	126 (35.1)
	High school graduate, non-civil-service career	79 (22.0)
	Unknown	21 (5.8)
Mayor's local popularity	First, rank order cities from highest to lowest in terms of number of times present mayor has been reelected. Then, rank order cities again according to difference in percentage points in most recent election between plurality attained and highest attainable plurality (with two candidates, $x - 50\%$, with three, $x - 34\%$, with four, $x - 24\%$, etc.), assigning the following points: 3 points = difference of less than 10; 2 points = 10–20; 1 point = 20 or more	
	Most popular group (overall ranking of 1 to 6)	83 (23.1)
	Very popular group (ranking between 7 and 9)	97 (27.0)
	Rather popular group (ranking of 10 or 11)	108 (30.1)
	Least popular group (lowest ranking)	71 (19.8)

II. Local Political Conditions

Name (Code name in parentheses)	Method of Calculation	Sub-Categories	Frequency (Percentage)
Mayor's vitality	Age in 1975	65 or younger 66 or older	262 (73.0) 97 (27.0)
City-assembly support for mayor	Progressive-conservative camp balance in city-assembly membership, 1975	Large majority in mayor's camp Small majority in mayor's camp Majority in opposition camp Not sure	189 (52.6) 80 (22.3) 70 (19.5) 20 (5.6)
Progressive local organization	Ratio of percentage Communist vote to percentage Socialist vote for city in 1972 Lower House Diet election $\times 10 \times$ total of percent Communist vote + percent Socialist vote	Low (100 or less) Medium (101–300) High (301 or more)	136 (37.9) 68 (18.9) 155 (43.2)
Citizen activity level	Total number of pollution complaints registered in city offices by citizens, 1973	Low (100 or less) Medium (101–200) High (201 or more)	77 (21.4) 163 (45.4) 119 (33.1)
City-assembly-citizen interaction	Total number of petitions submitted to city assembly by citizens, 1974	Low (50 or less) Medium (51–100) High (101 or more)	144 (40.1) 120 (33.4) 95 (26.5)
Neighborhood association as assertive local interest group	Response to question: Which groups in your city seem to be the most assertive of their particular interests? (multiple answer, no more than 5 from list of 19)	Respondents who selected "neighborhood associations" Respondents who did not select "neighborhood associations"	199 (55.4) 160 (44.6)
Communist party as assertive local interest group	Response to preceding question	Respondents who selected "communist party" Respondents who did not select "communist party"	178 (49.6) 181 (50.4)
Medical association as assertive local interest group	Response to same question as "jichikai"	Respondents who selected "medical association" Respondents who did not select "medical association"	121 (33.7) 238 (66.3)

Variable	Response to question	Response categories	N (%)
Citizens' movements as assertive local interest groups	Response to same question as "jichikai"	Respondents who selected "citizens' movements"	114 (31.8)
		Respondents who did not select "citizens' movements"	245 (68.2)
Mayoral involvement in budget process	Response to question: Which pattern most clearly describes your mayor's degree of personal involvement in the annual budget-drafting process?	Deep involvement	81 (22.6)
		Moderate involvement	264 (73.5)
		Weak involvement	9 (2.5)
		Other	4 (1.1)
City-assembly involvement in budget process	Response to question: Which pattern most closely describes your city assembly's degree of interest in their annual deliberation on the budget draft?	Vigorously debated	265 (73.8)
		Moderately debated	83 (23.1)
		Hardly debated	5 (1.4)
		Other	2 (0.6)
Mayor-city assembly balance of power	Response to question: During the course of your city's preparation of and deliberation on the annual budget draft, which pattern most closely describes the relationship between the mayor and the city assembly?	Mayor dominates assembly	113 (31.5)
		Assembly dominates mayor	62 (17.3)
		Relative power balance	138 (38.4)
		Other	33 (9.2)
Personal reaction to citizens' movements	Response to question: How do you react to the following statement regarding citizens' movements: "Citizens' movements interfere with our work"	Strongly disagree	18 (6.2)
		Disagree	141 (48.3)
		Agree	73 (25.0)
		Strongly agree	12 (4.1)
		Not sure	48 (16.4)
Public hearings and commissions as valued information source	Response to same question as "Ceninf"	Respondents who selected "public hearing and commissions"	141 (39.3)
		Respondents who did not select "public hearings and commissions"	218 (60.7)
City assembly as valued information source	Response to same question as "Ceninf"	Respondents who selected "city assembly"	155 (43.2)
		Respondents who did not select "city assembly"	204 (56.8)
Formal schooling of respondent	Response to question: What level of formal education did you complete?	Middle school	20 (5.6)
		High school	166 (46.2)
		University	170 (47.4)

Name (Code name in parentheses)	Method of Calculation	Sub-Categories	Frequency (Percentage)
III. Local Environmental Conditions			
Income differential	Per capita income index, where per capita national baseline = 100 (1975)	Low (0–90)	88 (24.5)
		Medium (91–110)	101 (28.1)
		High (111 or above)	170 (47.4)
Population density	Per k², 1973	Low (1,000 or below)	108 (30.1)
		Medium (1,001–3,000)	147 (40.9)
		High (3,001 or above)	104 (29.0)
Percentage population increase	1965–1970	Low (6.9% or less)	105 (29.2)
		Medium (7.0–15.0%)	148 (41.2)
		High (15.1% or above)	106 (29.5)
Percentage population employed in tertiary sector	1970	Low (50.9% or below)	83 (23.1)
		Medium (51.0–58.9%)	126 (35.1)
		High (59.0% or above)	150 (41.8)
Percentage corporation tax of total local tax revenues	1973	Low (12.9% or less)	131 (36.5)
		Medium (13.0–15.9%)	147 (40.9)
		High (16.0% or more)	81 (22.6)
Percentage public assistance of total expenditures	1973	Low (8.9% or less)	149 (41.5)
		Medium (9.0–13.9%)	116 (32.3)
		High (14.0% or more)	94 (26.2)
IV. Individual-Respondent Background Information			
Ideological disposition	Response to question: Do you consider yourself conservative or progressive, politically speaking?	Very conservative	10 (2.8)
		Moderately conservative	106 (29.5)
		Middle-of-the-road	148 (41.2)
		Moderately progressive	81 (22.6)
		Very progressive	5 (1.4)
		Not sure	2 (0.6)
Administrative experience	Response to question: How many years have you held the position of section chief or above?	Less than 3 years	17 (4.7)
		3–6 years	36 (10.0)
		7–12 years	142 (39.6)
		More than 12 years	148 (41.2)

13

Neighborhood Organizations and the Distribution of Public-Service Outputs in Britain

Alan D. Burnett and
Dilys M. Hill

British academic interest in the distribution of urban public services has grown in recent years. This chapter reviews this research, singles out the influence of neighborhood organizations on local political outputs, and concludes that citizens *react* to decisions taken in the public domain. Their impact occurs mainly in affecting local use of services, the location of facilities, and to a lesser extent the quantity and quality of service delivery.

British studies of urban political outputs show certain parallels with U.S. work (Burnett 1981a); for example, the interauthority ecological analysis of Boaden (1971) and Newton (1979). On the other hand, many of the British studies have focused on the evaluation of the extent to which resources are allocated according to need—the concept of *territorial justice*. This is in contrast to U.S. studies that focus on identifying whether patterns of service delivery discriminate against particular groups or areas (Lineberry 1977).

Opinions differ on the most appropriate theoretical approach to these questions: ecological, managerialist, Marxist, and other paradigms are all used (Saunders 1979; Dunleavy 1980). But all agree that a whole range of factors are significant: Pinch (1980) lists need, political (party) control, electoral marginality, size, resources, costs, attitudes of officials, the take-up of services, the influence of pressure groups, central-government intervention, and "personalities." Newton and Sharpe (1977) suggest that *specific* distributional decisions are explained in terms of the interactions between and within public agencies, whereas *broad* patterns of resource allocation are influenced by economic, social, and geographical characteristics. In addition, political outputs have been investigated (Kirby 1979; Bassett and Short 1980; Knox 1978; Lambert, Penny, and Webster 1980); and, as in U.S. studies, the impact of bureaucratic rules on service delivery was found to be a major explanatory factor in patterns of expenditure and service provision. There are, however, few studies of political influence in terms of individual contacting, the allocation of money by council candidates to win elections (the vote-buying model), or pressure from neighborhood or other groups.

Local Pressure Groups and Services:
Some British Examples

P. Lowe (1977) has argued that locality-based environmental pressure groups in Britain are primarily concerned with *amenity* and *accessibility*—that is, preserving and enhancing the quality of the environment. He maintains that amenity societies representing well-off, well-connected areas are more successful than tenants' associations representing working-class public-housing schemes. He argues, but does not fully substantiate, that as a result inequalities in political influence will exacerbate social and spatial variations in real income and life chances.

British case studies confirm that there is considerable variation in the type, longevity, issue orientation, and success of neighborhood groups (Humble and Talbot 1976). Cosgrove and his coworkers found that statutorily recognized community councils in Scottish cities raised a wide range of public-service issues during the first few years of their existence. They were concerned with housing, education, environmental issues, transport, and public utilities. Because Scottish community councils cover the whole city, are amply supported by local governments, and have some influence on service outputs, we can conclude that they are eliciting greater responsiveness and equality in service delivery.

S. Lowe (1978) showed that tenants' and action groups in Sheffield employed three main tactics to raise issues: writing to their local councillors, writing to public officials, and holding public meetings. Tenants' associations monitored welfare problems and environmental complaints (including street lighting, rents, police patrolling, and dog wardens). Action groups, by contrast, were concerned with redevelopment plans and similar issues affecting their areas. Both groups were active in exclusionary tactics against "noxious" intrusions—be they factories or university and hospital extensions or road developments—but also engaged in self-help provisions such as playgrounds, luncheon clubs for old people, garbage removal, community transport, and community centers. Other studies, however, are more ambivalent about if, and how, neighborhood organizations reduce or buttress service inequalities. They have found, however, that although they raise many issues, they play a relatively marginal role in policymaking (Gyford 1976).

Constraints on Neighborhood Action in British Cities

Britain has a concentrated system of power at the local level: the elected council and its committees administer a wide range of statutory services. Policy is made in the light of national legislation, party programs, professional advice, and perceived local needs. Central government has a tripartite role: national legislation makes services mandatory, central grants total some two-thirds of revenue expenditure, and directives lay down guidelines. Local representatives are elected on a ward (neighborhood) basis, but the key to power is control by party groups. The system is highly professionalized, with nonelected officers working closely with—some would say guiding—councillors, and contributing a large input to policy.

Policy outcomes, then, are dependent on national guidelines through central legislation and financial support, and on the local distribution of services through the council and its committees advised by full-time professional officers. Leading councillors and officers take decisions in the light of their own political and professional judgements, albeit influenced by party, constituency, and consumer. Lambert, Blackaby, and Paris (1975) showed that in Birmingham, England, councillors had only limited scope to translate constituents' areal demands into policy outputs because power was concentrated in the party group. This centralized power and the departmental, professionalized structure of administration means that policies are pursued on the basis of a citywide "public interest" and of professional values.

As a result, British neighborhood activism is a voluntaristic and episodic phenomenon. Whereas scholars outside Britain have stressed that political conflicts based on class are being permeated by conflict based on spatial aggregates (Dear 1980; Peterson and Kantor 1977), British commentators remain sceptical. Cockburn (1977) and Edwards and Batley (1979) argue that localized community action is at best marginal and at worst alienative and irrelevant. Again, the "fiscal mercantilism" (Cox 1976) of U.S. local governments is absent in Britain, and neighborhood issues tend to revolve around environmental and land-use problems rather than public safety, property values, and local schools (although this last may be changing). In Britain the exclusionary incentive to neighborhood activism is attenuated by three factors (Cox 1976). First, central-government grants form a high proportion of local-government spending. Second, these grants have a redistributional effect toward the standardization of services. Third, residential mobility is relatively low (half the rate in the United States). The result is a less vociferous local participation than is evident in community activism in the United States. Our purpose in this chapter is to explore the reasons for this difference.

Neighborhood Organizations and Service Distribution in South-East Hampshire

Here we are concerned only with *neighborhood organizations*—formally constituted, voluntary, environmental groups of residents. These include local residents', ratepayers' (homeowners), and tenants' associations, and one neighborhood council. The analysis excludes more ephemeral protest and action groups, residents' committees, and very localized block or street associations.

This study focuses on neighborhood associations because, although such groups have been studied elsewhere—for example, in North America (Rich 1980a; Getter and Schumaker 1978; Ley 1974; Zisk 1972; Cox and McCarthy 1980); in Latin America (Cornelius 1974); and in continental Europe (Castells 1978)—the field is relatively neglected in Britain. There are a multiplicity of neighborhood groups in Britain, but only a fraction have been examined systematically (Boaden 1971; Cousins 1976; Dearlove 1974; Dunleavy 1977). Our focus on South-East Hampshire provides a metropolitan example to set alongside previous studies of either individual cities—London, Birmingham, Liverpool, and Sheffield—or a heterogeneous national sample. This study includes the whole range of such organizations in an entire city region comprising both urban and suburban environments and several jurisdictions.

South-East Hampshire, a coastal subregion in south-central England, consists of the city of Portsmouth (population 200,000), the boroughs of Havant (115,000) and Gosport (80,000), and part of the Borough of Fareham (85,000) (figure 13-1). The area is divided physically between the coastal zone (including Portsea and Hayling Islands) and the chalk downs and Portsdown Hill to the north. There are marked contrasts, too, between the densely packed Victorian terraced housing in the inner-city areas and the modern private housing developments in the suburbs. In addition, there is substantial "overspill" public housing from Portsmouth into the neighboring jurisdiction of Havant Borough.

Since local-government reorganization in 1974, the borough and city councils have been responsible for functions such as housing, local plans, and leisure services, whereas Hampshire County Council (whose headquarters are to the northwest in Winchester) administers education, social services, libraries, and major environmental planning. Since 1945 the Conservative party has dominated the area, both locally and nationally. Because the location, age, socio-economic status, housing tenure, and amenity of the region's neighborhoods are so diverse, it provided an ideal area for the study of spatial variations in political participation and its consequences. The key questions were: Are neighborhood organizations correspondingly heterogeneous in form and function, and do they influence service outputs?

The Origins and Distribution of the Associations

Figures 13-1 and 13-2 indicate the location of the organizations' territories, which varied in population from a few hundred to 47,000 (Leigh Park). The majority of the twenty-one formal neighborhood associations came into existence in the 1970s. Some were initiated spontaneously in response to environmental threats (for example, the plan to build an oil refinery on the Solent

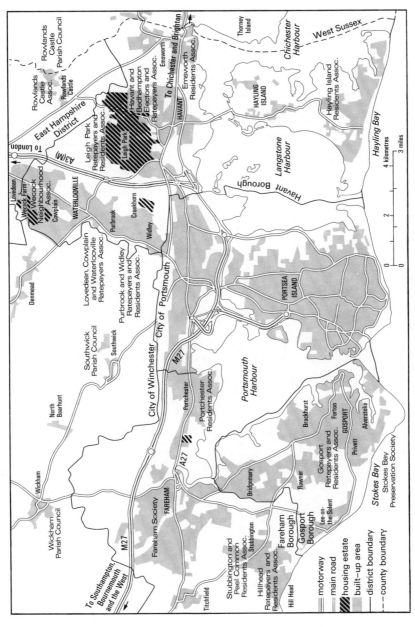

Figure 13-1. South-East Hampshire Communities

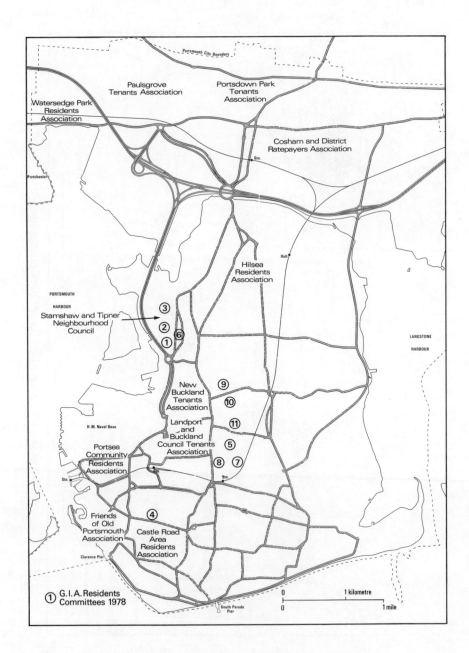

Figure 13–2. Neighborhood-Association Territories

coastline); others to press for amenities on new residential estates or to combat specific defects such as dampness in an architectural-award-winning public-housing estate (Portsdown Park). Two associations owed their foundation, at least in part, to Portsmouth's housing and leisure services' department officials who were anxious to have a recognized body of residents with whom to consult. A similar external impetus produced the Stamshaw and Tipner Neighborhood Council, formed on the initiative of a local minister of religion and the representative of a London organization—the City Poverty Committee—that was a part of the participatory-democracy movement of the early 1970s.

Research has shown that community activism is associated with clear physical boundaries, people's perceptions of the locality, and personal inter-action. The distribution shown in figures 13-1 and 13-2 reveals that the or-ganizations were concentrated on the western side of Portsea Island, with fuller coverage on the suburban mainland. Both private suburban residential areas and large council estates were well represented, as were high-status areas such as Old Portsmouth and Rowlands Castle. It was evident that these associations were correlated with neighborhoods with clear physical boundaries. Davidson (1979) found a similar pattern in a U.S. city. In Portsmouth, with one excep-tion, virtually all those perceived communities identified by Hall (1978) had organizational representation. Whereas in Detroit individual contacting was greatest in median areas of social well-being (Jones et al. 1977), in South-East Hampshire the reverse seemed to be the case. This form of collective action was concentrated in the western working-class zone of Portsmouth and in the more affluent suburbs.

Organization and Membership of Associations

Virtually all the associations had detailed written constitutions covering aims, elections, functions of committees and officers, meetings, subscriptions, and membership. The majority had executive committees of key officers who determined the organizations' ethos, role, and level of activity. They were (often reluctantly) recruited from the membership; and although a minority remained in office indefinitely, the general pattern was of a steady turnover. This turnover was even more marked among committee members, especially in tenants' associations on the council (public-housing) estates. Resignation from office was common because of disagreements on tactics, family and work commitments, movement out of the area, and personality conflicts. The costs of active participation frequently outweighed the benefits.

Areas differed in type of officers: whereas affluent areas had attorneys among their organization officials, in working-class neighborhoods it was trade unionists, ministers of religion, and local women who predominated. Officers were the key activists who directed the fortunes of the organizations and decided which issues should be pursued and by what means. The members, by contrast, played a much more passive role. For example, less than 10 percent of residents voted in the Stamshaw and Tipner neighborhood-council elections, although individual contacts with officers did occasionally take place. Few attended formal meetings. These patterns are similar to those reported by Rich (1980b) in a U.S. city.

Although there were contrasts between associations in type and size of area, membership, and socioeconomic composition of committees, the most striking feature of the sample was the similarity of the groups' aims and or- ganization. Thus one would expect to find a degree of uniformity in their political role, but some differences in the issues they raised, how, to whom, and to what effect. This indeed was the case.

Public Service and Other Issues

The British and American literature suggests that the prime issues for residents are not only the quantity and quality of public services, but also locational conflicts (disputes over land use and the location of public facilities), regulation of antisocial behavior, and a wide range of quality-of-life concerns. Their aim is to protect or enhance the use and exchange value of their property (Cox and McCarthy 1980). In South-East Hampshire, from inner city to outer suburbs, many "threats" to the neighborhood originated from proposed land-use changes. For example, in the prestigious Old Portsmouth area, residents resisted the extension of the YMCA, and demanded that the cross-Channel ferry terminal, which caused road congestion, be relocated and that a former electric-power- station site be rezoned for housing. The residents of deprived inner-city Portsea also pressed for a former factory site to be rezoned for public housing. In Buckland the community association opposed the widening of an urban high- way (because it would mean the demolition of houses and the loss of part of a grade-school playground), the rebuilding of a tavern, and the rezoning of residential land for factory units. The Stamshaw neighborhood council pressed for the conversion of a former factory into a leisure center and supported the city council's efforts to remove a group of garages, warehouses, and workshops that violated local zoning laws.

It was in the suburbs, however, that such conflicts had a major political significance. Agricultural lands and open spaces were defended against residential (especially public-housing), industrial, and even recreational use. For example, Hayling Island residents opposed large-scale house building, and those in Bed- hampton fought a proposed leisure complex, a hypermarket, and the construc- tion of an ornamental garden. In Havant industrial parks and public overspill housing projects planned by Portsmouth were vigorously resisted. In one major growth area (Fareham), residents' associations strove continuously to alter the scale and the location of urban developments in what was planned as a growth zone between Southampton and Portsmouth.

Neighborhood activists perceived the location of public facilities as major issues. Associations argued, predictably, that existing and new desirable facilities should be encouraged and that "noxious" ones should be diverted elsewhere. For example, Hayling Island residents resisted the closure of the Portsmouth-Hayling Island ferry, whereas the Lovedean, Cowplain, and Waterlooville Association supported a highway to divert traffic around their shopping center and pressed for the relocation of a leisure center away from the neighborhood (and closer to a nearby public-housing estate). Again, issues ranged from opposition to the garbage incinerator in Havant to demands for localized improvements (a pedestrian crossing over a major highway, a skateboard park) in Portsdown. Finally, two associations in Havant joined forces to intervene in the plan of the Health Authority (a separate national service) to build a centralized health center while closing several smaller facilities.

The quantity and quality of public services were particularly important in areas in which residents were more dependent on public, rather than on private, provision and in which there were, therefore, many complaints about the staffing, equipment, and siting of public buildings. Dissatisfaction was also evident over housing allocation and repairs, supervision by wardens, street cleaning, snow clearance, fire precautions, road maintenance, secondary-school reorganization, bus services, and garbage collection. These bread-and-butter issues lacked the drama of more politicized locational conflicts, but they were important to residents and took up much of the time of the associations' officers.

In the private sector, neighborhood associations tried to resist both commercial buildings and leisure facilities on such grounds as fumes, visual intrusion, and traffic congestion. An environmentally detracting boat-building yard in Old Portsmouth, a meat-products factory in Portchester, and a processed-food factory near Watersedge Park were all long-standing issues, as was a tavern on the Portsdown Park estate. In such cases those adversely affected sought the regulatory intervention and support of the local environmental-health and planning departments, and resorted to legal action.

Political and financial issues were also important. These included proposed changes in the boundaries of local electoral areas (Portsea and Hayling Island) and increases in public-housing rents, rates (property taxes), parking charges, and other fees. There was also the concern for status and, in two cases, resentment over stigmatization of an area by outside bodies. For example, the association in Portsdown Park reacted angrily when an unflattering report about the estate was prepared by a group of social workers, police, probation officers, and a child-care agency and was leaked to the press.

The significant variations in the issues that were raised by different neighborhoods arose from the character, age, and housing tneure of the different localities, and were concerned to protect the status quo as much as to affect the

distribution of public services. The mobilizations that did arise were mainly
defensive but were addressed a wider range of issues than those identified in
Canada by Janelle and Millward (1976), reflecting the wide range of public
intervention in the United Kingdom.

Links between Neighborhood Organizations and Authoritative Decision Makers

The organizations' agendas were drawn up by their officers and reflected local
issues as these emerged from the political environment via local newspapers,
public meetings, or informal acquaintanceships with local power holders. Organizations (in practice, their officers, though occasionally in consultation
with members) then had to decide what to do about the issue—or whether
to do nothing. Alternatively, though infrequently, they tried to alleviate
problems through their own personal efforts. Although the scope for such
self-help was limited, some minor campaigns and services were mounted—for
example, a litter campaign in Leigh Park and a club for mothers and babies in
Portsdown Park.

The majority of issues, however, were tackled by political demands on
public decision makers (councillors and city officers). Organizations, when
deciding on tactics, took past experience, contacts with officers, advice from
councillors and outside experts, the need to be *seen* as active, and the nature
and importance of the issue into account. In South-East Hampshire, associations
used the whole gamut of political tactics; but the overall impression was of a
middle way between the quiet persuasion of parish councils and the strident
tactics of protest groups (Burnett 1981b). The choice of tactics depended on the
individual organization, the issue, and the local authority's response.

In Portsmouth and Havant, housing and other public-service issues were
frequently channeled through the Joint Consultative Body, a forum in which
officials from the housing and other departments met public-housing tenants'
representatives on a regular basis. This is clearly an example of that structural,
official channel of demand access that, though difficult to establish, is crucial
to effective participation. In this case it was in fact the only official means of
representation that the overspill housing-estate residents had vis-à-vis the Portsmouth City Council—their landlord. In general, however, contacts with officials
were unstructured and included letters to chief officers of the council, telephone
calls, attendance at public inquiries, petitions, letters to the local press, and
stories leaked to local reporters. Only rarely would the unorthodox strategy of
taking legal action against the city council be used (as occurred over dampness
in public-housing apartments, stimulated by the success elsewhere in the city of
a Labour party community-action group). Three alternative actions were more

commonly used to seek assistance. First, there was the approach to national organizations or to other local groups for support. Second, there were approaches to local officials on minor issues. Third, there was the major tactic of petitions, letters to the editor, and visible protest for the prime issues (such as opposition to a planned freeway).

Ratepayers' associations channeled their grievances through their elected councillors (ward representatives), letters to the local newspapers, and attendance at public inquiries. Associations in more working-class neighborhoods of Portsmouth contacted their (Labour) Member of Parliament or local officials. Their councillors, however, were in the minority on the council and could only air their grievances rather than actually effect policy changes.

Responses and Outcomes: The Impact of Demand Making on the Distribution of Outputs

Public authorities respond in a number of ways to citizen demands. There was invariably a symbolic response, and there was no shortage of communications flowing between neighborhood and city halls. But who benefited? Undoubtedly there were some notable, if partial, victories. For example, the Havant Borough Council refused planning permission for a new leisure center, and the Portsmouth City Council was forced by the courts to remedy the dampness in the Portsdown Park housing estate. Other victories included the achievement of a more restricted ferry service and the vetoing of an oil refinery on the Solent shore. Public services—buses, street cleaning, tree planting—improved. Money and manpower were devoted to neglected areas or services. Some demands, however, were only partially successful. An industrial park is still planned in Havant, although stricter conditions have been imposed on its layout. On the other hand, there have been major defeats: the tavern was built in Buckland despite an appeal to the (national) ombudsman; no additional safety fencing was added to the balconies of Portsdown Park apartments despite a vociferous campaign following the death of a young child; a hypermarket is currently nearing completion in Bedhampton; Paulsgrove still has to suffer from the use of a substandard temporary building for a branch library; the central health center in Havant is still planned.

Victory and defeat were not the monopoly of any one type of neighborhood organization. The inequalities that S. Lowe (1978) attributed to differences in political clout between rich and poor neighborhoods were not apparent here. Ratepayers' groups from the affluent suburbs and tenants' associations in deprived inner-city areas were both successful on some occasions. Neither the scale of the proposed building development nor the tactics employed by the groups were decisive.

Two elements that were crucial, however, were *support* and *concessions*. A major tactic for community groups was to secure the support of their ward councillor, the local newspaper, and in certain cases the national parliamentary representative (the MP). This support in turn ranged from the nominal or passive, through the associative (with the group spearheading the campaign), to the active form of support (wherein the politician or other leader engaged in initiatives on the group's behalf at the citywide level). Support, even from political or community leaders, was not in itself a guarantee of success. This lack of certainty was attributable not to either the amount or the quality of such support, but to the parameters within which the game was played: the outcome was dependent on the willingness to make concessions of the council-dominated centralized power structure.

It was the capacity and willingness of power holders to make concessions in the light of their own definitions of need that affected outcomes—a finding parallel to that of Jones and Kaufman (1974) in the United States. This illustrates the elitist mode of British policymaking. As noted earlier, Pinch (1980) found that pressure from residents was only one—and not necessarily the predominant one—of a series of factors influencing the spatial distribution of services. The dominance of governing elites was paramount, and concessions were made on their terms.

Political actors, we found, made concessions in three situations: where demands did not challenge service-delivery rules (bureaucratic control); did not involve massive expenditure (resource-reallocation control); or did not counter clearly stated policy (value-allocation control). These were the three major determinants of the success of neighborhood organizations' petitioning efforts in this study. An associated factor was that some demands involved a zero-sum scenario. If authorities had acceded to these demands, there would have been other adverse consequences elsewhere in the system—in terms of loss of employment (the closure of a "noxious" factory) or loss of amenity (the relocation of a facility). In these cases it was the pressure from more powerful local interests—the Chamber of Commerce or the public-service unions—that took precedence over local residents' demands.

Conclusions

How, then, do service issues mobilize residents in British cities—and to what effect? Political demands are made when neighborhood problems are perceived as being the responsibility of public authorities and amenable to solution by them. Rich (1979b) has suggested a fourfold model: *defensive and exclusionary, demand-aggregating and articulation, resource reallocation,* and *concession seeking and supportive.* All were found to operate in our case study, with the first and last categories dominant. When neighborhood associations in South-East

Hampshire were threatened with negative externalities associated with unwanted facilities or land uses, they used exclusionary responses. Neighborhood groups aggregated, articulated their demands, and so resisted or altered official proposals that threatened environment and property. Some of these plans were withdrawn; others may well have been transferred to other locations; still others (the problems arising from existing noxious facilities, for example) were alleviated rather than removed.

Neighborhood associations claimed to be the legitimate voice of their area and its residents, a claim that was sometimes conceded by public officers. Many issues involved the reallocation of resources, predominantly rent, and municipal expenditures on services. In many cases, in fact, minor concessions were granted by planning authorities over the size and character of noxious facilities, if not their location. Likewise, areas represented by neighborhood associations were able to enjoy minor benefits in the shape of a more responsive bureaucracy. Although there is no doubt that streets were cleaned, snow cleared, vermin exterminated, playgrounds maintained, windows repaired, roads patrolled by dog wardens, police patrols increased, and so forth as a result of the organizations' intervention, nonetheless the overall allocation of resources remained substantially that which had already been determined by local-authority officials.

Would the distribution of public-service outputs in South-East Hampshire— or, indeed, any British city region—be different if neighborhood organizations did not exist? Do those areas that are represented get a better deal than they would otherwise? Are inequalities that may exist as a result of bureaucratic rules increased or reduced as a result of this form of collective political involvement? This case study provides some important clues. Given that neighborhood organizations do influence the distribution of public resources, albeit marginally, what political and administrative policies are desirable to enhance citizen access to policymaking and implementation? The case study suggests that three possible scenarios are feasible: the *laissez faire,* the *supportive,* and the *institutional.* In the first, tolerance—not the right of access—is the dominant feature. This form of political interaction has been condemned by some observers as a one-way consultation by public officials, on their terms, rather than genuine citizen input (Lambert, Blackaby, and Paris 1975). As has been shown, however, neighborhood organizations do spasmodically influence what happens in their city halls.

The second case, that of the supportive framework, envisages that, for example, the Portsmouth Consultative Committee would encompass all neighborhood groups, matched by officials from city-hall departments in a form of administrative decentralization. Administrative decentralization in Britain—the area-management schemes under the sponsorship of the Department of the Environment—remains limited to an advisory input rather than a decision mechanism of a true "little city hall" type (Webster 1980). These area-management schemes have had little part to play in broader policy or resource allocation (Harrop et al, 1978). Again, the dominant political norm is that of strong centralized governing authorities that consult,—on their terms—local groups. For this reason, perhaps the most that could be expected is for neighborhood groups to gain the right to be consulted over requests for residential development (planning applications). But councillors and bureaucrats still insist that they alone are democratically acountable to the whole electorate, whereas neighborhood groups are sectional and not always representative of the community for which they claim to speak.

Because of these deficiencies in the present system, some suggest that the national government legislate a system of neighborhood or community councils throughout the country. Such community councils would meet the call for elected bodies that were, therefore, truly representative of their areas. They could also claim wider powers than the present rural parish councils in England and Wales and the voluntary-based community councils in Scotland (Burnett 1976; Morton 1979). The danger of such a move, however, is that they would be merely minor administrative organizations. Further, the national political climate is unfavorable. Although the central government appeared to lend support to initiatives for urban neighborhood councils in the 1970s (Hill 1979), the Local Authority Associations (their national pressure-group organizations) and the major voluntary agencies all opposed the idea, and the government has retreated into suggestions for purely voluntary initiatives.

This chapter shows that in Britain area-specific inputs exist, but that they are episodic and largely based on single issues. They can result in successful exclusionary actions in locational conflicts and in minor changes in service provision. The local political system remains elitist, however, and councillors are more likely to rely on their own party caucus for policy guidelines than to seek out citizen opinion (Newton 1976; Lambert, Blackaby, and Paris 1975). This reflects the conflict at the heart of the claim for local-authority responsiveness to area needs in the British political culture. At the locality level there is a strongly centralized decision-making power, with councillors and officers acceding to area demands only when political and administrative costs are minimal. This attitude is justified by the power holders on the grounds of their electoral accountability for the whole jurisdiction and not just a part of it. The dominant style of citizen influence on policy outputs is thus the claim that local governments make for their own legitimate authority, on the one hand, and the reactive style that is adopted by local residents, on the other. In the British political culture, demands emerge as a result of groups *reacting to* issues generated in the official political arena rather than from the local expression of the spontaneous needs of citizens. This in turn reflects the generalized attitudes toward authority and the acceptance of long-standing public-service provision in a more or less standardized form, which are the mark of the British political system and of its more closed style of government generally.

References

Bassett, K., and Short, J. 1980. "Patterns of Building Society and Local Authority Lending in the 1970s." *Environment and Planning* A, no. 12:279-301.

Boaden, N. 1971. *Urban Policymaking.* London: Cambridge University Press.

Burnett, A.D. 1976. "Legislating for Neighbourhood Councils." *Local Government Studies* 2:31-38.

——. 1981a. "The Distribution of Local Outputs and Outcomes in British and American Cities: A Review and Research Agenda." In *Political Studies from Spatial Perspectives,* eds. A.D. Burnett and P.J. Taylor. Chichester and New York: Wiley.

——. 1981b. "Protesting over Public Outputs in Portsmouth." In *Conflict, Politics and the Urban Scene,* eds. C.R. Cox and R.J. Johnston. London: Longmans.

Castells, M. 1978. "Urban Social Movements and the Struggle for Democracy." *International Journal of Urban and Regional Research* 2:133-146

Cockburn, C. 1977. *The Local State.* London: Pluto Press.

Cornelius, W.A. 1974. "Urbanization and Political Demand Making: Political Participation among the Migrant Poor in Latin American Cities." *American Political Science Review* 68:1125-1146.

Cosgrove, D.F.; Sheldon, H.N.; Masterton, M.P.; and Masterton, E.M. 1978. *Community Councils Research Project: Interim Report.* Edinburgh: Central Research Unit, Scottish Office.

Cousins, P.F. 1976. "Voluntary Associations and Local Government in Three London Boroughs." *Public Administration* 54:63-81.

Cox, K.R. 1976. "Local Interests and Political Processes in American Cities." Working Papers in Public Policy, Center for Social and Behavioral Science Research. Riverside: University of California.

——. 1980. "Capitalism and Conflict around the Communal Living Space." In *Urbanization and Planning in Capitalist Society,* eds. M.J. Dear and A.J. Scott. Chicago, Maaroufa.

Cox, K.R., and McCarthy, J.J. 1980. "Neighborhood Activism in the American City: Behavioral Relationships and Evaluation." *Urban Geography* 1:22-38.

Davidson, J.L. 1979: *Political Partnerships: Neighborhood Residents and their Council Members,* Beverly Hills, Calif.: Sage Publications.

Dear, M. 1980: "A Theory of the Local State." In *Political Studies from Spatial Perspectives,* eds. A.D. Burnett and P.J. Taylor. Chichester and New York: Wiley.

Dearlove, J. 1974. "Councillors and Interest Groups in Kensington and Chelsea." *British Journal of Political Science* 1:129-153.

Dunleavy, P. 1977. "Protest and Quiescence in Urban Politics: A Critique of Some Pluralist and Structural Myths." *International Journal of Urban and Regional Research* 1, no. 2:193-218.

_____ . 1980. Urban Political Analysis. London: Macmillan.

Edwards, J., and Batley, R. 1979. The Politics of Positive Discrimination. London: Tavistock.

Getter, R.M., and Schumaker, P.D. 1978. "Contextual Bases of Responsiveness to Citizen Preferences and Group Demands." Policy and Politics 6:249-279.

Gyford, J. 1976. Local Politics in Britain, London: Croom Helm.

Hall, D.R. 1978. "Applied Social Area Analysis: Defining and Evaluating Areas for Urban Neighbourhood Councils." Geoforum 8:277-309.

Harrop, K.T.; Mason, T.; Vielba, C.A.; and Webster, B.A. 1978. The Implementation and Development of Area Management. Birmingham: Institute of Local Government Studies.

Hill, D.M. 1979. "Neighbourhood Councils." Planning and Administration 5:27-40.

Humble, S., and Talbot, J. 1976. Investigation into Neighbourhood Councils. Birmingham: Institute of Local Government Studies.

Janelle, D.G., and Millward, H.A. 1976. "Locational Conflict Patterns and Urban Ecological Structure." Tijdschrift voor Economische en Sociale Geografie 67:102-114.

Jones, B.D.; Greenberg, S.R.; Kaufman, G.; and Drew, J. 1977. "Bureaucratic Response to Citizen Initiated Contacts." American Political Science Review 71:148, 165.

Jones, B.D., and Kaufman, G. 1974. "The Distribution of Urban Public Services: A Preliminary Model." Administration and Society 6:337-360.

Kirby, A.M. 1979. Education, Health and Housing: An Empirical Investigation of Resource Accessibility. Farnborough: Saxon House.

Knox, P.L. 1978. "The Intra Urban Ecology of Primary Medical Care: Patterns of Accessibility and Their Policy Implications." Environment and Planning A, no. 10:415-435.

Lambert, J.; Blackaby, B.; and Paris, C. 1975. "Neighbourhood Politics and Housing Opportunities." Community Development 10:95-112.

Lambert, C.; Penny, J.; and Webster, B. 1980. The Impact of Services on the Inner City. Birmingham: Institute of Local Government Studies.

Lewis, J. 1975. "Variations in Service Provision: Politics at the Lay Professional Interface." In Essays on the Study of Urban Politics, ed. K. Young. London: Macmillan.

Ley, D. 1974. Community Participation and the Spatial Order of the City. Vancouver, B.C.: Tantalus.

Lineberry, R.L. 1977. Equality and Public Policy. Beverly Hills, Calif.: Sage Publications.

Lowe, P.D. 1977. "Amenity and Equity: a Review of Local Environmental Pressure Groups in Britain." Environment and Planning 9:35-58.

Lowe, S. 1978. "Community Groups and Local Politics." In Local Government and the Public, eds. R. Darke and R. Walker. London: Leonard Hill.

Morton, J. 1979. "Parish Politics." *New Society,* 25 January, p. 197.

Newton, K. 1976. *Second City Politics.* Oxford: Oxford University Press.

——. 1979. "Central Place Theory and Local Expenditure in Britain." Paper prepared for International Political Science Association Conference, Moscow.

Newton, K., and Sharpe, L.J. 1977. "Local Outputs Research: Some Reflections and Proposals." *Policy and Politics* 5:61-82.

Pahl, R. 1979. "Sociopolitical Factors in Resource Allocation." In *Social Problems and the City,* eds. D.T. Herbert and D.M. Smith. Oxford: Oxford University Press.

Peterson, P.E., and Kantor, P. 1977. "Political Parties and Citizen Participation in English City Politics." *Comparative Politics* 9:197-217.

Pinch, S.P. 1980. "Local Authority Provision for the Elderly: An Overview and Case Study of London." In *Social Problems and the City,* eds. D.T. Herbert and D.M. Smith. Oxford: Oxford University Press.

Rich, R.C. 1979a. "Neglected Issues in the Study of Urban Service Distributions." *Urban Studies* 16:143-156.

——. 1979b. "The Roles of Neighborhood Organizations in Urban Service Delivery." *Urban Affairs Papers* 1:81-93.

——. 1980a. "A Political-Economy Approach to the Study of Neighborhood Organizations." *American Journal of Political Science* 24:559-592.

——. 1980b. "The Dynamics of Leadership in Neighborhood Organizations." *Social Science Quarterly* 60:570-587.

Saunders, P. 1979. *Urban Politics: A Sociological Interpretation.* London: Hutchinson.

Webster, B.A. 1980. "Policymaking and Responsive Local Government: The Experiment of Area Management in England." Paper prepared for the American-European Conference on Neighbourhood Local Government, Florence.

Zizk, B.H. 1972. "Local Interest Politics and Municipal Outputs." In *People and Politics in Urban Society: Urban Affairs Annual Review,* vol. 6, ed. H. Hahn. Beverly Hills, Calif.: Sage Publications.

14 Administrative Linkages and Intermunicipal Service Distributions: The Case of Welfare and Education in Israel

Frederick A. Lazin

The effect of intergovernmental administrative arrangements on municipal-service distributions is often pondered by political scientists. Do such arrangements favor equity, foster recipient satisfaction, and enhance the quality of the service? This chapter deals with the role and function of local-national relations on intermunicipal service distributions. It studies the impact of administrative linkages between different levels of governmental jurisdictions involved in implementing policies and programs of the ministries of Welfare and Education in Israel.[1] It examines the consequences of these arrangements for provision, funding, and employment on the intermunicipal distribution of the respective services.

Israeli law and tradition both dictate that welfare and education are primarily the responsibilities of the national government and its respective ministries (Peled 1978). Both the Ministry of Welfare and the Ministry of Education are committed to an equitable distribution of services on the municipal level with the goal of fostering equality of opportunity within the population. To achieve this end both ministries delegate specific functions to local-government authorities and agencies. This chapter evaluates the extent to which these arrangements either foster equity or reinforce existing resource inequalities between the municipalities.

The findings are based on two studies. The first, in the summer of 1977, analyzed both education and welfare services in five cities and towns.[2] Though not a representative sample, the five are typical of the various kinds of Israeli communities in terms of geography, ecology, demography, and type. Gedera (1977 population: 5,900) is representative of small towns whose residents are mostly Oriental Jewish immigrants from the Moslem countries of North Africa and the Middle East, with a minority of more prosperous veteran settlers. Beersheva (101,000) has a municipal administration similar to those of the largest Israeli cities. Rechovot (57,600), a larger medium-sized veteran city located in the heart of the country, serves as a marketing and technological

---

The author wrote this chapter while on leave at the School of Architecture and Urban Planning, University of California at Los Angeles. He wishes to thank Professor Samuel Aroni for this generous support, and Mayumi Nakaoka for her able research assistance.

center. Ramle (37,900), a small medium-sized city that is poorer than neighboring Rechovot, has a mostly Oriental population with a 15-percent Arab minority. Finally, Kiryat Gat (22,400) is typical of the more than thirty new towns established as planned communities since 1950 (Ministry of Labor and Social Affairs 1978, pp. 15-17).

The second study, undertaken two years later, investigated municipal welfare services in the towns and cities of the Negev region, a peripheral development area in southern Israel.[3] The communities studied were Arad (1976 population: 9,400), Beersheva (98,900), Dimona (27,600), Eilat (16,600), Mitzpeh Rimon (1,900), Netivot (7,000), Ofakim (11,000), Sderot (8,500), and Yerucham (6,300).

Using an approach influenced by Grodzins's and Elazar's studies of municipal services in U.S. communities, I investigated the roles and functions of the municipality (elected and appointed officials, administrative personnel of staff and line agencies, and street-level bureaucrats); national ministries (Welfare, Education, and others); and public and private bodies in arrangements for provision, funding, and employment of the respective municipal services (Grodzins 1966; Elazar 1970). An open-ended questionnaire was used in extensive interviews with the mayors and the heads and senior staff of municipal departments of education and welfare of each community.

Although based on a single country during the late 1970s, the findings contribute to a better understanding of potential effects of institutional arrangements on intermunicipal service distributions. Israel's special characteristics and experiences in trying to achieve equity make it an excellent site for evaluating various proposals to achieve an equitable distribution of services within metropolitan areas of the United States. The formally unitary Israeli system, with its national political institutions and dependent municipalities, presents an almost ideal test case for proposals that favor a more centralized system in the United States, with greater roles for the federal and state governments. In addition, many of the smaller and poorer Israeli communities evidence the difficulties that would probably confront neighborhood governments that might be created in response to proposals for decentralization at the city level. Finally, despite its unitary and centralized political institutions, much of the decision making and policy implementation in education and welfare in Israel is decentralized and characterized by "widespread power sharing on a noncentralized basis (Elazar 1977, p. 49).

The findings reported here raise at least three questions about the likelihood of successfully implementing various reform proposals to achieve equity in service distribution in the metropolitan United States (Altshuler 1970; Lipsky 1973; Ostrom 1977; Rich 1977, 1979). These issues are:

1. How do we determine the needs of a particular unit (neighborhood); and what are the proper roles for citizens, elected and appointed officials, and street-level bureaucrats in doing so?

2. How do we provide sufficient funding to satisfy the objective needs of each unit when the units are in competition for insufficient funding from higher governmental jurisdictions?
3. How do we recruit the necessary number of trained professionals for local services, especially in the less attractive areas?

Welfare

Formally, the ministry sets welfare policy and establishes programs and services for the entire country. However, the task of provision is delegated to elected municipal authorities, who in turn are required to establish a local welfare agency. With the approval of the ministry, the local agency hires professional staff and provides services in accord with ministry programs, guidelines, and supervision. In addition, the ministry funds the entire cost of income maintenance and about 80 percent of the operating budget of the local agency, including staff salaries. Municipal social workers are paid on a national scale, with grade incentives provided in less attractive communities. Although the agency director and staff are legally employed by and responsible to the elected municipal council, programatically they are under the supervision and authority of the ministry.

Local welfare agencies; municipal officials; the ministry; and other governmental, public, and voluntary bodies are involved in many complex arrangements for the delivery of municipal welfare services. In administrating the ministry's income-maintenance program, the municipality and its welfare agency perform a technical function only: they process all eligible persons without limitation, who then receive monthly grants funded entirely by the ministry. Consequently, distribution of such funds is fairly uniform throughout the country, with eligible persons, regardless of where they live, receiving support in accord with ministry guidelines.

This is not the case with most social services, however. Because the ministry designates these services as discretionary and requires that local authorities provide matching funds, the local municipality decides what services to provide, the extent of provision, and the number of staff to assign to programs it adopts. In the case of material and partial financial assistance, for which provision is also discretionary and where ministry funding is insufficient to offer these services to all eligible recipients, the local authorities determine allotments and allocation procedures.

There is probably no single arena or process in which decisions are made about what services to provide. Agency heads operate within a "zone of indifference" bounded programatically by the elected municipal officials and fiscally by city budget personnel and the Ministry of Interior (Wilson 1969, p. 232; Antunes and Mladenka 1976, p. 163).

Formally, major decisions about service provision are made in municipal budget deliberations involving elected municipal officials and their budget personnel, the local agency head, and representatives of the ministries of Welfare and Interior. The local-agency head prepares a draft budget request based on existing programs approved the previous year. Before submitting it, he clears major modifications and changes with key elected officials and the Ministry of Welfare. The former are formidable, exercising a virtual veto over changes in program and funding. Their support can also be used by the agency head to offset potential objections by city budget personnel. In sharp contrast is the position of the Ministry of Welfare; despite its formal powers, organizational fragmentation makes it ineffectual. Its organization, rather than being hierarchical, is characterized by fairly independent divisions (line agencies), each of which is responsible for supervising a different category of services (family, youth, elderly, the retarded) on the municipal level. In practice, each lobbies to have the municipal agency expand the division's services even at the expense of other ministry services. Following clearance, the local agency head formally submits the proposal to the city budget personnel, whose primary concerns are fiscal. They in turn must justify all cost increases and new job lines to the Ministry of Interior, which by law must approve all municipal budgets.

Of lesser importance in determining intercity distribution patterns is the role of the street-level bureaucrats—the social workers. The research confirms earlier findings of the influence of social workers in providing actual services. The social worker, sometimes in consultation with ministry supervisors, clearly determines what services eligible clients will receive. Social workers' decisions are based either on discretion or on decision rules and routines. However, the conflicting loyalties of social workers to their profession, the ministry, the municipality, their agency, and their clients (Jaffe 1977) results in different rules and routines to govern the methods of service delivery among street-level bureaucrats in the same and different agencies (Jones 1977, p. 300; Lineberry 1977, pp. 66, 153–154). Insofar as the focus here is intercity distributions, however, the decisions made by elected officials, the agency head, and the budget personnel are more important. Nevertheless, the caliber and number of social workers of a particular agency are relevant in evaluating the quality of services it provides. Their education, training, experience, character, and attitude should be taken into consideration (Allbrandt 1973, p. 6). Evidence in both studies shows significant variations in the professional qualifications and experience of social workers and in the percentage of filled positions that are allocated by the ministry in accord with need.

If the municipality chooses not to provide a particular service, the ministry can offer to fund the entire cost. If the local refusal is based on considerations other than budget, however, the ministry exerts little leverage to alter local decisions. In practice, therefore, there is a wide variety in the type and scale of services offered in different communities. Conscious decisions, not necessarily related to need, are made about what to offer and what to neglect. Some communities, for example, emphasize community services, whereas others focus on individual care; one community has extensive birth-control programs, but another refuses to provide the service; one focuses its resources on services for the elderly, neglecting the more problematic services for youth and other groups (Lazin 1980).

To compensate for the imbalance in intermunicipal service distribution, the ministry sponsors regional and national facilities for problem youth, the retarded, and the elderly, and encourages some of the larger and better-developed local agencies to open up their facilities to other communities. However, the discretionary nature of these activities and the cooperation required by local authorities suggest that they may unintentionally reinforce existing inequalities between communities.

The absence of standard services can be viewed positively. The municipality may choose to provide those services that meet the needs of its particular constituency. Several of the communities of the Negev, for example, have very different social problems; each agency adjusts its services accordingly. In addition, the provider of services is responsible indirectly to the clientele being served; the latter help elect the municipal government that has authority over the local agency and its street-level bureaucrats. With few exceptions, however, the municipal electoral system is ineffective as a demand-registering system (Lineberry 1977, p. 72). First, most welfare issues involving the local agency and its programs have little salience in municipal elections, with the possible exception of those related to religion. Second, the small number of welfare recipients, together with the prevailing social values of the society, reduce the potential influence of welfare clientele over elected and appointed municipal officials.

A different interpretation is also possible, however. One can view the intermunicipal distributions of services as patterned inequality: the poorer, more problem-ridden communities offer fewer services, provided by less qualified professionals, than do the more established communities. Although size and location are relevant factors, with the smaller or more peripheral areas at a disadvantage, they are neither sufficient as explanatory variables nor consistent (Newton 1975, p. 256).

In summary, despite the ministry's commitment to equity, several of the administrative linkages result in the provision of services that reflect the existing level of social, political, economic, and professional resources of the particular community. First, the subsidies and resources obtained from the ministry are partly a function of the strength and abilities of the local political leaders. Despite apparent parity of national standards and regulations for subsidies to municipalities according to need, bargaining is still important; some municipalities are better organized and more adept than others. A dynamic director or mayor with national influence makes a significant difference (Rich

1979, p. 149; Sharkansky 1977, pp. 5, 10). Second, many of the ministry services require local matching funds. Despite ministry subsidies averaging 75 percent of the cost of provision including salaries, certain communities are unable to raise their contribution (Antunes and Mladenka 1976, p. 148). Moreover, in the case of most social services and material assistance, the level of all sources of funding is insufficient to meet the minimal needs of all persons eligible under ministry guidelines in each community. Third, some municipalities are more willing than others to accept the professional opinion of either their social workers or the ministry on the need to provide particular services. Finally and perhaps most significant, many communities, especially those with socially distressed populations, have difficulty attracting qualified social workers. Although the problem is most acute in peripheral areas, it also occurs in the center of the country. Many positions either remain unfilled or are filled by less qualified persons, and case overloading is a serious problem. As a result, some communities are unable to provide certain services regardless of financial resources. Ironically, these are usually the communities with the greatest objective need for social workers, as defined by the ministry.

Education

This system is more centralized and national in character than the welfare system with considerably less local input and influence. This reflects the value that social and political interests place on education as a means of redressing social inequality and of nation building (Peled 1978). A second feature is the large number of autonomous national systems that operate schools on the municipal level alongside the ministry systems. This centralized fragmentation reflects both historical circumstances and the continued lack of national consensus on important social values. The importance placed on education, combined with the salience of ideological cleavages, led political interests to demand the right to preserve their own existing educational systems after independence in 1948. In addition, as a result of the neglect of secondary education and particularly vocational training by national bodies of the Jewish community in Israel before 1948, private, philanthropic, and quasi-political organizations filled the gap. These groups later influenced the establishment of a national educational system that ensured their autonomous role and function in secondary vocational education.

The ministry is committed to fairly standard services on the municipal level, with adjustments for compensatory education. The ministry redistributes centrally collected financial resources to communities according to financial need so that "the quality of education should not depend on people's income and on their financial capability to support an educational system" (Peled 1978, p. 152); this is in marked contrast to the U.S. system.

For purposes of analysis municipal education services are best divided into two categories: the compulsory and free kindergarten and primary grades one through eight, and the noncompulsory secondary-school grades nine through twelve.[4]

In the compulsory schools the ministry offers and supervises two educational systems—State Secular and State Religious—both of which are operated locally by a municipal agency, responsible to the elected municipal council. Private systems, recognized by the ministry and sponsored by religious, philanthropic, and quasi-political groups, also operate national systems of private schools on the local level. The ministry sets national policy and programs for state systems; provides a standard curriculum for each grade and subject; pays most of the operating budgets for municipal education departments; issues regulations governing finance, administration, and pedagogy; and trains, hires, assigns, and pays teachers and principals for municipally operated kindergartens and primary schools. With respect to recognized primary schools, the ministry provides similar guidelines and services, certifies teachers, and may fund operating costs and teachers' salaries. However, in matters of staffing and curriculum the private systems enjoy virtual freedom within very broad guidelines.

The municipality chooses to establish either one or both state systems, for which it then builds, operates, and maintains the school. The ministry, in turn, arranges for grants and low-interest loans for construction. It does the same for private systems that build, operate, and maintain their own schools. The municipality may subsidize part or all of the maintenance and operating costs of private recognized schools.

There are also a number of required and optional supplementary and special educational programs and services in the primary-school system. All municipalities must provide special education for the mentally, emotionally, and physically handicapped; truant officers; and public-health nurses. Nevertheless, certain compulsory services may not be provided. Municipalities may also offer psychological counseling, dental care, lunch programs, a long study day, and other services. In both types of systems the ministry grants municipalities considerable freedom to determine the extent, level, quality, and allocation of the service.

In theory, the at-large, proportional-representation municipal elections and frequent coalitions that run local councils serve as effective mechanisms to provide local residents with an input into education policy. For example, should the majority choose a council whose members are affiliated with one of the national religious political parties, the schools will probably be State Religious. If there is a broad local coalition, then the council may support both state and private systems in order to satisfy the differing wishes of its constituents (Rich 1977, pp. 331, 332; Antunes and Mladenka 1976, p. 151).[5] Parents in turn choose a system for their children. Thus these arrangements may maximize parental satisfaction and respond to exceptional demands (Rich 1979, p. 152; 1977, pp. 331, 332). If able to influence their local council, numerical minorities can send their children to a state or private school (supported by ministry and municipal funds) with which they share important values.

Municipal secondary education is provided by different sponsors and takes one of three forms: academic, vocational, and comprehensive high schools (which have both a vocational and an academic program). In general the municipality provides either academic or comprehensive high schools affiliated with the State Religious or State Secular systems. These decisions are made by elected municipal officials. Private organizations and other ministries also operate national networks of vocational schools. In some communities, like Rechovot, the municipality together with private networks sponsors vocational schools. For their own respective secondary schools the municipality and private sponsors build, equip, and maintain the institutions, and hire and employ teachers and principals.

The ministry subsidizes the municipalities' operating expenses for secondary education and helps cover the cost of tuition for needy pupils. In development towns the ministry absorbs the entire cost, making secondary education tuition free. The ministry also provides guidelines for administration, finance, pedagogy, and hiring of staff. Although in principle the individual sponsors set policy for their independent vocational systems, in fact the ministry uses financial incentives and other means to influence their policies. Consider, for example, the ministry's matriculation exams. These are compulsory for all high-school students, regardless of system, who want to receive a diploma necessary for university entrance and for many jobs. The ministry grants grading advantages for these exams to pupils of systems and schools that comply with ministry regulations and inspection. Also, many schools gear classroom learning to the ministry tests. Municipalities also use similar means to influence private systems in their jurisdiction. For example, in exchange for cooperation, Beersheva keeps entrance requirements to its prestigious comprehensive schools high enough to guarantee students for the less desirable private systems.

Despite the standard school system and massive financial subsidies from the ministry, patterned inequality still exists. There is an unintentional class and cultural imbalance in the provision of municipal educational facilities and services (Lineberry 1977, p. 17). The difference between superior and inferior systems, cutting across the urban-rural and size divisions, is between regions and locales that are predominantly inhabited by old-timers and those that are almost exclusively populated by more recent Oriental Jewish immigrants from non-European countries. For example, rural kibbutzim, including many on the periphery, whose members are mostly veteran settlers or their offspring, generally have excellent school facilities and staff. In sharp contrast, the newer communities—often but not always located in the peripheral developing areas— have inferior educational systems: their teachers are less experienced, more transient, and less likely to reside in the community. The lack of adequately qualified personnel limits course offerings and results in the nonperformance of many administrative and pedagogical functions required by the ministry. Children thus receive very different educations depending on the municipality in which they live.

Within this context Israel shares problems faced by educational systems in other countries. First, there is the issue of economy of scale. In smaller communities attempts to satisfy local preference may result in the operation of several systems, none of which is adequately equipped or staffed. Even if these are combined into one system, the local education authority may be unable to match services provided by the larger municipalities and the regional schools of the agricultural settlements (Newton 1975, p. 256). A partial but unsatisfactory solution to this problem is provided by the boarding schools, attended by almost one out of four Israeli secondary-school pupils. These schools increase the options for parents and pupils and offer unusual opportunities to many gifted students. Scholarships guarantee equal access. The level and quality of these schools varies significantly, however. Moreover, by removing the better-qualified students from many poorer and peripheral communities, the boarding-school system unintentionally works to the detriment of the municipal educational systems.

Second, the ministry requires matching funds for some programs, including many of those designed to meet the needs of the culturally deprived students who are found in higher percentages in newer communities. Consequently, some communities either curtail or do not provide certain services. It is important to note that these arrangements indicate the lack of sufficient national resources to provide the minimum level of services deemed essential by the ministry. Thus there is a competition for limited resources between unequal communities. Third, the voluntary nature of many of these services allows municipalities and school principals not to provide them, despite the needs of pupils.

The most serious problem, however, concerns staffing and can impair the ability of some systems and schools to educate. The poorer communities, especially those catering to more socially and educationally handicapped pupils, face shortages of qualified, experienced teachers. This is the case despite financial incentives and the ministry role in hiring, firing, and assignment—even despite the fact of a standard national pay scale. One obstacle to improvement has been the pressure exerted by teachers unions. During the 1960s they successfully opposed attempts by the ministry to replace uncertified teachers with recent graduates from teacher colleges. In general the unions are very much involved in "formulating ... substantive policies" of the ministry and local departments of education (Antunes and Mladenka 1976, p. 152).

Conclusions

The findings on welfare and education services in Israel are relevant for evaluating proposals to make service distributions more equitable. They confirm the hypothesis that institutional arrangements do profoundly affect service distributions. Whatever institutional arrangements are proposed and implemented, therefore, should heavily influence the outcome of the interplay of resources, personnel, and local-preference characteristics. In particular, the Israeli experience indicates the need to be concerned with at least three issues that potentially impede successful implementation of reform proposals to make service distributions in metropolitan areas in the United States more equitable, including Rich's (1977) model for neighborhood government. The following comments emphasize the need to structure reforms in such a way as to ensure a greater degree of successful implementation.

First, there is the problem of needs. In the case of neighborhood governments or any other proposed units, who should decide what the needs are—an elected council, separately elected boards for each service, central or street-level bureaucrats, or the majority or some percentage of the citizenry? Should there be national, state, metropolitan, or municipal priorities and standards? A related issue is the question of the magnitude of election districts—at-large as opposed to single member—and the electoral formulation—plurality, majority, or proportional representation—to adopt. The answers to most of these questions will affect the choice of certain needs over others to be addressed by particular service systems.

Second, is funding a potential impediment to egalitarian distribution between municipalities or local units of allocation? Under certain circumstances, the highest relevant jurisdiction—the national government—may be unwilling to allocate sufficient fiscal resources to satisfy the minimum level of needs in social welfare and education of all its citizens (Lazin 1980; Wilensky 1975, p. 80). It is relevant to ask whether proposals for increased funding for social services in inner-city urban neighborhoods are feasible today (Banfield 1974, p. 260). The answer is, at best, "very unlikely."

Clearly, the problem of inegalitarian intermunicipal distribution of services, whether in Israel or the metropolitan United States, may well be more political than economic or bureaucratic in nature. In a system of neighborhood government, therefore, despite support and serious redistributive efforts at metropolitan, state, and national levels, and the probable difference in neighborhood preferences, funding will probably be inadequate to prevent patterned inequality between neighborhoods (Rich 1977, pp. 399–400). The problem is compounded by inequalities between neighborhoods and communities competing for the limited resources. Despite a commitment to fairness and equity in an unrigged system, some parties would compete better than others (Rich 1977, pp. 395; 1979, pp. 152, 153; Sharkansky 1977, p. 12). It is probably impossible to achieve Bish's ideal of "institutional fairness" whereby "the rules, law and structure of political organization should be fair, unbiased and designed so that all individuals (towns and neighborhoods) receive net benefits" (Bish 1975, p. 76) if we interpret the net to be what the recipient feels he deserves.

Of equal magnitude is the lesson of matching funds. The Israeli experience suggests that no matter how minimal the local contribution, the requirement reinforces the existing inegalitarian distribution of resources between communities because some can afford the small fees more easily than others.

Third, the most serious problem may well be with staffing (Chase 1979, p. 4). In both service areas studied here, the poorer and more socially distressed local communities experienced difficulty in recruiting certified teachers and social workers. The absence of qualified applicants make meaningless and ineffective national standards and regulations. In most democracies, governments cannot coerce professionals to work in communities against their will. Like their counterparts in many industrialized societies, Israeli professionals prefer to work and live in the more attractive communities. Financial incentives are usually insufficient to motivate them to work in communities they dislike. As long as there are alternative places of employment, they will prefer to work elsewhere. Unfortunately, when alternatives become nonexistent, many choose to leave their profession altogether. The situation is compounded by the fact that most service professionals are women, who may value their husbands' careers and their family responsibilities above their commitment to their profession. Such a woman will choose to work in an area determined by her family situation. In peripheral areas, where commuting to work is impractical, professionals often leave in search of a better school system for their own children.

The problem of staffing also affects the quality of services delivered within a particular jurisdiction. This is especially true in the case of social welfare and education, where the role of the professional is inseparable from the quality of the service itself. The education, training, and experience—as well as the character and attitude—of the street-level bureaucrat are all pertinent factors. If the Israeli experience is typical, it is not encouraging; the better qualified prefer to work in more socially desirable communities.

Notes

1. In October 1977 the ministries of Welfare and Labor merged into the Ministry of Labor and Social Affairs. The former Ministry of Welfare retained its organizational and programmatic identity and autonomy within the new ministry.

2. The Settlement Study Center of Rechovot Israel sponsored the research. Ms. Tora Banin and Ms. Lily Abraham assisted the author.

3. The Humphrey Center for Social Ecology of Ben Gurion University funded the project. Ms. Netta Ha-Ilan, Mr. Zvi Mintz, and Ms. Nitza Sibush helped with the research.

4. In 1977 free compulsory education included kindergarten, eight years of primary school and one year of secondary school. After 1977 the Begin

government extended compulsory education to the tenth grade and abolished all tuition fees for secondary education.

5. Antunes and Mladenka (1976, p. 151) do not consider proportional representation.

References

Allbrandt, R. 1973. "Efficiency in the Provision of Fire Services." *Public Choice* 16:6.

Altshuler, A. 1970. *Community Control.* New York: Western Publishing Co.

Antunes, G., and Mladenka, K. 1976. "The Politics of Local Services and Service Distributions." In *The New Urban Politics*, eds. L. Masotti and R. Lineberry, pp. 147–169. Cambridge, Mass.: Ballinger.

Banfield, E. 1974. *The Unheavenly City Revisited.* Boston: Little, Brown.

Bish, R.L. 1975. "Commentary." *American Institute of Planners Journal* 41:67–82.

Central Bureau of Statistics. n.d. *Standard Abstract of Israel 1977.* Jerusalem: Central Bureau of Statistics.

Chase, G. 1979. "Implementing a Human Service Program: How Hard It Will Be." *Public Policy* 27:385–403.

Elazar, D. 1970. *Cities of the Praries.* New York: Basic Books.

_____. 1977. "The Compound Structure of Public Service Systems in Israel." In *Comparing Urban Service Delivery Systems: Structure and Performance*, eds. V. Ostrom and F.P. Bish, pp. 47–82. Beverly Hills, Calif.: Sage Publications.

Grodzins, M. 1966. *The American System*, ed. D. Elazar. Chicago: Rand McNally.

Jaffe, E. 1977. "Problems of Loyalty in Social Work." *Social Security* 12–13: 174–179. (Hebrew).

Jones, B. 1977. "Distributional Considerations in Models of Government Service Provision." *Urban Affairs Quarterly* 12:291–312.

Lazin, F. 1980. "The Effects of Administrative Linkages on Implementation: Welfare Policy in Israel." *Policy Sciences* 12:193–214.

Lineberry, R. 1977. *Equality and Urban Policy: The Distribution of Municipal Services.* Beverly Hills, Calif.: Sage Publications.

Lipsky, M. 1973. "Street Level Bureaucracy and the Analysis of Urban Reform." In *Neighborhood Control in the 1970's*, ed. G. Frederickson, pp. 103–115. New York: Chandler.

Ministry of Labor and Social Affairs. 1978. *Social Profile of Cities and Towns in Israel.* Jerusalem: Ministry of Labor and Social Affairs.

Newton, K. 1975. "American Urban Politics: Social Class, Structure and Public Goods." *Urban Affairs Quarterly* 11:241–264.

Ostrom, V. 1977. "Structure and Performance." In *Comparing Urban Service Delivery Systems*, eds. V. Ostrom and F.P. Bish, pp. 19-44. Beverly Hills, Calif.: Sage Publications.

Peled, E. 1978. "The Case of Israel." In *Government in the Classroom*, ed. M. Williams, pp. 389-395. New York: Proceedings of the American Academy of Political Science.

Rich, R. 1977. "Equality and Institutional Design in Urban Service Delivery." *Urban Affairs Quarterly* 12:383-410.

———. 1979. "Neglected Issues in the Study of Urban Distributions: A Research Agenda." *Urban Studies* 16:143-156.

Sharkansky, I. 1977. "Local Government in the Welfare State." Paper prepared for the Workshop in Financial Problems of European Cities, European Consortium for Political Research, Berlin.

Wilensky, H. 1975. *The Welfare State and Equality*. Berkeley: University of California Press.

Wilson, J. 1969. *Varieties of Police Behavior*. Cambridge, Mass.: Harvard University Press.

15 Centralization, Bureaucracy, and Urban Services: A Comparative Perspective

Andrew Parkin

The spatial correspondence between intrametropolitan socioeconomic patterns and governmental jurisdictions—between de facto and de jure boundaries—is a crucial, yet often unrecognized, factor affecting the delivery of urban services. The demand (or "preference" or "need") for certain services is intimately connected with the socioeconomic characteristics of a population. Hence, because metropolitan areas comprise heterogeneous conglomerations of rather more homogeneous neighborhoods in class, ethnic, racial, status and life-cycle terms, there is an intimate connection between service demand and neighborhood characteristics.

This connection can be illuminated through a development of Oliver Williams's (1967, 1971) conceptual distinction between policies of *system maintenance* and those of *life style*. Whereas system-maintenance policies and services, such as communications systems and utility networks, bear little relation to socioeconomic characteristics, life-style policies and services are acutely sensitive to them. A listing of life-style services would begin with *public education*, for which class, ethnic, and life-cycle influences on policy preferences are well documented. Public policy on *urban development and land use* is another locality-sensitive area: neighborhood residents have a collective economic interest in prohibiting developments that would reduce market values for property and perhaps a collective sociocultural interest in preserving the population characteristics of the neighborhood. *Housing* policy is also localistic in focus. Housing within neighborhoods tends to come from a limited range of physical styles and market values; forms of tenure (such as renting) are more prominent in particular localities; public-housing units tend to be constructed en masse in certain areas. *Law enforcement and police* services also have life-style characteristics. The poor provide both the principal victims and the principal perpetrators of physical crimes. There are also documented social variations in conceptions of appropriate police behavior in maintaining order and combating crime. *Public-welfare* and *public-health* services are logically most needed in less affluent neighborhoods, whereas *public libraries* are more likely to be demanded in richer areas. There is also a distinct neighborhood interest in *taxation* arrangements: the degree of progressiveness in the tax structure, the extent to which it draws on propertied wealth, the degree to which localities are dependent on the local tax base, and so on.

Because life-style services and policies are so sensitive to locality-specific characteristics, Williams has suggested that there is a natural tendency for public responsibility for their provision to be decentralized to local-government units. Local government would be more likely to respond to the specialized life-style needs and demands of a fairly homogeneous local population. System-maintenance services, on the other hand, are "neutral with regard to life style values." Thus if other criteria, such as economies of scale, suggest the appropriateness of greater centralization of responsiblity, there would be no natural resistance to this.

This chapter examines the distribution of urban services from a comparative perspective, taking the Williams model as the point of departure. In particular, the experience of the United States, where the Williams assumptions seem especially pertinent, is contrasted with that of Australia, where the same assumptions seem remarkably miscast. The comparison produces some insights into the impact of governmental structure on patterns of urban-service delivery. It might also indirectly facilitate an assessment of proposals for the centralization of financing and management of services as a remedy for service inequalities in the United States.

The Decentralized Model: The United States

Urban government in the United States seems to confirm the logic of the Williams reasoning. Metropolitan areas are divided into a patchwork of local-government jurisdictions that embrace fairly homogeneous populations. Central cities are the most populous municipalities, and hence potentially the most socially diverse; yet even central cities have a residential population that is disproportionately lower-income, lower-status, and made up of ethnic and racial minorities. Suburban jurisdictions are smaller in area and population and even more internally specialized with respect to occupation, income, ethnicity, life-cycle, and housing-market values. These municipalities assume the major policy-making responsiblity for life-style services, including a significant dependence on a local property tax. This in turn produces packages of urban services more or less in response to specialized locality demands. As Williams et al. (1965, pp. 29-30, 294-295) observed in metropolitan Philadelphia:

> Community specialization with respect to class or status, life-style and economic function results in divergent interests and policies that operate to maintain a decentralized governmental structure. . . .
>
> What does local control mean to suburban municipalities? It means the ability—perhaps limited, but nevertheless available—to exercise preferences and enjoy resource advantages in the expression of a public personality, albeit within the confines of a physical environment largely determined by past decisions. . . .

[E]ach municipal ordinance and budget is, in a fashion, an announcement to the world of a particular attitude toward amenities, public education, and neighborhood development.

This is a pervasive pattern (Downes 1968). Central-city politics, for example, can be interpreted historically as reflecting a peculiar demographic basis that gave rise to political machines based on an immigrant and working-class constituency, to persistent ethnic symbolism in municipal elections, and more recently to some electoral successes for black politicians. The positive features of this model of urban government—responsiveness to citizen demands, greater opportunities for citizen participation in policymaking, a degree of competitive efficiency in the public sector—are expressed articulately by scholars of the influential public-choice school (Tiebout 1956; Ostrom, Tiebout, and Warren 1961; Warren 1964).

Studies of urban-service delivery in U.S. cities have generally taken for granted the de jure municipal boundaries within metropolitan areas and have concentrated on intramunicipal distributive patterns. The accumulated findings of these studies do not convincingly show any general tendency for service delivery *within* a municipality to favor particular social groups over others. As Rich (1979, p. 145) interprets the literature:

[T]he overall impression [is] that there is a good deal of equality in service distributions. Municipal services do not appear to be consistently manipulated by the affluent to the disadvantage of the poor. Nor are they clearly redistributive instruments through which government attempts to redress inequalities in private resources with public services for the less affluent.

Although significant in its own right, this literature overlooks the major dimension of service inequality in metropolitan areas, namely the intermunicipal disparities (Rich 1979). The decentralization of life-style services, particularly with a strong dependence on a local property tax, produces great variation between municipalities in the scope, quality, and cost of urban services. This variation results in part from genuine choice but also in part from variation in resources. Municipalities with poorer tax bases, generally the residential location of poorer residents, must levy higher rates of taxation to produce a given revenue return. In addition, their residents demand more public services in the welfare, public-housing, police, and public-health areas, making their overall revenue requirements greater. Perverse incentives exacerbate the disparities. Each municipality is rewarded for attracting net tax-producing new developments or residents and for excluding net revenue-consuming units. Local control over land use and development provides the mechanism, through exclusionary zoning, for pursuing this reward. Businesses and households that can scramble over the financial threshold imposed by exclusionary zoning are likewise rewarded for locating where the ratio of services to taxes is highest.

The outcome is a strongly regressive metropolitan pattern (ACIR 1967, 1976; Danielson 1976; Oakland 1979). Those municipalities (such as most older central cities) with low per capita tax base and/or high per capita demands for services feature higher rates of taxation, yet often lower levels of services (quantitatively and qualitatively), than their more privileged suburban counterparts. In such circumstances intramunicipal distributive patterns would seem to be of secondary importance.

This inequality (and injustice) has inspired various reform proposals, a common element of which has been a centralizing of governmental authority (Rich 1980). Voluntary arrangements entered into by some municipalities to coordinate or consolidate services serve only to reinforce the patterns of disparity and segregation (Marando 1968; Dye et al. 1963). Only by removing some decision-making power from the local and specialized level, the reformers have argued, can more broadly equitable (not to mention redistributive) patterns of service provision be facilitated.

The type of centralization envisaged has varied. One variant has been to propose metropolitan government—the consolidation of local jurisdictions into a large metropoliswide authority—or, alternatively, various forms of metropolitan federation. Given the economic and social advantages accruing to probably the majority of metropolitan residents under the decentralized system, it is not surprising that such proposals have been generally unsuccessful. Even in the few cases in which the federation option has been implemented, local jurisdictions have tended to retain responsibility for the key life-style policy areas (Erie et al. 1972). Another route to centralization is through the federal system, and certainly there has been an increasing involvement in urban affairs from state and particularly from federal governments over the past few decades—an involvement that has undoubtedly saved the overall system from collapse (ACIR 1978). However, it has not addressed the problem of horizontal inequities. The ethic of localism remains powerful and is still the key dimension in U.S. urban government.

The Centralization of Urban Services: Australia

Because of its pervasive and self-reinforcing pattern of localism, there has been little opportunity within the U.S. system to test whether the centralization of responsibility for urban services would produce more equitable outcomes and with what effect on other aspects of delivery. It is here that Australian urban government provides an especially instructive comparison.

Australia shares many characteristics with the United States: both are advanced industrial "New World" societies with an immigrant population base and degrees of ethnic differentiation, high levels of urbanization and home-ownership, basic ethics of privatism in urban development, and liberal-democratic political institutions within a federal system of government. Australia is a metropolitan nation. Over 70 percent of its 14.5 million inhabitants reside in five metropolitan areas ranging in population from 3.2 million (Sydney) to 850,000 (Perth).[1] Physically, these metropolises resemble those of California.

Australia's six state governments, like their U.S. counterparts, have created a third tier of local governments that divide most of the metropolitan areas into a familiar geographical patchwork.[2] There, however, the resemblance to the United States ends. Contrary to the "natural" pattern postulated by Oliver Williams, local governments in the Australian metropolitan areas generally have responsibility only for mundane system-maintenance services or for basic, uncontroversial services to property like road construction and maintenance, garbage collection and disposal, small-scale recreational projects, and parking.[3] Local government has not been the product of local self-governing sentiments. Its creation by the states in the nineteenth century was for the administrative convenience of the states; it was "foisted," as one historian describes it, "on an unwilling community" (Maiden 1966, p. 91). The weakness of Australian local government arises both from this apparent community indifference and from a traditional, unambitious property-related sense of mission. Although the municipalities derive much of their revenue from a local property tax, the narrow range of municipal functions means that these tax rates are very low both by international standards and in comparison with other taxes levied by the state and national governments. A few city councils of inner Sydney and Melbourne (where the general pattern of nonpartisanship is broken by Australian Labor party control) and a few amenity-conscious affluent suburbs generate some public interest, but their distinctiveness in policy-output terms is minimal and mainly symbolic. Local governments do retain some powers over development, but it is significant that these seem more likely to be exercised in acceding to development plans than in imposing constraints on development in accordance with the collective interests of local residents (Parkin 1980).

State governments are Australia's principal urban governments. The lifestyle services for which local variation in demand would be expected, as well as the system-maintenance services for which there are significant economies of scale, are state responsibilities. Matters such as public schooling (by far the largest single item in state recurrent budgets), public housing, police services and the administration of justice, hospitals and public health, metropolitan planning, environmental protection, public transportation, highway planning and construction, water supply, sewerage and drainage, and industrial location are generally within the jurisidctions of departments and statutory authorities operating at or responsible to the state level. State responsibilities are financed through uniform national income taxation and various indirect taxes.

The dominance by state governments is the product of several factors. The state governments are the linear descendants of the colonial governments. The adoption of Westminster parliamentary institutions, with their disciplined political parties, strong government, and unitary assumptions, is likewise a centralizing influence, particularly when allied with an Australian tradition of public intervention in matters of economic development.[4] There also appear to be pervasive national values supporting an allegiance to vague egalitarian ideals and to their application by the public sector. In a classic historical study, Hancock (1930, p. 72) observed that "Australian democracy has come to look upon the State as a vast public utility, whose duty it is to provide the greatest happiness for the greatest number." More recently, Encel (1970, p. 56) has noted a "conception of equality which prevails in Australia . . . [and] which places great stress on the enforcement of a high minimum standard of material well-being." Such observations are supported in some interesting comparative historical and sociological studies (Lipset 1967; Rosecrance 1964; Feather 1975; Broom and Jones 1977; Mayer 1964). The result is a prominent role not only for public organizations—as Encel (1970, p. 78) observes, "the quest for equality has been satisfied to a large extent by the establishment of bureaucratic institutions"—but also for centralized government. "Local discretion," as Atkins (1973, p. 243) argues, "must cut across the general policy of redistribution between poorer and richer areas that has become firmly embedded in the Australian government system."

Centralization and Bureaucracy

It was noted earlier that U.S. studies of the delivery of urban services were limited by the de jure boundaries imposed on the "urban" subject. However, these studies do provide illuminating perspectives on intrajurisdictional delivery patterns. After making the major adjustment for the expansion of the urban jurisdiction to encompass the entire metropolitan area, their findings are broadly consistent with the patterns of urban-service delivery by the Australian states. Overall, service delivery seems fairly indifferent to variations in socioeconomic characteristics within the metropolitan area, producing a generalized egalitarian effect. This may be partly an application of value assumptions: as Norton Long (1972, pp. 42–43 argues, "the logic of equal services to ensure the equality of equal citizens is difficult to avoid once the citizens are under one . . . government." Yet, as in U.S. municipalities, the key element seems less ideological than organizational: it lies in the nature of decision making and implementation within public-service-providing bureaucracies.

Particular policy areas—education, public housing, public transportation, highway construction, and so on—are allocated to particular departments or statutory authorities. These organizations are assisted in operationalizing their broad missions through the adoption of what have been variously termed "standard operating procedures," "service delivery rules," or "institutionalized decision rules" (Allison 1971; Jones et al. 1978; Antunes and Mladenka 1976).

As Allison (1971, p. 81) has observed, "the pre-eminent feature of organizational activity is its programmed character: the extent to which behavior in any particular case is an enactment of pre-established routines," and such rules provide standard responses and procedures. The rules may arise in various ways. They might represent "rational" or "professional" judgments about the mission, or a trade-off between some of the cruelly contradictory expectations suffered by public organizations (such as "efficiency" and the red-tape-producing "fiscal integrity," "accountability to superiors" and "responsiveness to clients"), or the institutionalization of the actual practices of adaptations of street-level employees (Lipsky 1976).

Consider the state-level organizations, known as housing commissions or housing trusts, established to provide public housing. These authorities have constructed about 15 percent of housing units in Australia in the postwar period, a proportion far greater than in the United States, though far less than in Britain. The two principal distributive decisions for these authorities concern the *geographical location* of public-housing units and the *social allocation* of units to households on their lists of applicants.

Decisions about geographical location seem to be guided largely by an effort to maximize the number of housing units constructed within the capital funds available. As Painter, Gibbons, and Brezzo (1975, p. 80) bluntly express it, the "overriding policy is to build as much as possible, as cheaply as possible, for as many as possible." There has been some variation between the states in the method adopted. The Victorian Housing Commission was created in 1939 primarily as a slum-clearance and redevelopment authority. The economics of such a program, with its high acquisition costs and space restrictions in the inner city, seemed to require public-housing redevelopment in the form of high-rise apartment blocks. The inner Melbourne skyline is now punctuated by these tall housing projects. The New South Wales Housing Commission and the South Australian Housing Trust, by contrast, have preferred to construct low-density outer-suburban estates. Peripheral land is cheaper, large expanses can be purchased, and mass construction techniques can be adopted. As a result, large suburban swathes of Sydney and Adelaide (and more recently of Melbourne) are occupied by public-housing estates, distinguishable perhaps only by the relative uniformity of designs and standards from the neighboring "private" suburban areas.

There has also been interstate variation in the criteria for public-housing allocation. The South Australian Housing Trust, for example, was created in 1936 not as a welfare agency but as a central element in a state-government strategy to promote industrialization. A large supply of publicly constructed housing helped to maintain low costs of living, which were then translated into lower wage levels: by this sort of public management, many multinational corporations were coaxed into locating in the Adelaide metropolitan area. Although the trust has more recently assumed some limited welfare responsibilities, it allocates housing units primarily on a first come, first served basis, and its housing estates retain a relatively diverse clientele. The New South Wales Housing Commission, in contrast, was established in 1942 by a Labor government to assist with housing low-income families; and it attempts to apply criteria of need before allocating its units. One result is that its suburban estates seem to have developed more of a stigmatized image as low-income ghettos (Stretton 1975; Brennan 1973).

Other services are also affected by organizational modes and rules of allocation. Deep drainage, sewerage, and water mains are provided by the responsible authorities basically in response to perceived demand, as indicated by new outer-suburban subdivision, tempered both by limitations on the capital funds available and by organizational priorities that seem to emphasize water supply at the expense of sewerage. Consider this analysis of Sydney's Metropolitan Water, Sewerage and Drainage Board:

> The M.W.S. and D.B. appears to disregard the possibility of inducing regular constraint on water consumption and to accept the largely unchecked water consumption trends as the determinant of supply needs. . . .
>
> By erring on the safe side, the Board appears to be somewhat lavish in committing large capital outlays for future water supply reservoirs and headworks. . . .
>
> It seems probable that commitment to capital works for water supply development was one factor in the increasing sewerage backlog that developed during the 1950s and 1960s. [Butlin 1976, pp. 138–139]

Highways departments have emphasized in their construction and routing plans such factors as traffic flow, congestion, highway safety, and least-cost routes. The New South Wales Department of Main Roads, for example, has been described as having had "a strong commitment to road-building, high technical expertise in the traffic and construction areas and a firm belief as to where roads should go, even where that conflicted with the views of land use planners and environmentalists" (Wilenski 1978, p. 81). Police services in Adelaide are distributed on the basis of sophisticated estimates of the geographical location of police work (such as the incidence of crime, disturbances of public order, or surveillance activities) and of constraints on patrol response (such as likely traffic congestion and the road network). This distribution is indifferent to any predetermined territorial or social considerations. As officially described:

> The structuring of Police territories within Metropolitan Adelaide has no relationship to existing Local Government boundaries. . . . Because of the peculiar nature of the Police Operation in servicing public needs, the most critical factor is the patrol area and patrol response time.

Efficiency dictates that Police territories must, therefore, be primarily predicated on the basis of patrol workloads rather than the arbitrary assessment of territory based on other criteria. [Killmier 1975, p. 27]

Public hospitals seem to have been located mainly in inner-city areas, where perhaps access from all points in the metropolitan area is at an optimum (Lawrence 1972, pp. 112-117). Public-bus transportation routes are provided according to estimates of the demand for radial trips into the central business district.

Such bureaucratic criteria and procedures eschew a priori considerations of locality characteristics, but this does not mean that their impact is neutral with respect to locality. Planning new freeways according to minimum-cost routes threatens "less valuable" working-class neighborhoods and parklands more than "more valuable" middle-class neighborhoods. The distribution of police patrols according to work load produces more patrols in poorer neighborhoods. If demand for radial trips to the central business district is the criterion for the provision of a bus route, then blue-collar neighborhoods where commuting is mainly to other destinations are disadvantaged. Providing the basic water-supply and sewerage infrastructure in response to demand (rather than in advance of, and guiding, subdivision), and emphasizing the former at the (unacknowledged) expense of the latter, means that outer-suburban dwellers may face a backlog (Wilson 1978, p. 200). Regulations that now require private developers to install such basic infrastructural elements help the service authorities keep up with demand but also impose direct costs on outer-suburban home buyers (onto whom developers transfer the cost) that were previously borne by the whole community. The central location of public hospitals has again been inconvenient to outer-suburban dwellers, especially those with low incomes. Public housing, on the other hand, redistributes welfare to low-income groups either as a matter of policy or (as in South Australia) by virtue of their disproportionate consumption of it. However, public-housing clients must generally face the choice of inner-city high-rise projects with their attendant problems of vandalism and crowding, or outer-suburban estates with long commuting distances.

The most costly and most revealing of the state-government services are the public school systems. They have epitomized the phenomenon of fairly rigid control by centralized state-level bureaucratic organizations in the face of undeniable social variation between schools and school catchment areas. As Cramer and Browne (1965, p. 113) observed in their comparative study, "Australia provides the only example of a nation in which the component states each have highly centralized systems of educational control, with practically no local participation by the parents and citizens."

Public-school costs are borne by the state government, and state departments of education are responsible for most aspects of school policy: location and design, equipment, attendance boundaries, broad curricula and textbooks, certificates of achievement, teacher training, teacher allocation, staff salaries, and so on. Although this centralized arrangement is often defended on the grounds of maintaining the standards of rural schools, its principal effect in a metropolitan nation is inevitably to impose a fairly uniform system throughout the metropolitan areas. Both admirers—those who believe that the school systems "by international standards reasonably successfully . . . achieve equal educational provisions for each child" (Committee of Enquiry 1971, p. 335)—and critics—those who stress the "homogenized education: bland and uninspiring . . . so equal that it is anaemic" (Anderson 1969, pp. 50-51)—seem to agree on the tendencies toward uniformity. A succession of visiting U.S. educationalists have reached similar conclusions (Butts 1955, pp. 16-17; Anderson 1966). Certainly some intrametropolitan variations in school standards persist. Older inner-city schools, now featuring a higher proportion of ethnic minorities, suffer from space limitations and aging physical plant. On the other hand, some of the most attractive, lavish, and progressive school facilities are located in working-class and public-housing suburbs, allocated through departmental procedures indifferent to local variations in wealth and power (Black 1977, chap. 3; Fensham 1970; Walker 1979).

The overall distributive pattern of urban-service delivery is thus complex and inconsistent. There may be variations between metropolitan areas. There is, however, a tendency toward organizational indifference to socioeconomic and locality factors, and thus toward a uniformity of treatment across such factors. Uniform taxation underlines this tendency. This finding is consistent with the U.S. studies of intrajurisdictional delivery patterns, with the crucial extension of the jurisdiction to include the entire metropolis.

Responsiveness and Coordination

Although centralization produces more egalitarianism, it also suggests some insensitivity to locally generated needs and preferences. This trade-off has been experienced in Australian cities, at least until quite recently. Neighborhood interests lacked formal channels of access to or influence over public decision making.

The construction of freeways and arterial roads by highways departments might be guided by the finest engineering principles; yet the impact on neighborhood amenity, community interaction, and the safety and health of residents were factors outside the departments' functional mission. Victorian Housing Commission urban-renewal projects disrupted viable inner-city communities and displaced long-established residents. The special needs in ethnic neighborhoods, both for material programs (such as bilingual education) and for symbolic recognition, seemed not to be recognized: in marked contrast to the United States, neither political parties nor public bureaucracies in Australia found it rewarding to appeal, even symbolically, to the residentially concentrated enclaves of Italians, Greeks, Maltese, Poles, Lebanese, Yugoslavs, and other ethnic minorities.[5]

Whereas insensitivity to locality might be an expected concomitant of centralization, lack of coordination probably would not. Indeed, a major criticism of decentralized systems, like those in the United States, arises from their fragmentation and lack of coordination. However, the same sort of factors that promote uniformity of service delivery in centralized Australian bureaucratic organizations seem also to militate against the coordination of service areas. In place of *geographical fragmentation*, centralization may offer *organizational fragmentation*.

Descriptions of the traditional administrative structure of state governments have stressed the organizational incoherence (Encel 1962; Holmes 1976; Paterson 1978; Wettenhall 1962). The situation results mainly from the definition of narrow functional missions within specialized organizations, for which the administration of the task seems to involve no policy matters at all. Highways departments have developed construction schedules without reference to the effect on public transportation. Housing-commission estates have created apparently unanticipated demands for education, welfare, recreation, and police services. Sewerage hookups could not keep pace with subdivision approvals. The traditional central institutions, such as the Treasury and the auditor general's department, seem to have been concerned primarily with the integrity of expenditure, not with its appropriateness or consistency.

One possible mechanism for coordinated public intervention is through statutory metropolitan planning. Each of the Australian metropolitan areas has been the subject of such plans, usually drawn up by a specially created planning authority. The plans typically sketch the broad outlines of preferred future development, with incompatible land uses carefully separated, and have permitted standards and zoning guidelines to be specified for redevelopment in established areas. However, the plans (which seem inherently passive, legalistic, and incremental) have not seriously affected private-market forces. Harrison (1974, p. 137) concludes that "there is little to suggest that planning has made any significant difference to the patterns of urban growth and change over the post-war period"; Neutze (1977, p. 237) agrees that "land use planning has been mostly responsive rather than positive and directive." There also appears to have been little coordinating effect, even on public organizations. The most ambitious of the plans, envisaging a green belt around metropolitan Sydney, was undermined as much by the activities of the New South Wales Housing Commission, the Department of Main Roads, and municipal councils as by opposition from landowners and developers (Harrison 1972).

Developments in the 1970s

This analysis suggests a mixed picture: the centralization of Australian urban
government has an equalizing effect on service distribution at the expense of
local responsiveness and without apparent advantages in coordination. A paper
written in 1970 might legitimately have stopped at that point. During the last
decade, however, a number of developments have suggested that deficiencies
in responsiveness and coordination were being seriously addressed by state
governments (Parkin and Pugh 1981). Some of the stimulus came from the
national level, where a Labor party administration, which held office for the
1972–1975 period after twenty-three years in opposition, provided encouragement and funding for the urban programs. The impact and sustenance of the
developments in the 1970s, however, has necessarily been most significant
for state governments.

Sensitivity to neighborhood interests was forcibly introduced by an unprecedented mobilization at the local level against perceived indifference and inatten-
tion by state-level authorities. Announced plans for freeways through established
neighborhoods and for clearance and "renewal" of inner-city blocks (for public
housing or commercial centers or luxury apartments) catalyzed resident opposition. Mobilization, modeled indirectly on U.S.-style community action, was
assisted by a "gentrification" movement of middle-class professional households
into the inner neighborhoods most threatened by such redevelopment. Some
outer suburbs, consisting disproportionately of young mortgage-ridden home
buyers, also serendipitously found themselves electing marginal parliamentary
seats at a time of close electoral competition between a rejuvenated Labor
party, anxious to appeal to middle-class voters, and its conservative opponents.
There were also signs of political activism among ethnic groups.

State policies in the 1970s responded. Freeways and large-scale urban-
renewal plans were deferred, curtailed, or abandoned in all metropolitan areas.
Concessions were made to the new maxim of "citizen participation" in planning
for roadways, redevelopment, public transportation, or regional centers. Open
space was retained in outer suburbs for community and recreational use. New
public facilities such as hospitals were located in areas most disadvantaged
by the central location of the old facilities. Some state departments introduced forms of intrametropolitan administrative decentralization. Education departments liberalized their procedures and regulations to allow more
autonomy to local schools and to the embryonic parent-teacher councils.
Ethnic needs were recognized in new bilingual education programs and funding for cultural institutions.

The 1970s also saw organizational developments aimed at greater policy
coherence within state governments. A new type of public official, familiar
to observers of U.S. government but unusual in a Westminster system, rose to
prominence: the professional policy expert, appointed laterally (and sometimes

only temporarily) to a high-level position in the bureaucracy and with primary loyalty not to the department but to the minister or "the government." Informal networks developed between the new "policy secretariats" in ministerial offices or at the top levels of statutory authorities. This reflected a change of emphasis away from administration (with its pretensions of neutrality, autonomy, precedent, and routine) and toward policy awareness (with its implication of political, even partisan, sensitivity and overall coherence). Another manifestation was the growth in importance of premier's departments (the premier being the head of the majority party in Parliament, the state-level equivalent of the prime minister) as a source of advice and bureaucratic power independent of established departments. Premier's departments attempted to act as clearinghouses, coordinators and sieves for activities and proposals generated elsewhere in the adminstrative apparatus. There was also some consolidation of departments and agencies with interdependent functions. In several states, for example, transportation commissions were created to place public bus, train, tram, and ferry services under a single authority.

Perhaps the most interesting of the changes was the drift into relative obscurity of the organizations involved in the drafting and implementation of metropolitan planning. Consistent with the new policy awareness, *urban management* seemed a more appropriate umbrella term, with its suggestion of discretionary, immediate, and project-oriented public intervention, than the necessarily long-term and abstract *urban planning* (Ryan 1978; AIUS 1973, 1980). New organizations took the limelight. With the help of federal funds, authorities were created in most states (with the widest powers and biggest impact in South Australia) to act as public "banks" of undeveloped outer-suburban land, thereby both to dampen the speculative element in the price escalation of such land and to expropriate some of the unearned increment in value for the public sector.

Conclusion

Whereas in 1970 the centralized system of urban government and service delivery in Australia featured a mixture of trade-offs and effects—tendencies toward equalization but reduced responsiveness and weaknesses in bureaucratic coordination—by the 1980s there is evidence that the negative features are being imaginatively tackled without retrograde impact on the positive features. State governments seem more aware of legitimate locality-specific needs and better equipped to coordinate their own organizational activities. Though not guaranteeing good policy, this removes impediments to it.

This reorientation reflects a general awakening of consciousness in Australia about urban and environmental issues. For a country that is arguably the most urbanized and metropolitanized in the world (apart from anomalous city-states like Hong Kong), Australia has displayed a curious intellectual ambivalence about urban living. Only in the last decade or so have the particular problems of cities begun to be recognized. This new awareness might allow Australian metropolitan areas to marry their relatively equitable patterns of service delivery with creative urban programs.

For U.S. policymakers and scholars, the overall lesson might be that the centralization of responsibility for urban services does facilitate more just and equitable distribution. Thus at least some of the inequality that exists in service delivery in U.S. metropolitan areas can be attributed to the decentralized structure of urban government in the United States. Recent Australian developments also suggest that an unhappy trade-off of centralization with responsiveness need not be inevitable. Centralization could just produce another and less sensitive form of fragmentation, but with skillful policymaking and administrative intentiveness it might promote better-governed as well as more equal cities.

Notes

1. The other three major metropolitan areas are Melbourne (2.7 million), Brisbane (1.0 million), and Adelaide (0.93 million).

2. The exception is Brisbane, where a metropolitan government was created in 1925, although urban growth now continues beyond the city boundaries into neighboring local-government jurisdictions. The six states, in order of population size and with their major metropolises in parentheses, are: New South Wales (Sydney), Victoria (Melbourne), Queensland (Brisbane), South Australia (Adelaide), Western Australia (Perth), and Tasmania (Hobart).

3. It should be noted that Williams has elsewhere (1975a) pointed out the complications involved in cross-national analysis.

4. As Lowi (1975, p. 276) discusses, "responsible, programmatic parties . . . tend to centralize authority."

5. The present demographic impact of ethnicity on Australian cities is arguably as dramatic as it has been historically in the United States (Parkin 1977). It would probably be more valid to specify subnational groupings: Macedonians, Calabrians, Serbians, and so on.

References

ACIR (Advisory Commission on Intergovernmental Relations). 1967. *Fiscal Balance in the American Federal System*, vol. 2: *Metropolitan Fiscal Disparities*. Washington, D.C.: ACIR.

_____. 1976. *Improving Urban America: A Challenge to Federalism*. Washington, D.C.: ACIR.

_____. 1978. "Federal Initiatives and Impacts." *Intergovernmental Perspective* 4:8-14.

AIUS (Australian Institute of Urban Studies). 1973. *Managing the Cities.* Canberra: AIUS.

_____. 1980. *Urban Strategies for Australia: Managing the Eighties.* Canberra: AIUS.

Allison, G.T. 1971. *Essence of Decision.* Boston: Little, Brown.

Anderson, D.S. 1966. "Australian Education in Viewed by Overseas Visitors." *Australian Journal of Education* 10:229-242.

_____. 1969. "Equality in Education." In *It's People that Matter: Education for Social Change,* ed. D. McLean, pp. 56-65. Sydney: Angus and Robertson.

Antunes, G., and Mladenka, K. "The Politics of Local Services and Service Distribution." In *The New Urban Politics,* ed. L.H. Masotti and R.L. Lineberry, pp. 147-169. Cambridge, Mass.: Ballinger.

Atkins, R. 1973. "Local Government." In *Public Administration in Australia,* ed. R.N. Spann, pp. 221-246. Sydney: Government Printer.

Black, J. 1977. *Public Inconvenience.* Canberra: Australian National University Urban Research Unit.

Brennan, T. 1973. *New Community.* Sydney: Angus and Robertson.

Broom, L., and Jones, F.L. 1977. *Opportunity and Attainment in Australia.* Stanford, Calif.: Stanford University Press.

Butlin, N.G. 1976. *Sydney's Environmental Amenity 1970-1975.* Canberra: Angus and Robertson.

Butts, R.F. 1955. *Assumptions Underlying Australian Education.* Melbourne: Australian Council for Educational Research.

Committee of Enquiry. 1971. *Education in South Australia.* Adelaide: Government Printer.

Cramer, J.F., and Browne, G.S. 1965. *Contemporary Education: A Comparative Study of National Systems,* 2nd ed. New York: Harcourt, Brace and World.

Danielson, M.N. 1976. *The Politics of Exclusion.* New York: Columbia University Press.

Downes, B.T. 1968. "Suburban Differentiation and Municipal Policy Choices." In *Community Structure and Decision-Making: Comparative Analyses,* ed. T.N. Clark, pp. 243-267. Scranton, Pa.: Chandler.

Dye, T.R., et al. 1963. "Differentiation and Cooperation in a Metropolitan Area." *Midwest Journal of Political Science* 7:145-155.

Encel, S. 1962. *Cabinet Government in Australia.* Melbourne: Cheshire.

_____. 1970. *Equality and Authority.* Melbourne: Cheshire.

Erie, S.P., et al. 1972. "Can Something Be Done? Propositions on the Performance of Metropolitan Institutions." In *Reform of Metropolitan Governments,* ed. L. Wingo. Washington, D.C.: Resources for the Future.

Feather, N.T. 1975. *Values in Education and Society.* New York: Free Press.

Fensham, P.J., ed. 1970. *Rights and Inequalities in Australian Education.* Melbourne: Cheshire.

Hancock, W.K. 1930. *Australia.* London: Ernest Benn.

Harrison, P. 1972. "Planning the Metropolis—A Case Study." In *The Politics of Urban Growth.* ed. R.S. Parker and P.N. Troy, pp. 61-99. Canberra: Australian National University Press.

———. 1974. "Urban Planning." In *Public Policy in Australia,* ed. R. Forward, pp. 127-156. Melbourne: Chesire.

Holmes, J. 1976. *The Government of Victoria.* St. Lucia: University of Queensland Press.

Jones, B.D., et al. 1978. "Service Delivery Rules and the Distribution of Local Government Services: Three Detroit Bureaucracies." *Journal of Politics* 40:332-368.

Killmier, R.E. 1975. "The Territorial Organization of Police in South Australia." *Bulletin of the Royal Institute of Public Administration (S.A. Group)* 2:25-30.

Lawrence, R.J. 1972. "Social Welfare and Urban Growth." In *The Politics of Urban Growth,* ed. R.S. Parker and P.N. Troy, pp. 100-128. Canberra: Australian National University Press.

Lipset, S.M. 1967. *The First New Nation.* Garden City, N.Y.: Anchor Books.

Lipsky, M. 1976. "Toward a Theory of Street-Level Bureaucracy." In *Theoretical Perspectives on Urban Politics,* ed. W.D. Hawley, pp. 196-213. Englewood Cliffs, N.J.: Prentice-Hall.

Long, N.E. 1972. *The Unwalled City.* New York: Basic Books.

Lowi, T.H. 1975. "Party, Policy and Constitution in America." In *The American Party System,* 2nd ed., ed. W.N. Chambers and W.D. Burnham, pp. 238-276. New York: Oxford University Press.

Maiden, H.E. 1966. *The History of Local Government in New South Wales.* Sydney: Angus and Robertson.

Marando, V.L. 1968. "Inter-Local Cooperation in a Metropolitan Area: Detroit." *Urban Affairs Quarterly* 4:185-200.

Mayer, K.B. 1964. "Social Stratification in Two Egalitarian Societies: Australia and the United States." *Social Research* 31:435-465.

Neutze, M. 1977. *Urban Development in Australia.* Sydney: George Allen and Unwin.

Oakland, W.H. 1979. "Central Cities: Fiscal Plight and Prospects for Reform." In *Current Issues in Urban Economics,* ed. P. Mieszkowski and M. Straszheim, pp. 322-358. Baltimore, Md.: Johns Hopkins University Press.

Ostrom, V.; Tiebout, C.M.; and Warren, R. 1961. "The Organization of Governments in Metropolitan Areas: A Theoretical Inquiry." *American Politcal Science Review* 55:831-842.

Painter, M.J.; Gibbons, R.P.; and Brezzo, H. 1975. *Sydney Strategic Study: Institutional Decisionmaking.* Sydney: Bureau of Roads.

Parkin, A. 1977. "Ethnic Politics: A Comparative Study of Two Immigrant Societies, Australia and the United States." *Journal of Commonwealth and Comparative Politics* 15:22-38.

———. 1980. "Who Governs Australia's Cities?" In *Government, Politics and Power in Australia*, 2nd ed., ed. A. Parkin, J. Summers, and D. Woodward, pp. 374-389. Melbourne: Longman Cheshire.

Parkin, A., and Pugh, C. 1981. "Urban Policy and Metropolitan Adelaide." In *The Dunstan Decade: Social Democracy at the State Level*, ed. A. Parkin and A. Patience. Melbourne: Longman Cheshire.

Paterson, J. 1978. "Urban Management: The Australian Context." In *Urban Management Processes*, ed. P.F. Ryan, pp. 7-14. Canberra: Australian Government Publishing Service.

Rich, R.C. 1979. "Neglected Issues in the Study of Urban Service Distribution: A Research Agenda." *Urban Studies* 16:143-156.

———. 1980. "The Complex Web of Urban Governance: Gossamer or Iron?" *American Behavioral Scientist* 24:277-298.

Rosecrance, R.N. 1964. "The Radical Culture of Australia." In *The Founding of New Societies*, ed. L. Hartz, pp. 275-330. New York: Harcourt, Brace and World.

Ryan, P.F., ed. 1978. *Urban Management Processes*. Canberra: Australian Government Publishing Service.

Stretton, H. 1975. *Ideas for Australian Cities*. Melbourne: Georgian House.

Tiebout, C.M. 1956. "A Pure Theory of Local Expenditure." *Journal of Political Economy* 64:416-435.

Walker, S.R. 1979. "Educational Services in Sydney: Some Spatial Variations." *Australian Geographical Studies* 17:175-192.

Warren, R. 1964. "A Municipal Services Market Model of Metropolitan Organization." *Journal of the American Institute of Planners* 30:193-204.

Wettenhall, R.L. 1962. "Tasmanian Local Government at the Crossroad." *Public Administration* 21:378-387.

Wilenski, P. 1978. "Review of New South Wales Government Administration." In *Urban Management Processes*, ed. P.F. Ryan, pp. 74-85. Canberra: Australian Government Publishing Service.

Williams, O.P. 1967. "Life Style Values and Political Decentralization in Metropolitan Areas." *Social Science Quarterly* 48:299-310.

———. 1971. *Metropolitan Political Analysis*. New York: Free Press.

———. 1975a. "Urban Politics as Political Ecology." In *Essays on the Study of Urban Politics*, ed. K. Young, pp. 106-132. London: Macmillan.

———. 1975b. "The Politics of Urban Space." *Publis* 5:15-26.

Williams, O.P.; Herman, H.; Liebman, C.S.; and Dye, T.R. 1965. *Suburban Differences and Metropolitan Policies*. Philadelphia: University of Pennsylvania Press.

Wilson, R.K. 1978. "Urban and Regional Policy." In *Public Expenditures and Social Policy in Australia,* vol. I, ed. R.B. Scotton and H. Ferber, pp. 179-211. Melbourne: Longman Cheshire.

Index of Names

Aaron, H.J., 32
Abraham, Lily, 217
Adams, C., 105, 112
Alcaly, R.E., 15
Alford, R.R., 9, 15
Allbrandt, R., 210–218
Allison, G.T., 226, 227, 235
Alol, F., 86, 97
Altschuler, A.A., 83, 97, 208, 218
Anderson, D.S., 230, 235
Anderson, Martin, 149, 155
Aqua, Ronald X., 13, 173, 183
Argyris, C., 59, 66
Arkins, R., 226, 235
Aroni, Samuel, 207
Austin, M., 28, 32
Autunes, G., 1, 4, 14, 32, 44, 50, 53, 63,
  66, 69, 73, 80, 81, 114, 123, 124, 209,
  212, 213, 218, 226, 235
Axinn, J., 26, 32

Babcock, R., 83, 86, 97
Bachrach, Peter, 128, 138
Balk, W., 57, 66
Banfield, E., 216, 218
Bangs, F., Jr., 24, 33
Banin, Tora, 217
Baratz, Morton S., 128, 138
Barnekov, T.K., 3, 14
Baron, H.M., 66
Barton, A., 41, 49, 50
Bassett, K., 189, 203
Batley, R., 191, 204
Benson, C., 56, 62, 66, 83, 97
Berk, R.A., 66
Bieri, K., 25, 33
Bish, R.L., 88, 97, 158, 168
Black, J., 230, 235
Blackaby, B., 191, 204
Bloch, P.B., 78, 81
Block, P.B., 83, 97
Boaden, N., 198, 203
Bollens, J., 62, 66
Boots, A., 4, 14
Bosselman, F.P., 84, 86, 97
Branfman, E.J., 88, 89, 97
Brennan, T., 228, 235
Breslow, S., 26, 32
Brezzo, H., 227, 236
Broom, L., 226, 235
Brown, L., 25, 33
Browne, G.S., 229, 236
Bunce, Harold, 155

Burchell, R.W., 15
Burkhead, J., 57, 67, 68
Burnett, Alan D., X, 13, 189, 203
Button, James W., IX, 11, 69, 75, 82
Butts, R.F., 230, 235

Campbell, D., 69, 82
Carrol, S.J., 62, 67
Case, 7, 14
Castells, M., 192, 203
Chapman, J.W., 67, 68
Chase, G., 218
Chin, S.P., 25, 33
Cinganelli, David L., X, 12, 157
Clark, G., 14, 15
Cloward, Richard A., 128, 138
Clubok, A.B., 82
Cockburn, C., 191, 203
Cohen, B.I., 88, 89, 97
Cornelius, W.A., 203
Cosgrove, D.F., 203
Coughlin, R., 25, 33
Coulter, P.B., 106, 107, 112
Cousins, P.F., 192, 203
Cox, K.R., 8, 14, 191, 192, 196, 203
Cramer, J.F., 229, 235
Crawford, R., 24, 35

Danielson, M.N., 8, 15, 224, 235
Davidson, J.L., 195, 203
Danziger, J., 115, 124
Dear, Michael J., 14, 15, 19, 24, 26, 33, 35,
  191, 203
Dearlove, J., 192, 203
DeGrove, J.M., 82
deLeeuw, F., 86, 98
Dommel, P., 130, 131, 138
Downes, B.T., 223, 236
Downs, Anthony, 130
Drewett, R., 115, 124
Duncan, O.D., 168
Dunleavy, P., 189, 192, 203
Dye, T.R., 224, 235

Edwards, J., 191, 204
Eisinger, P.K., 76, 82
Elazar, D., 208, 218
Encel, S., 226, 231, 235
Erie, S.P., 1, 13, 15, 224, 235
Esposito, L., 167, 169

Fainstein, N.J., 14, 15
Fainstein, S.S., 14, 15

239

Index of Subjects

About the Contributors

Ronald Aqua is staff associate at the Social Science Research Council in New York, where he coordinates the activities of scholarly committees dealing with Japanese and Korean studies. He has published a number of articles on local policymaking processes in Japan and on local government and rural development in Korea.

Alan D. Burnett is principal lecturer in geography at Portsmouth Polytechnic in England. He is coeditor of *Political Studies from Spatial Perspectives* (1981), and has written on the distribution of local public services in British and North American cities. His current research interests include political participation in British cities and residential structure in socialist cities.

James W. Button is associate professor of political science at the University of Florida. His research interests focus on race relations and social change in the United States. He has published several articles on the impact of the civil-rights movement in the South, as well as a book entitled *Black Violence: Political Impact of the 1960s Riots* (1978).

David L. Cingranelli received the Ph.D. from the University of Pennsylvania and is presently an assistant professor of political science at the State University of New York at Binghamton. As an affiliated faculty member of the Center for Social Analysis at that university, he has participated in evaluation research projects in a variety of policy areas, including medical education, nutrition, emergency medical services, and police and fire protection. His published research has been in the area of urban-service delivery and evaluation methodology.

Russell S. Harrison is chairman of the political science department at Rutgers University–Camden. He has written on the distribution of educational services in *Equality in Public School Finance* (Lexington Books, 1976), and on the distribution of housing opportunities as a function of exclusionary zoning and residential segregation. His research interests include intergovernmental fiscal relations, governmental organization in metropolitan areas, growth-management policies, and the political economy of metropolitan areas.

Dilys M. Hill is reader in politics at the University of Southampton in England. Her publications include *Participating in Local Affairs* (1970) and *Democratic Theory and Local Government* (1974), as well as articles in such journals as *Urban Studies* and *International Political Science Review*. Her research interests include both U.S. and British urban development.

E. Terrence Jones is professor of political science and director of the Public Policy Administration Program at the University of Missouri–St. Louis. He is the author of *Conducting Political Research* (1971) and of numerous articles on urban politics, public policy, and research methods.

Dennis R. Judd is head of the political science department at the University of Denver. He is currently completing a book on public policy and is also engaged in a research project on the political economy of the Denver metropolitan area. He has published *The Politics of American Cities, The Politics of Urban Planning*, and numerous articles related to the fields of urban politics and planning, and public policy.

Frederick A. Lazin is coordinator of the Urban Studies Program and senior lecturer in behavior sciences at the Ben Gurion University of the Negev, Ber Sheva, Israel. He is a student of Israeli social policy and urban administration.

Alvin H. Mushkatel is associate professor in the Center for Public Affairs at Arizona State University. His publications and research interests have focused on the effects of urban-redevelopment policy, state land policy, and housing-rehabilitation programs.

Andrew Parkin is lecturer in political theory and institutions at the Flinders University of South Australia; editor of *Government, Politics and Power in Australia* (1980) and *The Dunstan Decade: Social Democracy at the State Level* (1981); and author of journal articles on urban government, public policy, and ethnic politics.

John F. Sacco is associate professor of public affairs at George Mason University. Previously he was a faculty fellow and evaluation officer at the U.S. Department of Housing and Urban Development. Currently, he is working on a manuscript entitled *Program Evaluation—An Implementation Perspective.*

Mary Bryna Sanger is assistant professor of urban affairs and policy analysis in the Graduate School of Management and Urban Professions, New School for Social Research. She is the author of several articles and of *Welfare of the Poor* (1979). Her current research interests include the impact of charter revision on city services in New York City. She is currently engaged in identifying and analyzing opportunities for social-welfare initiatives in New York State.

Joseph P. Viteritti is research associate in the Administration, Planning and Social Policy Program at the Harvard University Graduate School of Education. He was formerly a special assistant to the chancellor of the New York City public-school system and has served as a management consultant to a variety of local-government agencies. He received the Ph.D. in political science from the City University of New York. He is author of *Bureaucracy and Social Justice* (1979) and *Police, Politics and Pluralism in New York City* (1973).

Jennifer R. Wolch received the Ph.D. in urban planning from Princeton University. She is currently assistant professor of urban and regional planning at the University of Southern California, Los Angeles. Her main interests include human-service-delivery systems, geography of service-dependent populations, and the role of public and nonprofit service provision in urban economic development.

Harold Wolman is senior research associate in the Public Finance Program at the Urban Institute in Washington, D.C. He received the Ph.D. in political science from the University of Michigan.

About the Editor

Richard C. Rich is associate professor of political science at Virginia Polytechnic Institute and State University. His primary professional interests are in the areas of urban politics and policy analysis (especially urban neighborhoods and citizen participation); and his articles on these subjects have appeared in such journals as *American Behavioral Scientist, Urban Affairs Quarterly, American Journal of Political Science, Urban Studies,* and *Social Science Quarterly.* He is deputy editor of the *Journal of Community Action,* coeditor of a series of books on urban public policy published by the State University of New York Press, and associate editor of the *Journal of Applied Behavioral Science.*